The God of the Bible and Other Gods

The GOD of the BIBLE and OTHER GODS

Is the Christian God Unique Among World Religions?

Robert P. Lightner

kregel
PUBLICATIONS

Grand Rapids, MI 49501

The God of the Bible and Other Gods: Is the Christian God Unique Among World Religions?

Copyright © 1998 by Robert P. Lightner

Published by Kregel Publications, a division of Kregel, Inc., P.O. Box 2607, Grand Rapids, MI 49501. Kregel Publications provides trusted, biblical publications for Christian growth and service. Your comments and suggestions are valued.

For more information about Kregel Publications, visit our web site at http://www.kregel.com.

Cover design: Alan G. Hartman
Book design: Nicholas G. Richardson

Scripture quotations are from the *New American Standard Bible,*© the Lockman Foundation 1960, 1962, 1963, 1968, 1971, 1972, 1973, 1975, 1977.

Library of Congress Cataloging-in-Publication Data
Lightner, Robert P.
    The God of the Bible and other gods: is the Christian God unique among world religions? / Robert P. Lightner.
        p.   cm.
    Includes bibliographical references and indexes.
    1. God—Biblical teaching. 2. Christianity and other religions. I. Title.
BS544.L54   1998   231—dc21   98-15293
                                                                    CIP

ISBN 0-8254-3154-9

Printed in the United States of America

1 2 3 / 04 03 02 01 00 99 98

Contents

Dedication

To MY FRIEND Charles C. Ryrie, who loves to speak and write of the God of the Bible as "the true and living God," whose love for and devotion to God has made a great and lasting impact upon me, and who first sparked my interest in writing.

Acknowledgments

MANY THANKS GO TO three of my student interns at Dallas Theological Seminary for their assistance in making this book possible. Bruce Bumgardner assisted me in grading, finding materials, and teaching so I could spend more time on the project. Henry Hastings did vital research for me on world religions. Paul R. Shockley did research on major cults and used the computer extensively. He also wrote the appendix dealing with postmodernism, a subject on which he has done extensive research. He holds a B.A. degree in Recent European History from Stephen F. Austin University.

In addition to these three interns I owe thanks to a Dallas Theological Seminary graduate, Wayne Bangs, for supplying me with bibliographic material.

Most of all, my thanks go to Pearl, my wife, who labored long and hard caring for all the details that go into making a work of this sort accurate and user friendly.

Preface

NOTHING IS MORE CENTRAL to the Christian faith than the belief that the God of the Bible exists. The reality of the existence of God and the personality of God are the most fundamental of all issues for the Christian and the student of Scripture.

Christians and non-Christians alike are concerned with the most crucial questions about God. One evidence of this interest in the past was the phenomenal success of the million-copy sale of Bishop John A. T. Robinson's book, *Honest to God.* Perhaps the book's widespread distribution disproved one of its major theses. The bishop seemed to build his whole argument around the idea that people are no longer asking, "How can I find a gracious God?" but rather are asking, "How can I find a gracious neighbor?"

No, the bishop was wrong. People everywhere are still asking the same questions about God that they have been asking from the beginning of time. The questions may be stated differently, but the burning issues are still the same. And the real answers to the perennial questions about God are found only in the Bible.

This book is all about the God of the Bible. Such a study is long overdue, for much of the recent dialogue in theology does not have a biblical orientation.

That all people everywhere acknowledge the existence of some power, person, or force greater than themselves is a generally accepted maxim. To be sure, Christians and non-Christians have different concepts about God. Even Christians have differing concepts and ideas about God. A poll representing all the various denominational bodies undoubtedly would indicate the disparity of beliefs between the groups and even between the people within each group.

This book does not present a case for belief in many gods. And it does not take the smorgasbord or potpourri approach to the divine. Rather, it presents the evidence for the existence of God in three Persons—namely, the Father, the Son, and the Holy Spirit

9

(see Matt. 28:19). The personal God of the Bible is the One about whom this book speaks.

Here is an overview of the book. In Part 1, I will set forth a brief presentation and defense for the inspiration and authority of the Bible. In Part 2, I will discuss the God of the Bible. This is the major portion of the book. In Part 3, I will provide information concerning the gods of major cults and world religions. I will use a chart to contrast these false gods with the true God of the Bible.

Ours is a highly secularized and computerized world. How, it may be asked, is it possible and furthermore why is it necessary to still believe in the personal and sovereign God of the Bible? Have we not come of age and outgrown the faith of our forefathers?

In response to these questions, note that much of the God-talk we hear these days is shallow and meaningless. God has become for many a pointless hypothesis; yet they still value using language about God because it produces for them an existential experience and creates a warm feeling of nostalgia.

But is God really necessary? Has not science made it possible for us to get along quite well without Him? Adler's observation in response to questions such as these is worth pondering: "More consequences for thought and action follow from the affirmation or denial of God than from answering any other basic question."[1]

Although there is much God-talk and a great deal of God-language in our day, there is still a tremendous dearth of useful study and helpful knowledge about the only true God—the God of holy Scripture. Does He exist? Who is He? What has He done for people? What is His plan for the world and mankind? If He is alive and active, why does He not do something about the terrible mess in the world?

In this book I will address these issues and many others. For some, the reading of it will make clear the dichotomy between their "god" and the God of the Bible. For others, my book will serve as a reminder of the Person and work of the God revealed in the Bible. And for them my book will produce a heart of submission, thanksgiving, praise, and worship to our Creator and Lord.

---

1. Mortimer J. Adler, *The Great Ideas, a Lexicon for Western Thought* (New York: Macmillan, 1990), 250.

PART 1

THE
BIBLE

CHAPTER 1

An Overview: Major Issues

BEFORE WE CAN BENEFIT from a study about the God of the Bible, we need to understand why we should even turn to the Bible in the first place to learn about the God presented there.[1] For some readers, the comments in this section will be familiar. There are others, however, who have never thought seriously about why Christians accept the Bible as the revelation of God and the true Word of God.

I will present here the most basic essentials of the historic orthodox doctrine of the Bible. It is not my intention to give a full discussion about these matters but only to set the stage for what follows.

I will present two primary reasons for believing that the Bible is God's infallible Word. One of these reasons is the Bible's own testimony to itself. The other reason is what Jesus taught about the Old Testament Scriptures of His day. Before exploring these two realities, however, I want to set forth six major issues that will help us see how God gave His written Word and how we are to apply it to our lives.

Revelation

The Bible is God's revelation of Himself to mankind. How wonderful it is that God has spoken to us! He has not been mute.

Revelation has to do with the giving of the divine message. It is God's communication to us. We understand the revelation—namely, the inspired message—from God through reason, which is a human activity. There can be no communication from God except through revelation, and there can be no understanding of His communication to us except through reason. Revelation and reason must not be confused, for the first is the work of God, while the second is the work of people.

God has revealed Himself in nature (see, for example, Ps. 19; Rom. 1-3). But our concern here is with God's revelation in His Word.

Inspiration

God's written Word was recorded by fallible men. How then did He preserve His Word from error and omission? He did it through the Holy Spirit's superintending work. This is the Spirit's perfect guidance in which He used the writers' personalities and styles but kept them from making mistakes and from omitting what He wanted mankind to know (2 Peter 1:21).

The term *inspiration* comes from the Greek word *theopneustos.* As used in 2 Timothy 3:16, it means the Scripture was "breathed out" by God. This means the Holy Spirit of God superintended the human writers in the production of Scripture so that what they wrote was precisely what God wanted to be written.

The historical Christian view of the inspiration of Scripture includes some important distinctions. For instance, only the words printed on the original documents of Scripture are inspired, not the copies and translations of these documents. Also, the actual words of Scripture are inspired, not just the divine concepts conveyed by them. Keep in mind that only some, but not all, of the words were inspired through a process of dictation.

Authority

Because the Bible is God's revelation, the conclusion follows naturally that it is therefore authoritative. Since Scripture was breathed out by God and recorded by humans who were guided and empowered by the Holy Spirit and kept from error, the Bible is just as authoritative as the God who gave it. This means that Scripture is His absolute standard of truth. Its content is the criteria for all judgment and evaluation. What the Bible teaches is binding. There is no higher court of appeal.

Canonicity

When the sixty-six books of the Bible were written, they were inspired. The content of those books was given to the human authors by God. He revealed to the authors by His Spirit what they should write, and He kept them from error as they wrote. When the sixty-six books were received as revealed and inspired by God, and therefore possessed His authority, they became part of the Canon, namely, the collection of inspired writings.

The term *canon* comes from the Greek word *kanon,* which in turn is thought to come from the Hebrew term *ganeh,* which means a measuring rod or rule. The term signifies that which measures or that which is measured by the rule or norm. In the fourth century A.D., the Greek Christians gave *kanon* a religious meaning and applied it to the Bible, especially to the Jewish sacred writings. The Canon, then, is the list of biblical books that are regarded as inspired and accepted as authoritative for all Christians.

The Old Testament Canon. The Jews divided the Old Testament into three parts of twenty-four books.[2] The objective historical evidence indicates that the Canon of the Jews of Christ's day included all the books of the Old Testament and only those books. Jesus often referred to these by using different titles, such as "Scripture," "Law, Prophets, and Psalms," "Commandment of God," "commandments," and "the Word of God."

The Savior not only taught the revelation, inspiration, and divine authority of the Old Testament, but He also embraced the Canon of the Jews of His day. Here is evidence to support this claim.

The pronouncement of woes that Christ made upon the scribes and Pharisees included His prophecy that they would murder some of His official representatives. As a result of this crime, the religious leaders would bear the guilt of murdering all upright people "from the blood of righteous Abel to the blood of Zachariah, the son of Berechiah, whom you murdered between the temple and the altar" (Matt. 23:35; see Luke 11:51). In using this expression, Jesus referred to all the books that are in the Hebrew Canon. This observation lends support to the fact that the third section of the Old Testament—namely, the Writings, or Psalms—contained all the books that are traditionally assigned to it.

F. F. Bruce offered the following explanation:

> It is almost certain that the Bible with which He was familiar ended with the books of Chronicles, which comes right at the end of the "writings" in the Hebrew Bible. . . . Now Abel is obviously the first martyr of the Bible, but why should Zachariah come last? Because in the order of books in the Hebrew Bible he is the last martyr to be named; in 2 Chron. 24:21 we read how he was stoned while he prophesied to the people in the court of the house of the Lord.[3]

Luke 24:44 is another passage that with equal force reveals Christ's acceptance of the entire Old Testament Canon of His day. Jesus spoke the words recorded in this verse after His resurrection. The Savior had finished a conversation with two disciples, who were walking to the village of Emmaus. Verse 27 says He quoted passages from the writings of Moses and all the prophets as He explained what the Scriptures said about Him.

After Jesus left these two disciples, they went back to Jerusalem and reported what they had seen and heard to the other followers of Christ. While the two were sharing their experience, Jesus appeared to the entire group. After eating a piece of broiled fish, He said to the disciples, "these are My words which I spoke to you while I was still with you, that all things which are written about Me in the Law of Moses and the Prophets and the Psalms must be fulfilled" (v. 44).

Jesus' statement is a clear recognition of the three divisions of the Old Testament. It is also His divinely inspired declaration that all things written about Him in the Hebrew Scriptures must be fulfilled.

The New Testament Canon. The twenty-seven New Testament books were written by at least eight, and perhaps by ten, human authors over a period of about two generations. Those to whom these writings were originally addressed received the books as God's inspired message to them. They treasured these books to the same extent that they valued their Old Testament Scriptures.

God did not see fit to preserve for us the original manuscripts of the New Testament writers. Undoubtedly if these documents had been preserved, some would worship them instead of the God who gave them. Nevertheless, we do have thousands of ancient manuscripts and fragments, some of which date back to within about fifty years of the originals. Through the science of textual criticism, experts have determined what those original autographs said.

The words of Christ and the apostles were precious to the early church. Believers would read the Scriptures in public worship (see 1 Thess. 5:27), for they knew that God's Word is inspired and profitable for teaching (see 2 Tim. 3:16–17). The mutilated canons produced by Marcion and others reminded the early Christians of the need for a true canon of Scripture. And the severe persecutions believers experienced at the hands of the Roman authorities encouraged them to collect their sacred writings and make official copies of them.

The Close of the Canon

There are four major reasons for believing that the Canon of Scripture is closed. The first reason is found in two passages of Scripture. Jude 3 mentions "the faith which was once for all delivered to the saints." "The faith" refers to the body of truth taught by the apostles and held in common by all Christians. This truth is more authoritative than one's personal beliefs.

Many New Testament scholars think the epistle of Jude was

written in the A.D. 60s or 70s. This means only the writings of the apostle John had yet to be penned.

In Revelation 22:18-19, John warned against adding to or taking from "the prophecy of this book." Revelation—like the rest of Scripture—is to be distinguished from mere human words. The biblical message is so important that God promises to judge those who might distort what it says (for example, by adding things to it or omitting things from it). This warning should prompt us to handle Scripture with care and respect, and to heed what it discloses (see Deut. 4:2; 12:32).

The second reason for believing that the Canon of Scripture is closed rests on theological grounds. It is clear that God wanted to reveal Himself to humanity. To guarantee the integrity of His message, He had to superintend the process in which His revelation was written, preserved, and collected.

The third reason is that the early Christians took great care in the selection of books for the New Testament Canon. In some cases the final decision to include a particular book was delayed while the question of the document's human authorship was resolved. Except for the Council of Trent (1545–63), no serious effort has been made to add books to the Canon that had been previously rejected by the early church. Those who lived closest to the time when the New Testament documents were written agreed on the books that now appear in our Canon. The saving power of these inspired writings has been attested time and again by Christians.

The fourth reason for believing that the Canon of Scripture is closed is that there are no more prophetic or apostolic spokespersons for God. Those who had these special gifts and abilities passed from the scene of history long ago (see 1 Cor. 13:10).

Illumination

Illumination is that ministry of the Holy Spirit that helps the believer to understand and apply the truth of Scripture. The Spirit sheds light upon the meaning of the biblical text so that the child of God can properly interpret and act upon it.

Only those who have the Holy Spirit can experience His work of illumination. In contrast, non-Christians are steered by their own natural inclinations. Because they depend solely on wisdom derived from the world, the things of the Spirit seem foolish to them. As long as they reject the assistance of the Spirit, they will remain spiritually blind to the revelation of God (1 Cor. 2:14).

After Jesus' resurrection, He shed light on the meaning of Scripture to the two disciples walking to the village of Emmaus (Luke 24:13-35). He enabled them to grasp the significance of the Old Testament and see how He fulfilled its prophecies about the Messiah (for example, passages such as Pss. 16; 22; and Isa. 53). The Holy Spirit continues this work of illumination (John 16:7-11).

Interpretation

Whereas illumination is the divine side of understanding the Bible, interpretation is the human side. The science of interpretation is called hermeneutics. Interpretation has to do with arriving at the meaning of and expounding Scripture.

Because of the multifaceted character of the Bible, the meaning of some of its passages is not immediately plain. That is why various methods of biblical interpretation have been set forth throughout the history of the church.[4]

Evangelicals generally agree on what it means to interpret the Bible, though the question of exactly how to interpret Scripture has led to some differences of opinion. They agree that every believer should be under the Spirit's control and guidance as they interpret Scripture (see Eph. 5:18; 2 Peter 1:20-21). However, evangelicals have not agreed on which method of interpretation to use consistently.

Generally speaking, evangelicals have favored a literal or normal approach to hermeneutics. But there are differences among them regarding the extent to which that method is applied. Within the broader Christian community, others have favored a spiritualizing or allegorizing method of interpretation. These two approaches are briefly discussed below.

The literal or normal method. Literal interpretation means, "interpretation that gives to every word the same meaning it would have in normal usage, whether employed in writing, speaking, or thinking."[5] This method is sometimes called the historical grammatical method.[6]

There are three reasons one can give in support of using a consistently literal hermeneutic—biblical, logical, and philosophical.[7] Concerning the biblical reason, it has been said, "The prophecies of the Old Testament concerning the first coming of Christ—His birth, His rearing, His ministry, His death, His resurrection—were all fulfilled literally. There is no non literal fulfillment of these prophecies in the New Testament. This argues strongly for the literal method."[8]

Concerning the logical reason, it has been argued: "If one does not use the plain, normal, or literal method of interpretation, all objectivity is lost." What check would there be on the variety of interpretations the imagination of people could produce if there were not an objective standard that the literal principles provide? And, "philosophically the purpose of language itself seems to require a literal interpretation. Language was given by God for the purpose of being able to communicate with mankind."[9]

Recently some who still wish to be classified as literalists and want to be identified within the fold of the grammatical-historical hermeneutic have embraced what they call "complementary hermeneutics." By this they mean, "The New Testament does introduce change and advance; it does not merely repeat Old Testament revelation. In making complementary additions, however, it does not jettison old promises."[10]

The spiritualizing or allegorical method. Allegorization is the method of interpreting a literary text by using the literal sense as the vehicle for arriving at a secondary sense, one that is supposedly more spiritual and more profound in nature. After arriving at this secondary meaning, the literal meaning is discarded.

Those who believe the Bible is God's infallible Word do not use the allegorical method as they interpret the text to better understand the great essentials of the faith. The spiritualizing approach is used mostly by some evangelicals in those portions of Scripture that deal with the doctrine of last things.

In summary, the six cardinal issues related to our view of the Bible that were discussed above are visualized below:

REVELATION

INSPIRATION

AUTHORITY

CANONICITY

ILLUMINATION

INTERPRETATION

Notes

1. Selected portions of this material have been taken from the author's *Handbook of Evangelical Theology* (Grand Rapids: Kregel, 1995) and *A Biblical Case for Total Inerrancy: How Jesus Viewed the Old Testament* (Grand Rapids: Kregel, 1998).
2. The threefold division of the Old Testament and the books included in each division are as follows:

    I. The Law (5 books)
       Genesis, Exodus, Leviticus, Numbers, Deuteronomy
    II. The Prophets (8 books)
       A. The Former Prophets (4 books)
          Joshua, Judges, Samuel, Kings
       B. The Latter Prophets (4 books)
          1. Major (3 books)
             Isaiah, Jeremiah, Ezekiel
          2. Minor (1 book) The Twelve:
             Hosea, Joel, Amos, Obadiah, Jonah, Micah, Nahum, Habakkuk, Zephaniah, Haggai, Zechariah, Malachi
    III. The Writings (11 books)
       A. Poetical (3 books)
          Psalms, Proverbs, Job
       B. Five Rolls (5 books)
          Song of Solomon, Ruth, Lamentations, Ecclesiastes, Esther
       C. Historical (3 books)
          Daniel, Ezra-Nehemiah, Chronicles

3. F. F. Bruce, *The Books and the Parchments* (London: Pickering and Inglis, 1950), 96. A problem exists in the reference to Zechariah by Christ. The passage in 2 Chronicles, to which Christ apparently makes mention, speaks of Zechariah as the son of Jehoiada, rather than the son of Berechiah, which is the New Testament statement. Lange lists several possible explanations for this difficulty (*Commentary on the Holy Scriptures*, VIII [Grand Rapids: Zondervan, 1960], 414–15). C. F. Keil also acknowledges the difference in the names of the fathers but still attributes Christ's reference to the 2 Chronicles 24 murder (*Chronicles*, 418). Gaussen, in his classic *Theopneustia: The Plenary Inspiration of the Holy Scriptures* (Chicago: Colportage, n.d.), also gives a detailed explanation of the difficulty (237–41).
4. See J. Dwight Pentecost, *Things To Come* (Findlay, Ohio: Dunham, 1958), 1–63, for an excellent survey of the interpretation of Scripture.

5. Charles C. Ryrie, *Dispensationalism* (Chicago: Moody, 1995), 80.
6. See Roy B. Zuck, *Basix Bible Interpretation* (Wheaton, Ill.: Victor, 1991), for extensive discussion on defense of this method of interpretation.
7. Ryrie, *Dispensationalism,* 81.
8. J. P. Lange, *Commentary on the Holy Scripture: Revelation* (New York: Scribner's and Sons, 1960), 98.
9. Ryrie, *Dispensationalism,* 81.
10. Craig A. Blaising and Darrell L. Bock, "Dispensationalism, Israel, and the Church: Assessment and Dialogue," *Dispensationalism, Israel and the Church* (Grand Rapids: Zondervan, 1992), 392–93.

An example of the complementary hermeneutic is the way progressive dispensationalists, who hold to this hermeneutic, understand the Davidic Covenant, which is recorded in 2 Samuel 7:4–17. While God originally gave the covenant to Israel alone, it is maintained that in the New Testament He also gave the covenant to the church. This view also argues that Christ's position at the right hand of the Father is the partial fulfillment of God's promises to David. According to this view, the Savior is now on the throne (see Heb. 1:3).

See also Ryrie, *Dispensationalism,* for a critique of the view.

CHAPTER 2

The Testimony of the Bible to Itself

IN THE HISTORY OF THE church a number of theories have been advanced regarding how the Bible came to be inspired.[1] All of these hypotheses attempt to answer the question of *how* the human writers were used by God so that errors did not come into the text, since all the human writers were members of Adam's sinful race.

It is clear that imperfect people committed the revelation of God to writing. The dual authorship of the Bible is stressed in passages such as these: "David in the Spirit" (Matt. 22:43); "The Holy Spirit rightly spoke through Isaiah the prophet to your fathers" (Acts 28:25); and, "men moved by the Holy Spirit spoke from God" (2 Peter 1:21). The question is this: How were the human authors kept from error and omission as they recorded God's infallible and inerrant message?

There is a view regarding the Bible's inspiration that does not attempt to answer the question of *how* God employed imperfect people to record His revelation without error. That view is called the verbal plenary inspiration view of Scripture. Instead of trying to find out *how* God did what He did, the view explains *what* resulted from God's use of fallible people.[2]

God supernaturally directed the writers of Scripture so that, without excluding their human intelligence, their individuality, their literary style, their personal feelings, or any other human factor, His own complete and coherent message to humanity was recorded with perfect accuracy in the words of the original manuscripts. The result was an infallible record of God's revelation.

This infallibility is *verbal,* which means it extends to the words the human authors used. This infallibility is also *plenary,* which means it extends to the whole of divine revelation. In summary, the inspiration of Scripture includes all its contents; and the total inerrancy of Scripture includes every word recorded on the original documents.

In this brief survey of the Bible's testimony to its own

inspiration, infallibility, and inerrancy, four key passages will be presented—2 Timothy 3:16-17; 2 Peter 1:19-21; 1 Timothy 5:18; and 2 Peter 3:16. Some reject the Bible's claims to be inspired by alleging that it is resorting to circular reasoning. These scoffers assert the passages are first assumed to be true and then what they claim is accepted as true. On numerous occasions conservative Bible scholars have painstakingly explored and rejected this objection to what God's Word says about itself.[3]

Surely our view of the Bible must be the view Scripture itself teaches. John Murray stated the issue clearly when he wrote the following:

> The nature of faith is acceptance on the basis of testimony, and the ground of faith is therefore testimony or evidence. In this matter it is the evidence God has provided, and God provides the evidence in His Word, the Bible. This means simply that the basis of faith in the Bible is the witness the Bible itself bears to the fact that it is God's Word, and our faith that it is infallible must rest upon no other basis than the witness the Bible bears to this fact. If the Bible does not witness to its own fallibility, then we have no right to believe that it is infallible. If it does bear witness to its infallibility then our faith in it must rest upon that witness, however much difficulty may be entertained with this belief. If this position with respect to the ground of faith in Scripture is abandoned, then appeal to the Bible for the ground of faith in any other doctrine must also be abandoned.[4]

2 Timothy 3:16–17

All Scripture is inspired by God and profitable for teaching, for reproof, for correction, for training in righteousness; so that the man of God may be adequate, equipped for every good work.

This passage teaches the divine origin of the Scriptures. The Greek term *pasa* may be translated "all" or "every." And the Greek term *grapha* means "writing" or a "written document."[5] Simply stated, Paul told Timothy that *all* Scripture comes from God and is inspired by Him.

The entire Old Testament is certainly involved, for that is what Timothy had been taught from his youth (v. 15). By application, the New Testament is also involved, for it too is called Scripture

(see 1 Tim. 5:18). Clearly, Paul was referring to the words of
Scripture, not just to ideas and oral proclamations based on them.

2 Peter 1:19–21

So we have the prophetic word made more sure, to which
you do well to pay attention as to a lamp shining in a dark
place, until the day dawns and the morning star arises in
your hearts. But know this first of all, that no prophecy
of Scripture is a matter of one's own interpretation, for
no prophecy was ever made by an act of human will, but
men moved by the Holy Spirit spoke from God.

These verses teach that as the human authors of Scripture wrote,
they were protected by the Holy Spirit from all error and omission.
The divine origin of Scripture is assumed here by Peter. The apostle
used this truth to help us understand how the Spirit kept the
human authors from making mistakes as they recorded God's
infallible message.

The writers were "moved," or borne along, by the Holy Spirit
of God as they penned their works. The message was not theirs
but God's. Those who wrote holy Scripture were not God-
breathed and were not inspired. But what they wrote while under
the Spirit's control was God-breathed and inspired.[6]

1 Timothy 5:18

For the Scripture says, "You shall not muzzle the ox while
he is threshing," and "The laborer is worthy of his wages."

In Paul's instruction to Timothy, he quoted Deuteronomy 25:4
and Luke 10:7. The significance of this observation is that the apostle
called both passages "Scripture," which implies that he assigned equal
inspiration to both the Old Testament and the New Testament.

When Christ used the term rendered "Scripture," He referred
only to the Old Testament (see, for example, John 7:38). After
Christ's resurrection and ascension, however, biblical writers used
the term to refer to the writings of both testaments. And early
church leaders made no distinction in their use of the term.[7]

2 Peter 3:16

As also in all his letters, speaking in them of these things,
in which are some things hard to understand, which the
untaught and unstable distort, as they do also the rest of
the Scriptures, to their own destruction.

In this verse Peter put the writings of Paul on par with the rest of Scripture. Because Paul's writings encompass a large portion of the New Testament, this is a major verse in support of the inspiration of the entire New Testament.[8]

When all these four key passages are taken together, they make a strong case for the truth that the New Testament Canon, along with the Old Testament Canon, is God's infallible and inerrant Word. There are also many more assertions recorded throughout the Bible that affirm its divine inspiration. We can rest assured that God's own complete and coherent message to mankind is recorded in Scripture with perfect accuracy.

In summary, we have seen that throughout the Old Testament there are claims to its divine authority. Each section of it (namely, the Law and the Prophets; see Matt. 5:17; Luke 24:27) as well as the entire Old Testament bear the inspiration of God. We have also seen that throughout the New Testament there are claims to the inspiration of the Old Testament. And there are specific claims for the inspiration of the New Testament itself.[9]

Notes

1. For a brief explanation of the major views—namely, the natural inspiration view, the mystical inspiration view, the mechanical dictation view, the partial inspiration view, the neo-orthodox view, and the inspired purpose or denial of total inerrancy view—see Charles C. Ryrie, *Ryrie Study Bible Expanded Edition, New American Standard Bible: 1995 Update* (Chicago: Moody, 1995), 2079-80.

2. See Norman Geisler and William Nix, *A General Introduction to the Bible,* revised and enlarged (Chicago: Moody, 1986), 45-47, for explanations of the process of inspiration.

3. John Gerstner sets forth the testimony of divinely commissioned messengers as the basis for Bible inerrancy. These are the steps of this argument:
   1. There is a God.
   2. People were made in God's image as rational creatures.
   3. As such, God designed people to make their choices on the basis of evidence.
   4. The evidence for the inspiration of the Bible is as follows:
      a. People have appeared in history with powers that only God could have given them (for example, the ability to perform miracles).
      b. Miracles are God's seal to mark people unmistakably as His messengers.

      c. God's message is indubitably true.

      d. Therefore, the inspiration of the Bible is indubitably true.

4. John Murray, "The Attestation of Scripture," *Infallible Word,* A Symposium by the Members of the Faculty of Westminster Theological Seminary, 3d revised printing (Philadelphia: Presbyterian and Reformed, 1946), 8–9.

5. For a thorough study of all the key words in this crucial passage, see Geisler and Nix, 34–36.

6. Ibid., 41–42.

7. See Homer A. Kent Jr., *The Pastoral Epistles* (Chicago: Moody, 1982), 176–78.

8. See Michael Green, *The Second Epistle of Peter and the Epistle of Jude* (Grand Rapids: Eerdmans, 1973), 146–48.

9. See Geisler and Nix, 65–97, for a thorough discussion of these points.

CHAPTER 3

Christ's View of the Scriptures

BEYOND THE GENERAL considerations given in the previous chapters for the Bible's testimony to its own inspiration, we will now examine the testimony of Christ to the revelation and inspiration of the Old Testament and to the promised work of the Holy Spirit in revealing and inspiring the New Testament.[1] We will begin by noting how extensively Christ used Old Testament Scripture in His ministry.

Christ's Use of Scripture

Our Lord used only the Hebrew Canon of His day, which consisted of the same thirty-nine books as our Old Testament, though they were arranged differently. Jesus rejected as authoritative the Apocrypha as well as the verbal and written teachings of the religious leaders.

Jesus often appealed extensively to the Scriptures available at the time. His use of the Old Testament extended to the whole of divine revelation then extant as well as to individual parts, words, and even letters that make up those words.

Christ's Teaching About the Origin of the Scripture

Did Christ have anything to say about the origin of Scripture? Indeed He did. He taught clearly, emphatically, and extensively that Scripture originated with God Himself. The Lord is the One who gave the revelation to people. This means the Bible did not come from the creative genius of men; rather, all Scripture came from God alone.

The way Christ referred to the Old Testament indicates that He believed it came from God. For instance, Jesus called the Old Testament the "Word of God." He also referred to it as "Law" and "Scripture." Jesus never questioned any of the Jews of His day about their high and exalted view that the Old Testament is indeed God's Word.

Jesus' acceptance of the historical factualness of people, places, events, and miracles recorded in the Old Testament supports the claim that He had a high view of its divine origin and inspiration. Noteworthy examples include God's creation of humanity (Matt. 19:4), the worldwide flood of Noah's day (Matt. 24:37–39), the burning bush that Moses saw (Mark 12:26), the historical existence of the prophet Elijah (Luke 4:25) and Naaman the leper (Luke 4:27), and the divine provision of manna (John 6:32).

Specific passages recording Christ's use of the Old Testament further substantiate the claim that He believed the sacred Hebrew writings came from God. For instance, on one occasion the Pharisees and scribes asked Christ why His disciples did not heed the rules and regulations of their Jewish ancestors (Matt. 15:1-2). In Jesus' response, He attributed to God the commandments that Moses had written (vv. 3–6; see Exod. 20:12; Deut. 5:16).

On another occasion the Sadducees—an important Jewish group in His day who did not believe in the Resurrection—questioned Jesus about His views concerning this doctrine. They asked Him to respond to a preposterous scenario they had concocted (Matt. 22:23–28). In his answer, Christ quoted from Exodus 3:6 (see Matt. 22:32–39). Although Moses was the human author of the passage, the Savior attributed the words to God.

Jesus quoted from the Pentateuch because the Sadducees particularly valued this portion of the Old Testament as being authoritative. Christ noted that the Lord's reference to Himself in the present tense—"I am the God of Abraham"—pointed to the reality of the Resurrection and the eternal life that all believers enjoy through faith in the Son. All this implies that the patriarchs continued to live in God's presence and in the future will be resurrected.

Christ's Affirmation of All Scripture Being Divinely Inspired

Christ's use of Scripture and His teaching that it came from God both verify that He believed it was inspired, or God-breathed. In addition to this, He also specifically addressed the *extent* of the inspiration of Scripture.

I will begin with Jesus' affirmation of the divine inspiration of the *entire* Old Testament. Christ viewed the sacred Hebrew writings as an organic whole. In His day the Old Testament was divided into three sections—the Law, the Prophets, and the Psalms. Jesus sometimes used this threefold designation (see, for example, Luke 24:44). On other occasions, He used the word "law" to refer to the entire Hebrew corpus (see, for example, Matt. 5:17–18). In both cases He affirmed the divine inspiration of the entire Old Testament.

Christ also affirmed the divine inspiration of *various parts* of the Old Testament. For instance, when He used the label "Law, Prophets, and Psalms" to refer to the entire Hebrew corpus, He was at the same time affirming the inspiration of these three individual sections. And in each of the many instances when Christ spoke about what had to be fulfilled concerning Him, He affirmed the inspiration of the particular passage He cited.

Christ further affirmed the divine inspiration of the *words* recorded in the verses throughout the Old Testament. I will present four examples to support this claim.

First, Christ's answer to the Sadducees, which I referred to above, shows that He believed Scripture came from God, not man. The Savior's response also makes evident His belief that the words of Scripture originated from God (Matt. 22:23–33).

Second, Christ's answer to the Pharisees, which is recorded in Matthew 22:43–45, confirms His view that the words of Scripture are God-breathed. Because the terms and phrases recorded in the Hebrew sacred writings came from God, they are infallible, inerrant, and divinely authoritative.

If this were not true, why would Christ have been so specific in His interpretation of Scripture? His response to the Pharisees rests, in part, on the presence of the second term rendered "Lord" in Psalm 110:1. His point was that the Messiah is both the human descendant of David and the divine Lord.

Third, Christ's answer to the Jewish authorities regarding His claim to be God, which is recorded in John 10:34–38, indicates that Jesus held the words of Scripture to be divinely inspired. To defend His assertion about His divinity, He quoted from Psalm 82:6. Note that His argument rests on the presence of the Hebrew noun translated "gods." In fact, Christ's logic hinges on the presence of the plural form of the noun, as opposed the singular form of it.

Fourth, Jesus' comments in Matthew 5:17–18 regarding the law of Moses verifies that He held to the divine inspiration of the entire Old Testament. In fact, He maintained that even the small markings, such as the stroke of a Hebrew character, were inspired by God.

Jesus solemnly affirmed that "until heaven and earth pass away, not the smallest letter or stroke shall pass from the Law until all is accomplished" (v. 18). "Smallest letter" might also be rendered "jot," and refers to the ninth letter of the Greek alphabet (ι). This is the nearest Greek equivalent for the Hebrew *yôdh* (ˑ), the smallest letter of the Hebrew alphabet.

The word translated "stroke" might also be rendered as "tittle." There is some uncertainty as to what the "tittle" refers. Most likely it relates to the tiny projections stemming off from Hebrew letters that distinguish one character from another one. An English illustration might be the dot appearing above the letter "i" or the line across the letter "t." The point of our Lord's words is that even the minutest portions of the Hebrew characters appearing in the words of the original autographs were divinely inspired.

I previously noted that Christ's teaching made provision for the divine inspiration of the New Testament Canon. This includes the individual books as well as the words and phrases appearing in those documents. For example, in John 16:12–15, Christ related that He had more truths He wanted to teach His disciples; however, they were not yet ready to receive them. That is why He would send the Holy Spirit to disclose and teach further truths He wanted them to know (see also John 14:26; 15:26–27).

It is clear that Jesus believed and taught that the Old Testament is the inspired Word of God. He also believed that the same Holy Spirit who inspired the Hebrew writings would superintend the process by which the inspired New Testament Canon would come into existence.

Summary

As Christians, we want to learn more about the God revealed in the Bible. Why do we believe this book is God's inspired Word? One reason rests on what the Bible says about itself. It claims that its words are God-breathed. Although Scripture was written by men, God is the source and ultimate author of what it reveals.

Another reason we believe the Bible is the Word of God rests on what Jesus said about Scripture. From the beginning of His public ministry to His death and resurrection He repeatedly affirmed that all Scripture is divinely inspired. Because the Bible is the infallible, inerrant, and authoritative Word of God, let us study it diligently and apply its truths to our lives.

Notes

1. For an extensive presentation of Christ's view of the Bible, see the author's *A Biblical Case for Total Inerrancy: How Jesus Viewed the Old Testament* (Grand Rapids: Kregel, 1998). See also J. W. Wenham, *Our Lord's View of the Old Testament* (London: Tyndale, 1953), 7.

PART 2

THE GOD OF THE BIBLE

CHAPTER 4

In the Beginning

THE BIBLE REFERS TO three different "beginnings." The first one opens the book of Genesis and concerns the beginning of time and God's creation of the world. The second "beginning" is mentioned in John 1:1. In this verse we learn that the Word—Jesus Christ—eternally preexisted before the dawn of time. The third "beginning" appears in 1 John 1:1 and echoes John 1:1. These two verses both reveal that the eternal Word became a flesh-and-blood man. This means Christ is fully human and fully divine.

The first of these three "beginnings" is fundamental to understanding everything else revealed in the Bible. Genesis 1:1 says, "In the beginning God created the heavens and the earth." Perhaps no more important words have ever been spoken or penned. Compton, the physicist, calls them the most wonderful words ever written.

All else in the Bible stands or falls upon the validity and truthfulness of the words of this verse. And the study of the Person and work of God is of inestimable value for all who would know the truth. Without a proper understanding of God and His plan, everything else in the Bible and in life becomes hazy and meaningless. A biblically defensible understanding of God provides a basis for understanding oneself and one's responsibility before the Lord and mankind.

If the first words recorded in the Bible are the most fundamental ones ever spoken or penned, it logically follows that the study of God is the most pertinent topic that could be investigated, for He is the primary subject of Genesis 1:1. This verse makes no argument for the existence of God. It is understood as an absolute fact.

But these days God's existence is either denied or His nonexistence is assumed in the classroom, the lecture hall, the pulpit, and the printed page. The anti-God philosophy of atheistic evolution undergirds all of modem education. We are told both directly and indirectly that "God" has died.

Given this prevailing mind-set, it follows that people on the street soon see no need for God and seek to get on with life without Him. From every quarter and in every walk of life people live and learn as though God did not exist. In this sophisticated and highly mechanized nuclear age in which we live, they see no need for the God of the Bible.

Many people feel they cannot believe in God since there is so much sin, suffering, and injustice in the world. One of their arguments is that if a sovereign and all-powerful God truly exists, He should do something to fix our troubled world. Another argument is that if a personal God exists and people are the product of His creative hand, He must be wicked and cruel, for there is so much evil in His creation.

The basic fallacy of these and similar arguments is the failure to take into account that people have willfully chosen to sin and break fellowship with their divine Creator. Though people still bear in themselves the image of God, that image has been marred terribly by sin. Thus, though God is personal and He made man in His image, His relationship with us has been broken by our sin.[1]

Based on what I have said, the dilemma facing humanity should be clear. At no time in history has there been a greater need for the people of God to stand up and be counted as His spiritual children. The One they worship and serve is the God of Abraham, Isaac, and Jacob, the God and Father of our Lord Jesus Christ, and the God revealed in Scripture.

Attempted Definitions of God

Definitions Without Scriptural Basis

Can God be defined? The answer is a qualified "yes." It is possible and necessary to use reasonable definitions of God to help us recognize His incomparable and exalted position above all other entities. And it is possible to affirm His characteristics and attributes, which are infinitely perfect in nature.

Of course, any and all such definitions we use will be imperfect and reflect our limited abilities to form them. That is why it is impossible for anyone to construct a statement that will adequately and completely define God. Such a declaration, were it possible, would so limit God that He would cease to be divine. For that reason we must say that God cannot be completely and perfectly defined.

Before attempting to present a definition of God that I believe is based upon Scripture, it will be good for us to consider briefly a sampling of some anti-biblical and therefore unacceptable definitions. The need for this is underscored in an article that appeared in the February, 1968 edition of *McCall's* magazine.

The author wrote about the widespread confusion and disbelief in the pulpits of the United States. The information in the article was based on a survey of 3,000 Protestant clergy concerning their theological beliefs. The results of this survey disclosed the following about what religious leaders believed concerning God: "A considerable number rejected altogether the idea of a personal God. God, they said, was 'the Ground of Being,' 'the Force of Life,' 'the Principle of Love,' 'the Ultimate Reality,' and so forth."

Clergy are not the only ones who affirm something about God. Virtually all people—loud demands to the contrary notwithstanding—believe in some kind of god. For instance, religious polls suggest that almost everyone believes in some kind of ultimate reality or power that everything else depends upon for existence. And people throughout the world often speak about "mother nature" or about "the man upstairs."

A large and powerful radio station regularly concluded its late night country music show with, "May the force be with you." It's clear this was intended to be a reference to deity. This aphorism and others like it are crude definitions of mankind's concept of the divine. Many people, of course, bow before any number of entities in "worship" without attempting to set forth a formal definition of God.

Other people, who are perhaps more sophisticated in their thinking, have attempted to set forth definitions of God. For example, the Church of Jesus Christ of Latter-day Saints—the Mormons—sets forth this definition: "God is perfect, exalted man with a literal flesh and bones body." The Christian Science definition is this: "God is eternal, impersonal Principle, Law, Truth, Spirit, and Idea. All that really is, is divine. God is spirit; there is no matter. God is good; there is no evil, sin, sickness or death."

Rationalistic philosophers have defined God as "a self existing being, in whom the ground of the reality of the world is found." Others have said, "God is a being who has the ground of his existence in himself." Those who embrace a false and unbiblical mysticism have said, "God is totally unlike man, nature, or abstract principles. God is not like anything we know. We can only say, 'God is not this,' and 'God is not that.' We cannot say what God is."

Definitions with Scriptural Basis

When we carefully examine the above definitions of God and compare them with biblical truth, they are found wanting and in serious error. Perhaps the best and most biblical definition of God is to be found in the Westminster Confession of Faith of the Reformed Churches. Chapter two of the Confession begins:

> There is but one only living and true God, who is infinite in being and perfection, a most pure spirit, invisible, without body, parts, or passions, immutable, immense, eternal, incomprehensible, almighty, most wise, most holy, most free, most absolute, working all things according to the counsel of his own immutable and most righteous will, for his own glory; most loving, gracious, merciful, long-suffering, abundant in goodness and truth, forgiving iniquity, transgression, and sin; the rewarder of them that diligently seek him; and withal most just and terrible in his judgments; hating all sin, and who will by no means clear the guilty.

This classic and orthodox definition has much to commend it. But because it is somewhat cumbersome, it cannot serve as an easy-to-remember definition. The one serious flaw in the above definition is its reference to God as "a most pure spirit." God is not a spirit in the way the above quote defines it. John 4:24, from which the Westminster statement comes, should be translated "God is Spirit." The indefinite article does not appear in the Greek New Testament.

With full recognition of the impossibility of giving a complete and exhaustive definition of God and using the old Westminster definition as the basis for a new one, I suggest the following: God is Spirit. He is a living and active divine Person who is infinite, eternal and unchangeable in His being, wisdom, power, holiness, justice, goodness, truth, and love. He can enjoy fellowship with persons He has created in His own image and redeemed by His grace, and He always acts in harmony with His perfect nature.

The Importance of Communion with God

Far more important than coming up with a perfect definition for God is the enjoyment of communion with Him. Faith in what Christ did at Calvary is the basis for our fellowship with God (see 1 John 1:1–3). We learn to draw near to God as a result of knowing and understanding Him better from studying His Word, the Bible (see Ps. 19:7–14).

These days society constantly pressures us to stockpile material things, and there is a prevailing anti-God sentiment within our communities. These factors can distort our understanding of God. In a world filled with sin, corruption, and injustice, it is easy for us to become insensitive to God's absolute holiness and His love for us.

In some ways the problems of our age are not much different from those that existed in the days of Isaiah the prophet. For instance, people living near Israel were forsaking the God of the Bible. Even the Lord's own people were turning away from Him and worshiping deities of their own making. The idolatrous culture in which they lived had its effect upon them as much as ours can have upon us.

Isaiah undoubtedly was discouraged by what he saw. It would have been natural for him to feel alone and perhaps begin to wonder whether God had not forgotten him and His chosen people.

God revealed Himself to Isaiah in a life-transforming vision (Isa. 6:1-4). There are three observations worth mentioning. First, the prophet "saw the Lord sitting on a throne," and His long robe filled the temple. God was ruling in the affairs of mankind and was in perfect control of the universe. Mighty seraphim hovered around His throne and described Him as the absolutely holy One.

We can only imagine what went through Isaiah's mind as he experienced this vision. Though Isaiah's world was filled with evil and though he may have felt perplexed about the enigmas of life, he had to acknowledge that God was in absolute control. The prophet could also see that the Lord had not forsaken His chosen people.

Second, Isaiah's encounter with the Lord proved to be a life-changing experience for him. God's presence made him realize the depth of his sinfulness. Seeing even the seraph humbly covering themselves before the Lord must have reminded the prophet of his moral imperfection (Isa. 6:5).

The prophet was brought to this view of himself because he had seen "the King, the Lord of hosts." The prophet did not physically see God's innermost nature with the naked eye. Rather, Isaiah was able to perceive the Lord in appearance seated upon a throne. By comparing himself with God, not with others around him, Isaiah came to a deeper awareness of himself as a sinner. There is nothing that will remove pride and a faulty view of sin quicker than a fresh appreciation of the absolute holiness of God and our utter fallenness as people.

Third, after the Lord cleansed Isaiah of his iniquities, He commissioned him to his prophetic ministry. We do not know how Isaiah heard the voice of the Lord (v. 8). What is important is that when the triune God called him, he responded with a clear and immediate answer. Isaiah's faithful response indicates that a real change had occurred in his life.

How every child of God could benefit from such a life-transforming encounter with the Lord! But God no longer reveals Himself in this way. In times past, He spoke in different ways "to the fathers in the prophets," but now with finality He has "spoken to us in his Son" (Heb. 1:1-2). Thus through Christ, the living Word, and through the Bible, the written Word, we too can know and commune with God, the God of the Bible.

Placing Our Study in Perspective

Every Christian doctrine has its foundation in the doctrine of God—namely, the teaching about His existence and work. It is impossible to truly understand any of the other great truths of Scripture apart from a proper understanding of the Person and work of the God of the Bible. All other truth is related in one way or another to Him. To try to understand any other truth in the Bible without first coming to firm and biblical convictions about God would be like trying to construct a building without a proper foundation.

The following diagram is intended to depict visually what I have been saying about the importance of the doctrine of God and its relation to all the other doctrines. This diagram should not be taken as recommending a sequential order in which to study the doctrines of the faith. The diagram should also not be seen as an attempt to elevate one particular doctrine or to minimize others.

| Doctrine of Christ |
| Doctrine of Last Things |
| Doctrine of the Holy Spirit |
| Doctrine of the Church |
| Doctrine of Salvation |
| Doctrine of Humanity, Angels, and Sin |
| Doctrine of Scripture |

Instead, the diagram's primary purpose is to show that all other biblical studies depend upon one's understanding of God and His Word for their validity. Additionally, the diagram is intended to show that the Person and work of Christ is like the capstone of a superstructure, with God and the Bible being the foundation.

Doctrines of God and the Bible

The Doctrine of Scripture. The relationship that exists between the doctrine of the written Word and the doctrine of God is easily discerned. Beginning with the doctrine of holy Scripture, it is surely true that without belief in the God of the Bible that book becomes just an ordinary text and the fabrication of disillusioned people. A proper understanding of God causes one to see that it was He who controlled the writers of Scripture, keeping them from all error and omission. And it was He who inspired what the human authors wrote.

The Bible is the only written revelation from God. Without this holy book, people would be woefully ignorant of God, themselves, and all else that exists. They would not even be able to interpret God's revelation of Himself in creation without His revelation of Himself in Scripture. Biblical Christianity finds its bedrock in the doctrines of God and the Bible. A denial of the inspiration of the Bible—a book that claims to come from God— is to call God, the giver of Scripture, a liar. His character is impugned when His inspired Word is not believed.

The Doctrine of Humanity. Since God is the Creator of humanity, there is a definite relationship between them and Him. Scripture not only reveals that God brought Adam and Eve into existence but also that He created them in His own image (Gen. 1:26-27). Thus the existence of the human race presupposes the existence of God.

The Doctrine of Angels. The Bible reveals that God created the angels (Ps. 148:2, 5). They are His ministering spirits (Heb. 1:14). The only inspired source of information about angels appears in Scripture, which came from God and possesses His authority.

The Doctrine of Sin. Unquestionably the doctrine of sin depends upon the doctrine of God, if it is to be properly understood. In order to define sin there must be a standard, a norm, or criterion of judgment. God Himself is that criterion.

Sin means, among other things, "missing the mark." It is

anything that does not conform to God's holy character. Sin could not be recognized as such apart from God and His standard.

When the archer takes up his bow and arrow, he seeks to hit the bull's-eye. If he misses it, we say he missed the right mark. Of course, this means he also hit the wrong mark. But the point is that he missed the true mark. So it is in the experience of people. God is the mark, and we sin when we fail to meet His absolutely perfect moral standard.

The Doctrine of Salvation. What about the doctrine of salvation? Is it also related to and dependent upon the doctrine of God? It goes without saying that if there were no God, there could be no deliverance from sin. God the Father sent God the Son to provide salvation for sinners. All would be hopelessly lost apart from the God of the Bible and the Lord Jesus Christ, His Son, whom He sent to redeem the lost (John 17:3).

The Doctrine of the Church. The church, which is Christ's body (1 Cor. 12:27; Eph. 1:22–23), is composed of sinners God has called out from a life of iniquity and condemnation and has redeemed by His grace. Scripture similarly defines a local church as a group of called-out ones who have organized and meet regularly in a given area to carry out the purposes of God, as they understand them.

Thus, both the local and universal church are dependent upon God. From eternity past He planned for the existence of these institutions. God the Son is the resurrected Head and God the Spirit is the life-giving power of the church, which is Christ's body. Both these members of the Godhead occupy the same position relative to the local assembly as they do with respect to the universal body of Christ.

The Doctrine of the Holy Spirit. The Holy Spirit is the third Member of the blessed Trinity. Everywhere in Scripture the Person and work of the Holy Spirit are dependent upon belief in the God of Scripture. A denial of God's existence would, at the same time, mean a denial of the existence and ministry of the Holy Spirit.

The Doctrine of Last Things. If the world were run by chance or happenstance, there would be no possibility of believing in future events with any degree of certainty. The Bible's testimony is that God, who has revealed Himself in Scripture, controls and will consummate history. Thus it is possible to speak intelligently about last things when we understand that the God of the Bible is working out His wise and all-inclusive plan in the affairs of mankind.

The Doctrine of Christ. The Lord Jesus Christ is God manifest in the flesh (John 1:18). Through the incarnation, God became perfect man. He clothed Himself with humanity in the Person of Jesus Christ. Failure to embrace the God of the Bible makes it impossible to believe in the Christ whom Scripture reveals.

Summary

It should be clear from this brief survey that it is absolutely essential to think rightly about God, for all of our doctrinal beliefs depend upon our doing so. In addition, maintaining a proper view of God is basic to practical living. What we think about God reveals much about what we think about ourselves. Further, a proper understanding of the God of the Bible will affect all that we do and say. Moreover, holding to a correct doctrine of God will determine what we accomplish in our lives and what we will become for His glory.

Either people worship the God of Scripture or they venerate some false god. Idolatry involves far more than kneeling before a visible object that people have made. Idolatry also involves our thinking, for it begins in the mind before it ever leads to an act of worship. Corrupt thoughts about God result in the committing of corrupt deeds (see Rom. 1). Many professing Christians who are repulsed even by the thought of bowing before an image that people have made do in fact worship false gods—for example, success, material gain, a friend or lover, and so on.

Is God Necessary?

One of Augustine's famous pronouncements was that the human heart is restless until it finds its rest in God. The celebrated church father of the fifth century was right. People the world over are incurably religious. All, from the least educated and sophisticated to the highest educated and sophisticated, insist on worshiping someone or something. Because of this, I honestly do not believe there is such a thing as a genuine atheist, for those who profess to be one have made their mind their god.

The words of some of the most adamant deniers of God's existence often make the strongest case for humanity's need for Him. Here is a sampling to illustrate my point.[2] Voltaire, the French skeptic, is reported to have said, "If there were no God it would be necessary for man to invent one." Jean-Paul Sartre, a present-day atheist philosopher, conceded, "I reached out for religion, I longed for it, it was the remedy. Had it denied me, I would have invented it myself."[3] He went on to admit, "I needed God."[4]

Albert Camus, a French atheist, said, "Nothing can discourage the appetite for divinity in the heart of man."[5] Walter Kaufmann, another liberal thinker, put it well when he said, "Religion is rooted in man's aspirations to transcend himself. . . . Whether he worships idols or strives to perfect himself, man is the God-intoxicated ape."[6] Julian Huxley, the evolutionary humanist, wrote about enjoying religious experiences, and about inner peace that transports people above their problems. In fact, Huxley spoke about life as intolerable without such experiences.[7]

Norman Geisler, a contemporary evangelical apologist, summarized his discussion of humanity's need for God with these words:

> In a frank interview with the Chicago Sun-Times, the famous atheist Will Durant admitted that the common man will fall to pieces morally if he thinks there is no God. "On the other hand," said Durant, "a man like me . . . I survive morally because I retain the moral code that was taught me along with the religion, while I have discarded the religion, which was Roman Catholicism." Durant continued, "You and I are living on a shadow . . . because we are operating on the Christian ethical code which was given us, unfused with the Christian faith. . . . But what will happen to our children . . . ? We are not giving them an ethics warmed up with a religious faith. They are living on the shadow of a shadow."[8]

A Case for Theism

Reasonable Evidence for the Existence of God

In the history of the church and in the study and development of doctrine, various arguments have been presented to defend the existence of God. The first ones to be set forth here were developed by Thomas Aquinas and have been called the naturalistic theistic arguments. This means they are arguments derived primarily from nature and reason rather than from Scripture. I will later set forth the defense for the existence of God based on the teaching of Scripture.

Some think rational arguments for the existence of God are convincing and provide irrefutable evidence. However, others (some of whom believe in the God of the Bible) do not consider rational arguments valid. It must be admitted that these arguments do not scientifically *prove* the existence of God. However, it seems fair to insist that they do *demonstrate the reasonableness* of the Christian faith's belief in God's existence. These arguments certainly present some disturbing and, it would seem, unanswerable questions to the unbelieving mind. Surely, these arguments provide reasonable evidence for the existence of the God presented to us in holy Scripture.

Evidence from the existence of the world. Traditionally, this has been called the cosmological argument.[9] *Kosmos* is the Greek word for world; thus there is the argument from the world itself for the existence of God.

Employed also in this argument is the rule that every effect must have an adequate cause. The universe, it is argued, is an effect that demands an adequate cause. Observation of the creatures and things in the world raises the question, From where did these come? How did they get here?

Reason insists that whatever was responsible for bringing the world and the things in it into existence must have been greater than the world itself. The first cause or first mover must have had enough power and wisdom to bring the present world into existence. Just as surely as a watch implies a watchmaker and a car an automobile manufacturer, so surely the existence of the universe implies a Creator and provides strong implications for the existence of a first cause—namely, God (Ps. 19:1; Rom. 1:20).

As Terry Miethe and Gary Habermas said so well, there are only two options when it comes to answering the question of where the world came from. "Either the universe and all that exists within it can be explained by some materialistic, naturalistic, or mechanistic principle, i.e., the physical universe as we now know it is eternal; *or* there is a first uncaused cause, i.e., what theists call God who is eternal behind the physical universe."[10]

Evidence from the order and design in the world. I am considering here the teleological argument. It builds on the previous one and does a more careful and thorough examination of the world. This argument reasons that if the existence of the world argues for a first cause, then it surely follows that the intricate design in the world provides further support for that cause. This argument also contends for a rational and purposeful first cause (Rom. 1:18-20).

William Paley (1743-1805) is usually credited with popularizing the teleological argument. Long before Paley, however, the Spirit of God spoke through the psalmist about the Lord's order and design. "For You formed my inward parts; You wove me in my mother's womb. I will give thanks to You, for I am fearfully and wonderfully made; Wonderful are Your works, And my soul knows it very well" (Ps. 139:13–14).

Anyone who examines a watch or an automobile would not only conclude that a watchmaker and a car manufacturer exist somewhere, but also that they exercised intelligence in designing and producing their products. Only fools would look at the mechanism inside a watch (for example) and conclude that it just came together by chance. They would notice how the springs, wheels, and gears are coordinated so that the large hand travels precisely twelve times faster than the small hand. If they had enough sense to open the watch in the first place, they would be forced to conclude that an intelligent watchmaker existed.

Like the watch and the automobile, the universe is filled with intricate design, and it is far more complex and precise than what belongs to any single object on earth. Because of the obvious order and design in the universe, the teleological argument not only insists that there was a first cause—a world-maker—but also that the first cause was intelligent beyond description or comparison.

Consider this point. Not all who are involved in the United States space program believe in the existence of the God of the Bible. Nevertheless, all who ever were put out into space or had occasion to be directly involved in the program are quick to acknowledge the order and design of the universe.

Here's another thought. Even though Carl Sagan did not come to the logical conclusion that God exists, he marveled at the intricate design of the human brain.

> The information content of the human brain expressed in bits is probably comparable to the total number of connections among neurons—about a hundred trillion, 1014 bits. If written in English, say, that information would fill some twenty million volumes, as many as in the world's largest libraries. The equivalent of twenty million books is inside the heads of every one of us. The brain is a very big place in a very small space. . . . The neurochemistry of the brain is astonishingly busy, the circuitry of a machine more wonderful than any devised by humans.[11]

It's hard to believe that after Sagan admitted all this, he would still say, "The Cosmos is all that is, or ever was, or ever will be."[12]

Such a conclusion in light of the evidence for God's existence defies reason. Cosmologist Allan R. Sandage's quote from John Noble Williford in the *New York Times*, gives a totally opposite conclusion from that of Sagan:

> Science cannot answer the deepest questions. As soon as you ask why there is something instead of nothing, you have gone beyond science. I find it quite improbable that such order came out of chaos. There has to be some organizing principle. God to me is the explanation or the miracle of existence, why there is something instead of nothing.[13]

Robert Bork summarized as follows the argument for God's existence from the order and design in the universe:

> Evidence of a designer is not of course, evidence of the God of Christianity and Judaism. But the evidence, by undermining the scientific support for atheism, makes belief in that God much easier. And that belief is probably essential to a civilized future.[14]

Evidence from mankind. This is known as the anthropological argument for God's existence. Human existence is a specific and particular example of the design and order referred to above.

People are not robots; rather, they are self-aware beings who possess an intellect, will, personality, and emotions. To put it another way, people have the unique ability to think, feel, and determine. No other creature in the world can do these things.

In light of the above facts it is ridiculous to argue that people came from some impersonal source or force. Surely mankind, the effect, could not be greater than God, the cause. Never has it been demonstrated that an impersonal, unintelligent power brought into existence a personal, intelligent being. Since humans are personal and intelligent beings, they must have had a Creator who is also personal and intelligent (see Gen. 1:26-27; Acts 17:29).

Immanuel Kant, the German philosopher, insisted there was no way for people to have absolute knowledge about God. He thus rejected all the traditional arguments for God's existence. Kant, however, did acknowledge the value and validity of the moral or anthropological argument to show that without God there is really no basis for moral living. The moral argument may be stated by means of this syllogism:

1. All people are conscious of an objective moral law.

2. Moral laws imply a moral Lawgiver.

3. Therefore, there must be a supreme moral Lawgiver.[15]

In recent years, C. S. Lewis gave widespread credibility to the moral argument for God's existence. He built on the foundation laid by others before him and provided additional support for the argument.[16]

Evidence from the idea of a Supreme Being. This is known as the ontological argument (from the word *ontos,* which means "being"). It states that most, if not all, possess in their minds the idea that a most perfect and necessary Being exists. John Calvin's affirmation of the idea in every person of God's existence and his support from Cicero are much to the point here:

> That there exists in the human mind, and indeed by natural instinct, some sense of the existence of Deity, we hold to be beyond dispute, since God himself, to prevent any man from pretending ignorance, has endued all men with some idea of his Godhead, the memory of which he constantly renews and occasionally enlarges, that all to a man, being aware that there is a God, and that he is their Maker, may be condemned by their own conscience when they neither worship him, nor consecrate their lives to his service. Certainly, if there is any quarter where it may be supposed that God is unknown, the most likely for such an instance to exist is among the dullest tribes farthest removed from civilization. But, as a heathen [Cicero] tells us, there is no nation so barbarous, no race so brutish, as not to be imbued with the conviction that there is a God. Even those who, in other respects, seem to differ least from the lower animals, constantly retain some sense of religion; so thoroughly has this common conviction possessed the mind, so firmly is it stamped on the breasts of all men. Since, then, there never has been, from the very first, any quarter of the globe, any city, any household even, without religion, this amounts to a tacit confession, that a sense of Deity is inscribed on every heart.[17]

The argument from the idea of a Supreme Being to His actual existence was first advocated by Anselm of Canterbury. He was a devoted monk living in the eleventh century. There have been a number of variations of the argument since its origin. Philosophers such as Descartes, Spinoza, and Leibnitz all set forth different forms of the argument. Charles Hartshorne (1897-1988) was very sympathetic to it and reformulated what Anselm said about it.[18]

Those who use this argument ask the question, Where did this idea of a most perfect and necessary Being come from? It is maintained that this notion could not have come from civilization or even education, for people all over the world possess this idea, whether or not they are civilized and educated. Thus the idea of a most perfect and necessary Being did not originate with people.

Human beings do not normally make the claim of perfection. The universe has many imperfections in it; so the universe could not have produced such a notion of perfection in people. Some perfect and necessary Being must have planted this idea in them. The ontological argument contends that this perfect Being could only be God. In fact, no matter how hard people try, they cannot rid their minds of this idea of a most perfect and necessary Being, and of a sense of right and wrong based on His existence.

Summary

To varying degrees the arguments discussed above are limited in their ability to convincingly establish the fact of God's existence. For example, they cannot prove beyond all question the existence of the triune God of Scripture.

It must be remembered that the thinking processes of people have been affected by their fall into sin. Thus, though God's revelation of Himself in the world is real, sin has impaired humanity's ability to properly interpret the data. This places definite limitations on the relative benefit of natural arguments for God's existence.

The problem is not in God's revelation of Himself in nature but in the receiver of the revelation. Only after the Holy Spirit brings new life to believing sinners are they able to understand what God makes known in the world through natural revelation. Apart from the Spirit's work in the individual heart, people take the knowledge of God that He has given to all humanity and distort it. They end up worshiping and serving the creation instead of its Creator (Ps. 19:14; Acts 14:15-17; Rom. 1:19-23; 2:14-15).

Biblical Evidence for the Existence of God

Clark H. Pinnock makes the following observations concerning the relation between the naturalistic theistic arguments for God's existence presented above and the biblical evidence:

> It has been observed that nowhere does Scripture attempt
> a deductive argument for the existence of God like those

of Thomas Aquinas for example. This fact ought not to be taken to imply, however, that such an effort is unjustifiable and necessarily useless. The distinctiveness of the biblical approach is its immediacy. The theistic proofs for God's existence constitute a laborious, painstaking, and patient justification of theism. . . . But for the Bible the deepest proof of God's existence is just life itself.[19]

The knowledge of God and the knowledge people have of themselves are closely intertwined. If only God could be written off neatly and cleanly, how simple things would be. But the Hound of Heaven pads after us all. He does not let us go. There is no escaping Him. At the moment when least expected, He closes in.

The explanation for this is God's creation of humanity in His image (Gen. 1:26). Mankind's identity is known and understood theologically in relation to the eternal God. The human race in its true significance cannot survive permanently in isolation from its Maker, for without God people are the chance product of unthinking fate and of little worth. The current loss of identity and the emergence of seemingly faceless people in today's culture is a testimony to the effects of denying the existence of God. The knowledge of God is given in the same movement in which we know ourselves.

For the Scripture, then, the existence of God is both a *historical* truth (namely, God acted in history) and an *existential* truth (namely, God reveals Himself to every person). His existence is both objectively and subjectively evident. It is necessary *logically*, for our assumption of order, design, and rationality rests upon it. His existence is necessary *morally*, for there is no explanation for the shape of morality apart from it. His existence is necessary *emotionally*, for the human experience requires an immediate and ultimate environment. His existence is necessary *personally*, for the exhaustion of all material possibilities still cannot give satisfaction to the human heart.

Apart from historical truth, the deepest proof for God's existence is the reality of life itself. God has created people in His image, and people cannot elude the implications of this fact. Everywhere their identity pursues them. Ultimately there is no escape. "Where can I go from Your Spirit? Or where can I flee from Your presence? If I ascend to heaven, You are there; If I make my bed in Sheol, behold, You are there" (Ps. 139:7–8).

Holy Scripture everywhere assumes the existence of God. Nowhere does it seek to use formal logic and argumentation to prove His existence. The Bible begins with the assumption that God eternally existed (Gen. 1:1). Scripture teaches us that faith precedes reason when it comes to believing in God (Heb. 11:6).

Scripture does not call upon us to cast out reason, for it too is a gift of God (see Isa. 1:18). The fact remains, however, that reason cannot function properly without faith. For example, in all areas of learning, certain basic facts must be believed, or accepted as true, before any progress can be made in learning. In a similar way, God begins His revelation to humanity, not with an airtight defense for His existence, but with the sublime declaration that He eternally existed at the dawn of time. This is an absolute truth that we must accept and believe.

Since God did not seek to provide in His Word a logical defense for His existence, perhaps people should not try to prove His existence either. We have been given the Bible which, while it does not seek to defend God's existence before the skeptic or the unbeliever, does assume God's existence. And Scripture presents irrefutable evidence that He eternally exists, that He has worked in the past, and that He is still working today.

In the Old Testament, for example, God's existence and presence in the world is established by appeal to historical evidence (see Exod. 4:1ff.; 14:30f.; Num. 14:11; Josh. 2:8-11). Also, in the New Testament we are told about God's Son, who came to earth to reveal the Father to people (John 1:18). Surely no one can read the Word with any degree of seriousness and go on denying the reality of God's existence. Either God is all that Scripture makes Him out to be or the Bible is the biggest and most deceptive hoax ever compiled.

In both the Old and New Testaments the existence of God is everywhere evident, as I will seek to demonstrate. The Old Testament presents Him primarily as the God of all nations and peoples and the One who is all-powerful (see Gen. 17:1; Isa. 40:12-17). In the New Testament He is presented as the God and Father of our Lord Jesus Christ (1 Peter 1:3) and as the God of the individual who trusts in Christ for salvation from sin (Gal. 1:4; Phil. 1:2). The New Testament repeatedly emphasizes the intimacy that exists between the Father and the Son as well as between the triune God and believers (see John 17:23-26; 1 John 3:1-2). All who would come to God must first believe that He exists and is the rewarder of those who diligently seek Him (Heb. 11:6).

No doubt the strongest evidence in the Bible for God's existence comes from the testimony and teaching of the Lord Jesus Christ. By way of introduction, I want to clearly state here again that to deny the existence of the God of the Bible is to repudiate the Christ of Scripture. No one can have the one without the other.

The Son of God is the great Revealer of God. He is also the revelation of God to people (see Heb. 1:3). John wrote that as the revelation of God, Christ exposed the Father to human scrutiny. In a literal sense, God the Son laid bare the existence and essence of God the Father. No human has ever seen God in all His fullness, but Jesus has made Him fully known (John 1:18). Thus, Christ is God's revelation.

God also revealed Himself in the words of Scripture and in the miraculous deeds recorded therein. In addition to these evidences of His revelation, I also want to point out that God reveals Himself to the believing heart through the personal presence and ministry of the Holy Spirit. Romans 8:16 says that the "Spirit Himself testifies with our spirit that we are children of God."

The revelation of God in the Bible makes known His infinite love and grace to humanity. But like His revelation in nature, apart from the illuminating ministry of the Holy Spirit, the divine message can neither be believed nor fully comprehended.

The following diagram shows something of the comparison between the evidence from reason and the evidence from the Bible for the existence of God. The diagram also explains the intended results of these two revelations.

REASON IMPLIES	BIBLE REVEALS
1. Cosmological—First cause 2. Teleological—Rational first cause 3. Anthropological—Personal first cause 4. Ontological—Perfect first cause	1. All that reasonable arguments imply 2. Plus: God's love in Christ
Result: Man without excuse (Ps. 19; Rom. 1:20)	Result: Salvation through faith in Christ alone (John 3:18)

Notes

1. For a thorough treatment of the reality of God's existence and the effects of humanity's sin upon their understanding of God's existence, see Francis A. Schaeffer, *He Is There and He Is Not Silent* (Downers Grove, Ill.: InterVarsity, 1968).

2. These examples were selected in part from Norman L. Geisler's, *Is Man the Measure?* (Grand Rapids: Baker, 1983), 169–75.
3. Jean-Paul Sartre, *The Writings of Jean-Paul Sartre,* M. Contat and M. Rybalka, comp., R. C. McCleary, trans. (Evanston, Ill.: Northwestern University Press, 1974).
4. Ibid., 102.
5. Albert Camus, *The Rebel* (New York: Alfred Knopf, 1956), 147.
6. Walter Kaufmann, *Critique of Religion and Philosophy* (New York: Doubleday, 1965), 354–55, 397.
7. Julian Huxley, *Religion without Revelation* (London: Watts, 1941).
8. Geisler, *Is Man the Measure?* 170–71.
9. The cosmological argument has been stated variously in its history. Norman Geisler's restatement and explanation of it is commonly held among evangelicals (see his *Philosophy of Religion* [Grand Rapids: Zondervan, 1981], 190–226).
   1. Some limited, changing being exists.
   2. The present existence of every limited, changing being is caused by another.
   3. There cannot be an infinite regress of causes of being.
   4. Therefore, there is a first Cause of the present existence of these beings.
   5. The first Cause must be infinite, necessary, eternal, single, unchangeable, and one.
   6. This first uncaused Cause is identical with the God of the Judeo-Christian tradition.
10. Terry Miethe and Gary Habermas, *Why Believe? God Exists!* (Joplin, Mo.: College Press, 1993), 35.
11. Carl Sagan, *Cosmos* (New York: Random House, 1980), 278.
12. Ibid., 4.
13. *Readers Digest,* Dec., 1995.
14. Robert Bork, *Slouching Towards Gomorrah* (New York: Regan, 1996), 295.
15. Norman Geisler and Ron Brooks, *When Skeptics Ask* (Wheaton, Ill.: Victor, 1990).
16. C. S. Lewis, *Mere Christianity* (New York: Macmillan, 1953).
17. John Calvin, *Institutes of the Christian Religion,* vol. 1 (Grand Rapids: Eerdmans, 1962), 43.
18. Charles Hartshorne, *Anselm's Discovery: A Re-examination of the Ontological Proof for God's Existence* (LaSalle, Ill.: Open Court, 1965).
19. Clark H. Pinnock, *Set Forth Your Case* (Nutley, N.J.: Craig, 1968), 75, 76–77.

CHAPTER 5

The God of the Bible and His Critics

SATAN, THAT OLD DRAGON and father of lies (see John 8:44; Rev. 12:9), was the first creature to rebel against God. He voiced his criticism and rejection of the Person and plan of God when in pride he said, "I will make myself like the Most High" (Isa. 14:14).[1] From the time of the Devil's fall until the day he will be cast into the eternal lake of fire, he has sought to blind the minds of those who refuse to believe the Gospel. Satan also tries to keep them from turning to the true God in faith (see 2 Cor. 4:4).

Atheism is not new! Godless philosophers and philosophies of one sort or another can be traced to the earliest times. Satan was the first creature to question the right of the Creator to rule and to be the self-sufficient One above all others and all things. The Devil's plan was nothing short of an attempt to eliminate the Creator as the sovereign God of the universe.

But something new and different has occurred in recent days. Denials of God's existence are coming not only from skeptics and those outside the church but also from so-called theologians, bishops, and ministers. Anti-biblical views of God crept into the church long ago but they were camouflaged for the most part. Of late, however, contemporary church leaders have become brazen enough to voice their atheistic views, which really constitute attacks against Christianity itself.

Transaction, a monthly journal published at Washington University, St. Louis, Missouri, carried an article entitled "Will Ethics Be the Death of Christianity?" This article discussed the beginnings of the modern trend by theologians to deny God. Both of the authors of the above article, Rodney Stark and Charles Glock, were in the sociology department of the University of California in Berkeley. The report said:

> While many Americans are still firmly committed to the traditional, supernatural conceptions of a personal God,

a Divine Savior, and the promise of eternal life, the trend
is away from these convictions. Although we must expect
an extended period of doubt, the fact is that a
demythologized modernism is overwhelming the
traditional Christ-centered, mystical faith. . . . For the
modern skeptics are not the apostates, village atheists, or
political revolutionaries of old. The leaders of today's
challenge in traditional beliefs are principally theologians—
those in whose care the church entrusts its sacred
teachings.[2]

Old liberal theology, which developed from Friedrich Daniel
Schleiermacher (1768–1834) and which soon captured all the
mainline denominations, flourished until two world wars and Karl
Barth dealt death blows to it. This classic liberalism had embraced
a dreadfully weak view of God. Because the Bible was rejected, a
weak view of God was a natural corollary.[3]

Theologians of classic liberal theology emphasized the
immanence of God. By this they meant that God is actively present
within His world and much like mankind. The God of the Bible
had certainly been dethroned by the liberals. Along with this
dethroning of God, of course, there came the elevation and
exaltation of humanity and human reason. God, for the liberal,
was a purely human God who was not much above or greater than
the creature.

With the dawn of Darwin's theory of evolution in the mid-
nineteenth century, a new approach to theism arose. Liberals began
to believe God was present in all the processes of evolution. A
humanized God developed from their view. Since liberals accepted
the theory of evolution, they were forced to deny the literalness of
the account of creation in Genesis. Instead of accepting the account
of *fiat* creation given there, they maintained that God had been
working slowly or had turned His work over to the forces of nature
for eons of time to build the universe as we know it today.

The purpose of my book is not to present an exposé of
liberalism. Suffice it to say that the liberals of previous days had
built an anti-Christian and anti-biblical system of theology that
was based on humanistic reason and philosophy. That system
collapsed because of inner conflicts and because of devastating
wars that proved the liberal utopian idea to be false. (In recent
years there has been a concerted effort on the part of some to
revive classic liberalism, and there has been a measure of success
in this attempt.)[4]

The collapse of old liberalism or classic liberalism created a theological vacuum. Into that vacuum came what is now known as neo-orthodoxy. This system of thinking was built upon the same premise of the Higher Critical view of the Bible that liberalism had embraced. However, neo-orthodox adherents did seek to take the Bible more seriously than did their liberal predecessors.

Nevertheless, neo-orthodox theologians also rejected the Bible's inspiration and authority. As they promoted their agenda, they claimed to be restoring God to His rightful place. Pinnock argued that the total subjectivity of modern non-evangelical theology is the result of "the big sellout." "'Slopsism' is a nice way to describe modern theology. 'Insanity' is appropriate but less kind."[5]

The absolute futility of talking about the God of the Bible as an objective reality without accepting the Bible's total and objective propositional authority soon became evident. And so it was that neo-orthodoxy slowly began to lose ground in Europe, its birthplace.

The theology of Rudolf Bultmann soon replaced neo-orthodoxy. Bultmann did not believe it was necessary to return to the errors of old liberalism or to adopt the alternative that Karl Barth's neo-orthodoxy had offered. It is worth noting that Barth and his colleagues were not concerned about the facts of Christianity but with what they called the faith of the early church.

Demythologization

Historians will probably remember Bultmann most for coining the term "demythologize." He maintained that all the New Testament should be demythologized. In other words, everything that is miraculous and supernatural in the Bible should be rejected. Many of the students of the Bultmannian school of thought believed what their teachers asserted. In fact, these second and third generation adherents went beyond their professors, as is often the case with students.

Bultmannian followers have now produced the post-Bultmannian theology.[6] Numbers of them have taken Bultmann seriously, and they see no reason to believe in God at all. One must admit that they are entirely logical in their conclusions. Why believe in God or anything supernatural if the Bible is not authoritative? Unwittingly, the "God-is-dead" theologians have demonstrated the utter inconsistency of rejecting the Bible while at the same time attempting to believe in a God who is related in some way to the Bible.

The late Harry Emerson Fosdick is perhaps the best known

representative of the contemporary liberal school of thought. Fosdick spoke for the majority of present-day liberals when he criticized the old liberalism for its weak view of God. (Fosdick had once embraced liberalism.) Classic liberalism, he maintained, had adjusted itself too much to a man-centered culture. God had been deposed from His throne and was merely assigned to an advisory capacity with respect to mankind and the human enterprise.

As a reaction to this old liberal view of God, the contemporary liberal view emphasizes the need for a quest for an ideal, a source of help, or an object of devotion. The new liberals traced the Christian idea of God from what they call the Hebrew tribal god, Yahweh, through the prophets, especially Amos with his God of mercy, to Isaiah and Jeremiah, whose God was to preserve a remnant.[7]

G. Bromley Oxnam, another representative of the new liberalism, refused to believe that God is characterized by anything but love. He maintained that the Bible gives us an honest, though by no means inerrant, record of the ideas that people had about God. However, God was really not what the sincere but unenlightened Old Testament writers made Him out to be. Oxnam even believed that the God presented by the Old Testament may rightfully be viewed as a "dirty bully."[8] The true God, he believed, is purely and only a God of love and not to be identified with the God of the Old Testament at all.

The new liberal view of God is often expressed by speaking about God as the "absolute being" or "being itself." God's being should not be understood, we are told, as the existence of a being alongside or above other beings. Paul Tillich is representative of this viewpoint. He saw difficulties in the phrase, "personal God." This phrase, he insisted, does not mean God is a Person. Rather, it means that "God" is the ground of everything that is personal. Since "God" is "being itself," whatever can be said about Him is only symbolic. Tillich believed God is above all beings and is at the same time the complete totality of those beings. Tillich's God is not individual and personal; rather, it is the totality of individuality and personality, and thus not the God of the Bible.[9]

Within the general context of new liberal theology there has risen a "theology of hope."[10] My main intent here is to present a brief summary of this view of the concept of God. On the surface it would appear that those who embrace this theology are seeking to emphasize what the Bible teaches about future events. This is not the case, however.

Adherents to the theology of hope view God as subject to time and the process of time. Instead of being concerned with a defense of the existence of God, those associated with this approach are seeking to discover when God will become fully divine. God is said to be a part of time and not the Creator of time.

Definite limits are placed upon God by this view. People are not encouraged to trust in the wisdom and power of God, but instead to participate in the social structure so as to assist God in consummating all things. God is not seen as existing in a supernatural realm outside, above, and beyond His world but as being bound by time and circumscribed by the world.

In summary, the theology of hope is another version of pantheism, which equates God with the forces and laws of the universe. This view falls dreadfully short of a true and accurate presentation of the God of the Bible. Scripture teaches that He is infinite in His being and independent in His self-existence (see Exod. 3:14; 6:3; John 4:24).

With all the attempts of present-day liberals to update their view of God, there remains a cataclysmic gulf between their god and the God of the Bible. And why should that not be the case since they have rejected the absolute authority of Scripture and seldom even pretend to buttress their view with what the Bible teaches. The result is many gods for the liberal, and not one of them approximates the God of the Bible.

God Is Dead

The first "God-is-dead" theologians arose in the early and mid-1960s. They and all subsequent variations of their philosophy represent in the name of Christian religion and theology what is the logical result of an earlier rejection of the absolute, inerrant authority of the Bible. Even though the "God-is-dead" movement is not in the news as it once was, the philosophy behind it is very much alive.

Students of history and the Bible should not be surprised that such a radical and heretical theology would arise. Instead of asking why the death-of-God philosophy became so prevalent, especially among theologians and ordained clergy, we ought rather to be asking why ministers who are liberal, Bible-rejecting, and Christ-denying have not been heralding the death of God? After all, denying the God of the Bible is the result when one repudiates the Bible as God's infallible Word. Having set aside the written Word as less than God-breathed and the living Word as less than God incarnate, it is only logical to take the next of an endless number of steps and call for the burial of the God of the Bible.

Much of the present dilemma and chaotic conditions in both the secular and religious world today are caused by clergy who have spurned the divine pronouncements of Scripture. A long series of rejections and subsequent attendant conditions follow their rejections of the Bible as God's Word.

Along with this repudiation has come the rejection of the God of the Bible. After this usually follows a renunciation of the Bible's presentation of people as those who are spiritually dead, and living in rebellion against God. Following this there comes the repudiation of biblical morality and ethics. Having rejected all of these things, the next step is a short one—the rejection of biblical obedience to the laws of God and society. And of course many more items of rejection can be added to the list. But the crucial point here is that all of these steps can be traced back to the initial rejection of the absolute authority of holy Scripture.

Contemporary people have substituted other things to replace all the supernatural realities they have discarded or denied. All of these replacements find their source in, or at least depend upon, people for existence. Mankind is a natural and in fact the only possible substitute for God when it comes to authority. After all, there are really only two sources of authority in the world. Either we bow before the sovereign authority of God or we bow before human authority. There simply are no other choices unless, of course, one worships and serves Satan, and some are admittedly doing just that.[11] For the most part, however, authority either rests with God or people.[12]

When people replace the authority of God's Word with humanly derived authority, there is no other recourse but to embrace atheism. Tampering with the foundation and contaminating the source of the supply can only lead to a potential collapse of the building and the contamination of what flows from the supply. By placing themselves on the throne of God, people lead themselves to believe in their own inherent goodness. This in turn prompts them to embrace the whole evolutionary hypothesis. The human race is viewed, not as a product of the creative hand of God, but as the highest creaturely development in the survival of the fittest.

In summary, life loses all meaning and reality apart from God. Rushdoony has stated and illustrated this fact in a most concise and pointed way:

> Wherever man asserts his independence of God, saying in
> effect, that, while he will deny God, he will not deny life,
> nor its relationships, values, society, its sciences and art,

he is involved in contradiction. It is an impossibility for man to deny God and still to have law and order, justice, science, anything, apart from God. The more man and society depart from God, the more they depart from all reality, the more they are caught in the net of self-contradiction and self-frustration, the more they are involved in the will to destruction and the love of death (Prov. 8:36). For man to turn his back on God, therefore, is to turn towards death; it involves ultimately the renunciation of every aspect of life.[13]

To deny God, one must ultimately deny that there is any law and any reality. The full implications of this were seen in the last century by two profound thinkers.

The German philosopher Nietzsche recognized fully that all atheists are unwilling believers to the extent that they have any element of justice or order in their lives, and to the extent that they are even alive and enjoy life. In his earlier writings, Nietzsche first attempted the creation of another set of standards and values. He affirmed life for a time, until he concluded that he could neither affirm life itself nor give it any meaning and value apart from God. Thus Nietzsche's ultimate counsel was suicide; only then can we truly deny God. Ironically in his own life, this brilliant thinker—one of the clearest in his description of modern Christianity and the contemporary issue—did in effect commit a kind of psychological suicide.

The same concept was powerfully developed by the Russian novelist Dostoyevsky, particularly in his work entitled "The Possessed," or, more literally, the "Demon Possessed." A thoroughly Nietzschean character named Kirilov is preoccupied with denying God, asserting that he himself is God, and that people do not need God. But at every point, Kirilov finds that no standard or structure in reality can be affirmed without ultimately asserting God, and that no value can be asserted without being ultimately derived from the triune God. As a result, Kirilov committed suicide as the only apparently practical way of denying God and affirming himself, for to be alive was to affirm this ontological deity in some fashion.

The barnyard morality so prevalent today is clearly and closely related to the acceptance of biological evolution. When we teach people that they are biologically related to and have evolved from the amoeba, the slime on some ancient bank, the ape, or some common animal ancestor, it is only natural to expect them to live like a subhuman creature or even worse. The so-called "new morality" and "situation ethics" of our day are the result of the philosophy of evolution and the rejection of biblical authority. When the sanctity, dignity, and uniqueness of human life are eroded, violence and disobedience in all areas of life result. These are simply the natural outworkings or the fruit of the seed of unbelief sown long ago.[14]

The so-called "Christian atheists" or "Christian radicals" came from various religious backgrounds and affiliations. Here is a brief overview of a few of the prominent leaders of the "God-is-dead" movement of the 1960s.

- Dr. Michael Scriven, an Indiana University professor, was brazen enough to style himself as an evangelist for the cause of atheism. He said, "I seek to convert people to the belief that there is no God."
- William Hamilton, Professor of Theology at Colgate-Rochester Divinity School, said the objective of the "God-is-dead" movement—with which he was in sympathy—was to present "a godless Christianity."
- Thomas J. J. Altizer, Associate Professor of Religion at Emory University, Atlanta, Georgia, boldly said, "Christian theology must proclaim the death of God. . . . God has disappeared from history. . . . He is truly dead. . . . We must recognize that the death of God is an historical event; God has died in our time, in our history, in our existence."
- Episcopal Bishop John A. T. Robinson in his book *Honest to God* called for an outlawing of the word *God* "for at least a generation." He went on to say that in the space age "men can no longer credit the existence of God as a supernatural person."
- Gabriel Vahanian of Syracuse University, Anglican David Jenkins, Harvey Cox of Harvard Divinity School, and Paul Van Buren of Temple University of Philadelphia were other "death-of-God" spokespersons.

Two prominent viewpoints existed within the "God-is-dead" scheme of thought. One viewpoint, of which Bishop Robinson and Professor Vahanian would be representative, argued that a personal God had become meaningless to vast numbers of people. This group wished to change the Christian image of God, or at least to find new terminology for talking about Him. They spoke about getting rid of "excess theological baggage," by which they meant many of the biblical descriptions of God. Robinson, for example, in his book says that preaching must be adapted to what modern people are prepared to accept, and that means personal references to God as a "Father in heaven" should be abandoned.

The second viewpoint was even more radical and was represented by Altizer and Hamilton. They not only wanted to change the image of God that people have and find new and better ways of talking about Him, but also they boldly proclaimed the actual death of God. God, they said, is truly absent from history. He has disappeared from human experience. The loss of God, Hamilton said, is "final and irrevocable."

As John Warwick Montgomery pointed out in his helpful critique of the "God-is-dead" theology, there have been some efforts to resuscitate God. Montgomery was certainly correct when he observed the following:

> In general, it must be said that the attempts to counter "Christian atheism," though occasionally helpful in pointing up weaknesses in the theothantologists' armor, do not cut decisively to the heart of the issue. In most instances, the reason for the critical debility lies in the dullness of the theological swords the critics wield.[15]

As Montgomery indicated, not all the critics of the "God-is-dead" theology have been evangelical Bible-believers. Even some liberal theologians reject the death-of-God proposal. Some have scornfully ridiculed those who would try to bury God.

Christian Century, a mouthpiece of liberal theology, featured an article titled "Death-of-God: Four Views" in the November 17, 1965, issue. The editor explained that these four views represented the many responses that came to his desk as a result of the death-of-God debate. The four views and most of the letters the editor received were critical of the death-of-God theology.

Defenses Against "Christian Atheism"

Process theology[16] and neo-orthodoxy are often said to be defenses against so-called "Christian atheism."[17] The fact remains, however, that all who reject the absolute authority of the Bible have no right to argue for God's existence. All the arguments against "Christian atheism" from those who do not accept the full inspiration of Scripture fail to deal with the real issue.

Such affronts against the God of the Bible in the name of religion and Christianity arouse righteous indignation in the people of God. The blasphemous "God-is-dead" spokespersons resemble the unbelieving legalists of our Lord's day when they accused Him of being Beelzebul (or Beelzebub), the ruler of the demons (Matt. 12:24).

The God of the Bible needs no defense. Nevertheless, believers are commissioned in Scripture to be prepared to defend their faith, and to do so with gentleness and respect (1 Peter 3:15; see Jude 3). Keeping several crucial facts in mind will help us to do this. Although I introduced these truths earlier, I am reviewing them here for the sake of emphasis.

Before people rejected the God of the Bible, they rejected the authority of the Word of God and the Christ of Scripture. Thus when people spurn the Bible and therefore the Christ of the Bible, it is only a short and necessary step for them to spurn the God of the Bible.

This is pertinent information when considering the "God-is-dead" clan. They never really believed in the God who is revealed in Scripture. To them the God of the Bible is dead because He never really existed. The concept of God, which the Bible-deniers set forth, is not simply a variation of the one true God of the Bible. The false god they invented and the entire system that is associated with that pagan deity is totally foreign to the God of the Bible and the Christian faith based on belief in Him.

It is perfectly natural for the unregenerate to disbelieve in God and His Word. Paul, under the inspiration of the Spirit of God, observed that "a natural man does not accept the things of the Spirit of God; for they are foolishness to him, and he cannot understand them, because they are spiritually appraised" (1 Cor. 2:14).

We cannot expect those who are spiritually dead in trespasses and sins to embrace the God and Father of our Lord Jesus Christ, the God of the Bible (see Eph. 2:1–3). The Spirit of God must work in their hearts before they can receive by faith the God of the Bible and the Christ of Scripture (see John 16:8–11).

Those who have the witness of the Holy Spirit of God in their hearts can never be convinced that the Bible is not God's Word, that the God of the Bible does not exist, or that the Christ of Scripture is not fully divine as well as fully human. However, those who do not have this ministry of the Spirit will not and cannot truly believe what Christians affirm about God, His Son, and His Word.

No amount of clever arguments or restatement and reworking of Christian truth will convince the unbeliever that the truths of holy Scripture are reliable and authoritative. Only the Spirit of God can bring enlightenment to such a sin-darkened mind (see 1 Cor. 2:10). Of course, He often uses a well-thought-out defense of the faith along with the inscripturated Word to bring people to a knowledge of the truth.

Notes

1. Not all agree that Satan is in view in Isaiah 14:12–17 and Ezekiel 18:11–19. Some think the references are to historical figures. For a discussion on these passages, see Franz Delitzch, *Biblical Commentary on the Prophecies of Isaiah* (Edinburgh: T & T Clark, 1875), 1:314f.; Charles L. Feinberg, *The Prophecies of Ezekiel* (Chicago: Moody, 1969), 158–63; Charles C. Ryrie, *Basic Theology* (Wheaton, Ill.: Victor, 1987), 141–45.

2. Will Oursler, *Protestant Power and the Coming Revolution* (Garden City, N.Y.: Doubleday, 1971), 192.

3. For a brief presentation of the old or classic liberalism and the new or contemporary liberalism, see the author's *Neo-Liberalism* (Nutley, N.J.: Craig Press, 1970).

4. Compare Henry P. Van Dusen, *The Vindication of Liberal Theology* (New York: Charles Scribner's Sons, 1965).

5. Clark H. Pinnock, *Set Forth Your Case* (Nutley, N.J.: Craig Press, 1968), 15.

6. See Carl F. H. Henry, *Frontiers in Modern Theology* (Chicago: Moody, 1966).

7. Walter Marshall Horton, *God* (New York: Associated Press, 1937), 16–22.

8. G. Bromley Oxnam, *A Testament of Faith* (Boston: Little, Brown & Co., 1958), 3–31.

9. Paul Tillich, *Systematic Theology* (Chicago: University of Chicago Press, 1951), 245–84.

10. Representative of this movement would be Wolfart Pannenberg of Munich, Germany; Ernest Benz of Marburg; and Jurgen Moltmann of Tubingen. The latter is rightfully considered the "theologian of hope." For an excellent article on Moltmann's theology by David P. Scaer and a listing of those presenting the theology of hope, see the *Journal of the Evangelical Society* XIII (spring 1970): 69–79.

11. In San Francisco there is a Church of Satan founded by Anton La Vey. Satan is worshiped there openly. La Vey also wrote the *Satanic Bible,* which for a time outsold the holy Bible on some college campuses.

12. Norman L. Geisler gives an exposition of eight different kinds

of humanism in his book entitled *Is Man the Measure?* (Grand Rapids: Baker, 1983), 11–107.

13. Rousas J. Rushdoony, *Intellectual Schizophrenia* (Nutley, N.J.: Presbyterian and Reformed, 1961), 25f.

14. See Joseph Fletcher, *Situation Ethics* (Philadelphia: Westminster, 1966) and *Situation Ethics* a debate between Joseph Fletcher and John Warwick Montgomery (Minneapolis: Bethany, 1972).

15. John Warwick Montgomery, *The "Is God Dead?" Controversy* (Grand Rapids: Zondervan, 1966), 36–37. This little volume is an excellent summarization of the "God-is-dead" movement.

16. Process theology is related to process philosophy. As the name implies, this system of thought explains reality, including God, as a process rather than as something unchangeable. See John B. Cobb, *Living Options in Protestant Theology* (Philadelphia: Westminster, 1962), and John C. Cobb, *Process Theology* (Philadelphia: Westminster, 1976) for further explanations of this view's emphasis from those who subscribe to it. For an excellent critique from an evangelical point of view, see two articles written by Carl F. H. Henry, *Christianity Today*, 14 March 1969 and 28 March 1969.

17. See Longdon Gilkey, "Is God Dead?" *The Voice: Bulletin of Crozer Theological Seminary*, LVII (January 1965).

CHAPTER 6

Knowledge of the God of the Bible Found in His World

God the Revealer

GOD IS NOT MUTE. He has spoken! This chapter and the next one are designed to present God as the Revealer. God, in His grace, has made Himself and His will known. How desperate the plight of the human race would be if God had not extended this grace to them. The creature is always at the mercy of the Creator. Thus, apart from God's revelation, people would have never known about Him or be able to come to know Him personally.

As Francis A. Schaeffer insisted, unless God's revelation in nature and in the written Word is accepted, people indeed are below the line of despair. And apart from God's revelation, life has no meaning.[1] Furthermore, between God and mankind there is an impassable gulf, a wide chasm, which would never have been bridged had God not taken the first step by revealing Himself and His plan of redemption to people.

Holy Scripture does not minimize the distance between God and the human race. Rather, God's infinity and humanity's finiteness as well as God's holiness and humanity's sinfulness are everywhere emphasized. The Bible also stresses God's condescension to reveal Himself and His plan.[2] His will for mankind is evident throughout Scripture.

It is clear that in this life we will never know God fully. In a real sense He is incomprehensible. As people, we possess all the limitations common to humanity. As God, the Lord possesses perfections and completeness to an infinite degree. Nevertheless, God can be known sufficiently for salvation and for living the Christian life. God has made Himself known through nature and also in the written Word. Because He has revealed Himself, He holds people responsible for the knowledge He has given them about Himself. And because God has spoken, people are without excuse for not knowing Him (see Rom. 1:18-20).

63

To distinguish between the different forms of God's revelation, theologians have called His self-disclosure in nature *general revelation* and His self-disclosure in His written Word *special revelation*. This chapter primarily deals with general revelation. In the following chapter, I will discuss God's revelation of Himself in His written Word.

God the Creator

That God created people and the universe cannot be denied by those who believe the Bible. The divinely inspired Word talks about God's creative work with solemn and sublime simplicity. Life and the entire universe itself did not come into existence through some mysterious process, or by the survival of the fittest, or even by a big bang, but by God's direct and authoritative decree. The Bible teaches that the Lord, by the word of His command, brought our world into existence. He spoke and it was done!

God's Purpose in Creation

Why does the world exist? Why are people here? Why did God create anything at all? Why do we need salvation? Some might think it is not the creature's right to ask such questions. Yet they often lurk in the mind. It is possible to address them while remaining reverent to God. And pondering such questions can be a spiritually healthy experience.

Some have said God's goodness and desire for communication prompted Him to create creatures on whom He could display His love. While this view appears at first to exalt God's goodness and love, it really promotes the idea that happiness is the most important purpose in God's creative activities. God, it would seem in this view, exists for people rather than people existing for God.

We should not think that the love of God was dependent upon creatures for its manifestation and fulfillment. The relations within the Godhead among the Father, the Son, and the Holy Spirit would have satisfied the love of the Lord, even apart from the creation of anything. Thus God did not create people and the world so that He would be happy. Similarly His intent in creating the world was not to bring people happiness.

The happiness of people in this life is not God's main concern. Rather, it is the exaltation of His glory. This means that people do not exist to glorify themselves. As the Westminster clerics rightly noted in their catechism, "The chief end of man is to glorify God and to enjoy Him forever" (Q1, *Westminster Shorter Catechism*).

If God's primary purpose in creation was not to bring into being creatures on whom He could bestow His love so that they might be happy, then what was His chief purpose? The biblical testimony is abundantly clear. God created all things, including people, to display His glory and that through the manifestation of His glory He might receive praise and honor.

Of course, God's secondary purposes in creation include such things as the salvation of the lost and their eternal joy in communion with Him. But His foremost and ultimate purpose is to display His glory and to receive glory and praise from His creatures, including people (see Isa. 43:7; 60:21; Ezek. 39:7; Rom. 11:36; 1 Cor. 15:28). Though we will not always understand the purposes and ways of God, we must humbly acknowledge that He does all things well and to the praise of His glory (see Eph. 1:3–14; 3:9–10).[3]

God's Creative Activity

Recent space explorations have served to remind Bible believers that those who accept the theory of evolution are still seeking an explanation of how the universe came into existence. Despite all the advances in technology and all the knowledge gained from scientific research, the experts remain stumped. When God's revelation in Scripture concerning the origin of the universe is rejected, such a search is understandable. An unbelieving mind has no other choice but to use imagination and to postulate theories about the origin of the world.

The evolutionary hypothesis presents two basic views to explain how the universe came into existence. Some say there never was a beginning and there never will be an end of the universe. This is often referred to as the *steady-state theory*. According to this hypothesis, matter is eternal. Supposedly it is continually being created out of energy. Thus the universe has always been as it now is. For many years Professor Fred Hoyle was a proponent of this view. In recent days he has admitted that he was probably wrong for espousing such a theory.

The second view presented by the evolutionary hypothesis now prevails. Adherents of it contend that the universe came into existence by a gigantic explosion. This view, which is popularly known as the *big bang theory*, provides an explanation for the movement of earth's galaxies away from each other.

Such farfetched explanations find no support in the Bible. There the account concerning the creation of the universe is simple, clear, and concise. The Lord, through His verbal command, not through natural laws, brought this complex universe into existence (see Gen. 1; Exod. 20:11; 31:17; Neh. 9:6; Ps. 33:6, 9; 2 Peter 3:5; Rev. 14:7).

I admit that the Bible's testimony to God's work in creation defies rationalization and natural explanation. The creation of the universe must be accepted by faith as a supernatural act of the God of the Bible. There are some—and the number seems to be increasing, especially at the present time—who attempt to adjust and accommodate the biblical testimony to the unbelieving and godless viewpoints of evolutionists. This is a futile attempt and signifies nothing less than the surrender of God's truth to pagan theories.[4]

It is imperative to remember that not everything that purports to be scientific is so in reality. The one who embraces the Bible need not fear science. When correctly interpreted, God's revelation in nature and His revelation in the Bible never contradict each other. These two sources of divine revelation are not in conflict; rather, they complement each other.

We must never sacrifice the truth of Scripture at the altar of so-called "science." It is true that God did not give us the Bible to make people scientists. Instead, He has graciously given us His written Word to make saints out of sinners. Thus the main thrust of the Bible is not in matters pertaining to science.

Nevertheless, Scripture does have a considerable amount to say about the origin of the universe and life on earth. Wherever the Bible addresses subjects that are relevant to science, it does so with the same authority as when it addresses subjects that are relevant to salvation. If God's Word cannot be trusted to be reliable and accurate when it deals with scientific matters, how do we know when Scripture can be trusted?

It is true that all parts of the Bible were penned by fallible human authors. And yet every portion was produced while the fallible writers were under the superintending control of the Holy Spirit. He supernaturally directed them so that the divine message was recorded with perfect accuracy.

As might be expected, what evolutionists say about the origin of the universe they also say about people. Humanity's origin and existence is explained apart from God's existence and sovereign involvement. The theory is basic to and controls modern thought in the natural sciences, the social sciences, philosophy, and religion.

Instead of making humans the direct descendent of the ape, most contemporary evolutionists assert that humanity and higher forms of apes have a common ancestry. We should not assume, however, that these evolutionists are viewing the God of the Bible with more respect. The point of contention remains the same with all variations and degrees of Darwinian evolution.

Regardless of how nuanced and sophisticated an evolutionary viewpoint might be, its advocates still believe that millions of years ago natural forces somehow acted upon lifeless matter to gave rise to living organisms. Over billions of years these primitive creatures then supposedly evolved into all living and extinct plants and animals, including the human race.

Thus all forms of evolutionary theory maintain that life began by the random interaction of impersonal forces. Ironically no one, including evolutionists, can carry the implications of such a philosophy to its logical conclusion in their personal lives, for to do so would produce unbearable chaos and despair.

There are some, of course, who embrace what is called *theistic evolution*. Advocates of this theory insist that God used the processes of organic evolution to create humans. Theistic evolutionists do believe in God, and many of them are sincerely seeking to communicate their faith.

Nevertheless, two facts are worth mentioning. First, atheistic evolution removes God completely from the process of the creation of the universe and the human race. Second, *all forms* of evolutionary theory hold to *organic* evolution (from molecule to man) and *macroevolution* (from ape to man). Therefore, it is a contradiction in terms to speak of theistic evolution, unless these terms are invested with new meaning, which is usually the case.

One does not honor God by associating Him with the concept of evolution. And one shows a fundamental misunderstanding of evolutionary theory by associating it with God. As the terms "theism" and "evolution" have been normally understood, they are mutually exclusive. Thus, the attempt to harmonize biblical creationism with evolutionary theory by speaking of theistic evolution is little short of a semantic delusion.

Conceding the authority and teaching of Scripture regarding the origin of life for a naturalistic theory such as evolution is a real and prevalent danger. And asserting that the God of the Bible used an evolutionary process represents a major unnecessary concession, especially in those portions of Scripture that speak about His fiat creation.

Theistic evolution has been stated variously and is expressed in different ways. Perhaps the most popular and influential forms of this theory are "threshold evolution"[5] and "progressive creationism."[6] Carl F. H. Henry questions both of these attempted explanations of the origin of life, for he believes these theories result in a semantic delusion, engender a false hope, and are attempts to gain a truce between science and religion.[7]

It makes little difference what name one might give to such naturalistic views in order to avoid the evolution stigma. The fact remains that these theories are in direct conflict with Scripture, which teaches that "by the seventh day God completed His work which He had done" (Gen. 2:2). When we interpret this verse plainly and straightforwardly—as we would normally interpret any other piece of literature—we must reject all attempts, such as the theistic evolutionist makes, to portray God as using an evolutionary process to create life.

Here are some other Scripture passages that, when interpreted literally, contradict *both* theistic and atheistic evolution. God formed man out of the "dust from the ground" (Gen. 2:7). Scripture declares that the Lord took woman "out of man" (Gen. 2:23). The Bible says that God completed the entire work of creation in six days (in other words, six twenty-four-hour periods; Exod. 20:11; 31:17).

Scripture enjoins us to worship the Lord, our Creator, for "He spoke and it was done; He commanded, and it stood fast" (Ps. 33:9). The Bible flatly contradicts *all* forms of evolution when it declares, "All flesh is not the same flesh, but there is one flesh of human beings, and another flesh of beasts, and another flesh of birds, and another of fish" (1 Cor. 15:39). A normal, historical, grammatical interpretation of these and many other passages of Scripture substantiates the fact that the God of the Bible is the Creator of humanity and the universe.

In contrast with the other entities that God brought into existence in the six literal days of creation, His creation of humanity was altogether unique. The Lord formed the body of man from small particles of the earth. But man's life came from the breath of God. Man thus became a living person, or more literally, "a living being" (Gen. 2:7).

The triune God created people in His image (Gen. 1:26-27), in contrast to the rest of the creatures of the world which God created "after their kind" (v. 21). Humans in their entire self reflect the glory of God, giving each person dignity. Their ability to reason, to be creative, to speak, and to exercise volition comes from God. He has also given people dominion over the earth and its creatures (v. 28), and that responsibility sets the human race apart from all the other entities in the world.

A careful study of the Word of God will indicate that each member of the holy Trinity had a definite part in the creation of the universe and mankind. In Genesis 1:1, Moses used the Hebrew term *Elohim,* which is plural, to refer to God. Surely this is an indication of plurality within the divine unity and hints at the later New Testament revelation of the one God existing as Father, Son, and Holy Spirit.

Elsewhere in Scripture the creation of the universe is said to be the work of the Father (Pss. 33:6, 9; 102:25), the Son (John 1:3; Col. 1:16), and the Holy Spirit (Gen. 1:2; Job 26:13). The Bible also ascribes the creation of the human race to each member of the Godhead—namely, the Father (Gen. 2:7), the Son (John 1:3-10), and the Holy Spirit (Job 33:4).

God's Revelation Through His Creation

Students of the Bible are not all agreed on the content or the validity of God's revelation in nature. Some think God cannot be known at all through natural revelation, while others insist that God can be known through nature and that such knowledge of Him has redemptive merit. Still others insist that even though God has spoken through the things He has made, the non-Christians' lost condition keeps them from knowing God in any sense.

Finally, evangelical Christians are on good biblical ground when they insist that God has made Himself known through nature and that He has also enabled all people to know about His eternal power and divine nature by examining and studying the world (Rom. 1:19-20). This being the case, the awfulness of the sin of worshiping and serving the creature rather than the Creator becomes apparent (see Rom. 1:25).

Evangelicals would reject the notion that the knowledge of God acquired through the observation of nature can lead to salvation. Nevertheless, God's disclosure of Himself in nature is sufficient to hold people guilty for rejecting and rebelling against Him. Thus God is righteous in making people accountable for their heinous acts (see Rom. 1:21-32).

Scripture is abundantly clear in teaching that God has disclosed His existence through the world He created (see Ps. 19:1-6; Acts 17:22-34; Rom. 1:18-20). However, it must be remembered that apart from the Bible and the work of the Spirit, the sin-darkened mind of fallen humanity would not even be sure that God had revealed Himself in nature.

David, the psalmist, understood that the "heavens" and the "expanse" continually declare "the glory of God" and "the work of His hands" (Ps. 19:1). David also said concerning the extent of God's revelation in nature, "There is no speech, nor are there words;

their voice is not heard. Their line has gone out through all the earth, and their utterances to the end of the world" (Ps. 19:3-4).

It light of these verses, it's clear that God's disclosure of His existence in nature is available for all people to see and consider. To be sure, not all understand or accept God's revelation of Himself as He intended. Only the redeemed can grasp the full meaning of the divine revelation in the world. Nevertheless, God has given it to all people, though some willfully distort it and choose to worship the creature and humanly-made objects rather than the Creator (Romans 1).

The universal scope and extent of God's revelation in nature is set forth in the message of Paul to the people of Lystra. As a rebuke to those who tried to worship the apostle and his associate Barnabas, these missionaries declared that God not only made heaven, earth, the sea, and all the things in it, but He also gave humanity rain and fruitful seasons. Paul maintained that this was sufficient evidence that God had not left Himself without a witness in the world (Acts 14:15-17).

Paul argued strongly for the fact that God manifested Himself in all people and to all people through the creation of the world. For example in Romans 1:19-20, the apostle discussed the relationship between this universal revelation of God and the universal condemnation of all people. Paul argued that God's "invisible attributes, His eternal power and divine nature, have been clearly seen, being understood through what has been made."

This natural revelation of the power and deity of God renders all people who have rejected the truth of His existence without excuse before Him (Rom. 1:20). This divine disclosure in nature is universal. In other words, it extends to all people, even those "who suppress the truth in unrighteousness" (Rom. 1:18) and "did not honor Him as God" (Rom. 1:21). The fact that multitudes distort this revelation from God and serve the creature rather than the Creator does not change the fact that God has made Himself known by the things He has made.

God's revelation in nature may be compared to a great concert or symphony. Some hear only the instruments. But those who are familiar with the composer and know the words hear more than the music. They interpret what they hear by what they know about the music. In much the same way, only the one who has a personal relationship with the Creator through faith in Jesus Christ can really see in nature the fullness of what God intended to reveal about Himself through it.

David, a man after God's own heart (see 1 Sam. 13:14), also

affirmed the Lord's disclosure of His existence through the world He had created. As a lad alone on the Judean hills, David cared for his father's sheep. The boy had a lot of time to gaze at the marvelous craftsmanship of God evident all around him.

In Psalm 19:1 David wrote, "The heavens are telling of the glory of God; and their expanse is declaring the work of His hands." It's worth noting that in this verse, David used the Hebrew term *Elohim* to refer to God. This is the same word that Moses used in Genesis 1:1, a verse that talks about the eternal power and might of God in creating the world.

David cited specific things in nature through which God made His existence known to people. In addition to the heavens, the expansive skies, and all they contain, the former shepherd boy, who was rightly related to God, also saw evidences of His existence in the light of day (Ps. 19:2). Each day gave silent but eloquent testimony to the presence of the Creator. And the stately procession and regulated continuance of each day was a reminder of God's abiding faithfulness in sustaining the world.

Even the darkness of night was a silent witness to the existence of God. David wrote, "Night to night reveals knowledge" (Ps. 19:2). The orderliness of the stars in their courses and the moon in all its radiant splendor proclaimed a wordless message that God existed and had created everything. The Lord did not intend this message only for David. It was a universal declaration for all people to receive and contemplate (vv. 3–4).

Several prominent facts stand out concerning humanity and God's revelation of Himself in the world. *First,* all people everywhere have some knowledge of God for which He holds them accountable (Rom. 1:19). *Second,* nature's testimony to the existence of God leaves people "without excuse" (v. 20) before Him when they reject the truth.

Third, though God has made His existence universally known through nature, all people are still dead in trespasses and sins (Eph. 2:1). *Fourth,* the knowledge of God from general, or natural, revelation is insufficient by itself to bring people to salvation, for it cannot make people aware of their lost condition and of God's provision of a substitutionary atoning sacrifice through Christ.

Fifth, people in their unregenerate state often distort natural revelation and fail to live up to the knowledge or light they have from it (see Paul's argument to this effect in Rom. 1:18–32). *Sixth,* God's revelation in nature corresponds perfectly with His revelation in the written Word. *Seventh,* the questions that people have as a result of contemplating what God has disclosed in nature about

Himself are answered in the Bible, God's special revelation. *Eighth,* believers can use the reality of God's existence, which is evident in nature, as a starting point in witnessing to the unsaved (see Acts 17:15–34, where Paul did just that).

Notes

1. Francis A. Schaeffer's, *The God Who Is There* (Downers Grove, Ill.: InterVarsity, 1968). See also the revision in *The Complete Works of Francis A. Schaeffer: A Christian World View,* 5 vols. (Wheaton, Ill.: Crossway, 1982).
2. See Robert Lightner's *Sin, The Savior, and Salvation* (Grand Rapids: Kregel, 1996). Here you will find a study of the relationship between humanity's sin, the divine Savior, and God's saving grace.
3. A fuller discussion of the major goal, or purpose, of God in the world is given in Charles C. Ryrie, *Dispensationalism* (Chicago: Moody, 1995), 79–95, 183–95. See also Charles Hodge, *Systematic Theology,* vol. 1 (Grand Rapids: Eerdmans, 1993), 535–49.
4. The following works represent scholarly presentations of biblical creationism and therefore serve to refute all forms of evolution: Bolton Davidheiser, *Evolution and the Christian Faith* (Nutley, N.J.: Presbyterian and Reformed, 1969); Jobe Martin, *The Evolution of a Creationist* (Rockwall, Tex.: Biblical Discipleship Publishers, 1994); Henry Morris, *Biblical Cosmology and Modern Science* (Nutley, N.J.: Presbyterian and Reformed, 1970); Henry Morris, *The Twilight of Evolution* (Nutley, N.J.: Presbyterian and Reformed, 1963); John Whitcomb and Henry Morris, *The Genesis Flood* (Nutley, N.J.: Presbyterian and Reformed, 1961); John Whitcomb, *The Origin of the Solar System* (Nutley, N.J.: Presbyterian and Reformed, 1964); Paul S. Taylor, *Origins Answer Book* (Mesa, Ariz.: Eden Productions, 1993); and Paul Taylor and Van Bebber, *Creation and Time* (Mesa, Ariz.: Eden Productions, 1994).
5. E. J. Carnell, *An Introduction to Christian Apologetics* (Grand Rapids: Eerdmans, 1948), 239, 242.
6. Bernard Ramm, *The Christian View of Science and the Scripture* (Grand Rapids: Eerdmans, 1954), 116.
7. Carl F. H. Henry, ed., *Contemporary Evangelical Thought* (Grand Rapids: Baker, 1968), 247–57.

CHAPTER 7

Knowledge of the God of the Bible Found in His Word

IN SUBSEQUENT CHAPTERS I will deal with the biblical teaching concerning God's person and work. It is my intent here to contrast the knowledge of God in His written Word with the knowledge of Him found in the world (which we considered in the previous chapter). I also intend to make clear the harmony and relationship between the written Word and the living incarnate Word.

The Need for the Written Revelation

God has not only *done* certain things to make Himself known. He has also *said* certain things concerning Himself. God has given a direct and divine disclosure of Himself through the human authors of Scripture and in the Person of the Lord Jesus Christ, His Son.

The flood in Noah's day, the experience at the tower of Babel, and the Israelites' miraculous deliverance from Egypt through the Red Sea were all spectacular ways by which God revealed Himself to His people. But He wanted them and all the world to have a written record of these and other miracles.

Before God gave the Ten Commandments and the whole Levitical system to the Israelites, He first introduced Himself as the Lord God who had brought His people out of Egypt (Exod. 20:1-2). He then gave them His inscripturated Word, for He knew that it would be essential for the spiritual survival of His people.

The Word of God is equally essential for those today who trust in Jesus Christ, the living Word, for salvation. Just as people need physical food to sustain their bodies, so too they need spiritual nourishment from the Bible to sustain their souls. The Lord Jesus knew this. That is why He appealed to the written Word when the Devil tempted Him in the wilderness (Matt. 4:1-11; Mark 1:12-13; Luke 4:1-13). Since the incarnate Word relied on the written Word of God for spiritual sustenance and strength, surely we should do the same.

The basic difference between God's revelation in nature and His revelation in His Word is that the former is general while the latter is specific. Also, the first is made known through what exists in nature, while the latter is made known through objective, propositional declarations of truth.

General revelation—namely, God's disclosure of His existence in nature—is restricted in what it makes known. For example, its message does not include anything about the love of God revealed in Jesus Christ. Only special revelation—God's disclosure of Himself in Scripture—reveals truth about His Son.

God never intended general revelation to be sufficient to lead people to salvation. Rather, He wanted it to be a silent but powerful witness of His existence, eternal power, and infinite glory. Special revelation (namely, what is recorded in Scripture) is built upon God's revelation in nature; in other words, the former presupposes the latter. The divine corrective for humanity's distorted view of God is found in Scripture, His written Word, and in His Son, the living Word. Natural revelation substantiates the truth that people are exceedingly sinful, while special revelation makes known the divine remedy in and through Jesus Christ. A great scholar of the past put it this way:

> On the plane of nature men can learn only what God necessarily is, and what, by virtue of his essential attributes, he must do; a special communication from him is requisite to assure us what, in his infinite love, he will do for the recovery of sinners from their guilt and misery to the bliss of communion with him. And for the full revelation of this, his grace in the redemption of sinners, there was requisite an even more profound unveiling of the mode of his existence, by which he has been ultimately disclosed as including in the unity of his being a distinction of persons, by virtue of which it is the same God from whom, through whom, and by whom are all things, who is at once the Father who provides, the Son who accomplishes, and the Spirit who applies, redemption.[1]

Though the Bible does not set out to prove the existence of God, it certainly presents Him in all of His fullness and glory. He is everywhere evident throughout the pages of Scripture. Contrary to the opinions of many, the unregenerate do not and cannot seek after God (Rom. 3:11). For this reason, revelation from God is needed—both general and special. And also for this reason, God must be the One who takes the first step if there is to be any communication with mankind. The fact that God the Creator seeks to make Himself and His will known to His creatures is an act of pure grace on His part.

What B. B. Warfield said about the Old Testament concept of God is equally as true about the New Testament revelation of Him:

> The Old Testament does not occupy itself with how Israel thought of God. Its concern is with how Israel ought to think of God. To it, the existence of God is not an open question; nor His nature, nor the accessibility of knowledge of Him. God Himself has taken care of that. He has made Himself known to his people, and their business is not to feel after him if haply they may fumblingly find him, but to hearken to him as He declares to them what and who he is. The fundamental note of the Old Testament in other words is revelation. Its seers and prophets are not men of philosophic minds who have risen from the seen to the unseen and, by dint of much reflection, have gradually attained to elevated conceptions of Him who is the author of all that is. They are men of God whom God has chosen, that he might speak to them and through them to his people. Israel has not in and by them created for itself a God. God has through them created himself a people.[2]

God's revelation of Himself in the world is neither less accurate nor less authentic than His revelation of Himself in the Word. Nevertheless by divine design, natural revelation is inadequate by itself to meet humanity's spiritual needs. God never intended that His revelation in nature should constitute the totality of His message to the human race. And He did not intend His revelation in nature to be sufficient to lead to a saving knowledge of Him.

God's revelation in the world does not possess any power to alter the sinful conduct of people. Also, God has limited the extent and purpose of natural revelation. He did not provide it to correct people but to communicate to them their need for correction. And the revelation of God in the world does not provide any information about how sinful people might be spiritually cleansed from their sin. Only God's revelation in the written Word provides this necessary information.

Natural revelation and humanity's inner awareness of moral right and wrong are both limited in what they make known. For instance,

these sources of information do not say anything about the
spiritually lost condition of the human race, about their need for
a divine Substitute for sin, and about God's provision of Jesus
Christ as the only Savior from sin. God has revealed these truths
on the pages of Scripture.

General revelation also does not tell people how to live. Only
special revelation contains directives for living uprightly. God even
had to tell our first parents the proper ways to think and act. The
beauty and splendor of the garden did not communicate such
important information to them.

In summary, God's revelation in His Word was made necessary
because of humanity's sin. As a result of the disobedience of Adam
and Eve in the garden, humanity broke fellowship with God and
stopped communicating with Him. Instead of meeting with the
Lord, people sought to hide from Him (see Gen. 3:8).

The message of the Bible is about God reaching out to the lost.
Scripture does not portray the lost as searching for God while they
grope in the darkness of their sin. Rather, Scripture reveals that
God, in His infinite love and compassion, reached out to those
who were spiritually dead and had no desire to know Him (see
Isa. 65:1; Rom. 10:20).

It is important to remember that because of humanity's sin, God
subjected the creation to futility (Rom. 8:20). This means the
creation as well as the creature came under the curse of God. The
Lord originally created the world to glorify Him. But as long as
humanity lives in a state of sin, the world cannot achieve its divinely
intended goal. God will emancipate creation from its present state
of imperfection and decay when the believers' position as adopted
children in God's family is culminated in the Resurrection state (see
vv. 19, 21). But until that glad day "the whole creation groans and
suffers the pains of childbirth together" (v. 22).

The Revelation of God in Christ

Jesus Christ is the supreme and final revelation of God to
humanity. Hebrews 1:1 says, "God, after He spoke lone ago to
the fathers in the prophets in many portions and in many ways, in
these last days has spoken to us in His Son." This verse teaches
that the revelation of God to humanity before the incarnation of
Christ was piecemeal and anticipatory. In Old Testament times
God's inspired revelation came through dreams, visions, laws,
institutions, ceremonies, kings, judges, and prophets.

A marked change is introduced by the phrase, "in these last
days" (Heb. 1:2a). This refers to the messianic age, which began

with the coming of Christ. The Father sent His Son to bring His saving message to us. Jesus' superiority over the prophets is underscored in verses 2 through 4.

Though the revelation of God given before Christ and the revelation of God in Him are different, this does not mean they contradict each other, that they are foreign to each other, or that the one is more accurate than the other. Both revelations came from God and therefore both are completely accurate and reliable; yet the Son—who is "the true God" (1 John 5:20)—complements and consummates the divine revelation in the Old Testament. While God's revelation in ancient times was fragmentary and occasional, it is complete and final in Jesus Christ.

Hebrews 1:2-4 presents eight facts about Christ, the living Word, that confirm His status as God's complete and final revelation to humanity. (1) Jesus is "heir of all things"; (2) God made the world through Him; (3) Jesus is the radiance of God's glory; (4) Jesus is the exact representation of His nature; (5) Jesus upholds "all things by the word of His power"; (6) Jesus "made purification of sins"; (7) Jesus "sat down at the right hand of the Majesty on high"; and, (8) Jesus "has inherited a more excellent name than [the angels]."

God the Son revealed many truths about God the Father. In fact, He not only revealed truths about the Father, He *is* the incarnate Revelation of the Father (John 1:14). Scripture abounds with evidence about how Jesus revealed God and helped people understand Him more fully (see 14:8-10).

Christ revealed the *Person* of God in ways He had never been made known before. For instance, Jesus unveiled the Father to mankind (see John 1:18; 1 Tim. 3:16). Christ also made known the *glory* of God (Isa. 40:5; John 1:14; 2 Cor. 4:6). Additionally, God the Son revealed the *power* of God the Father on many occasions and in many different ways (John 3:2; 1 Cor. 1:24).

The Person of Christ made known the *wisdom* of God (John 7:46; 1 Cor. 1:24). Jesus also declared the *life* of God (1 John 1:1-3). Further, the Savior disclosed and demonstrated the boundless *love* of God (John 3:16; Rom. 5:8; 1 John 3:16). Moreover, the Lord Jesus unveiled the *grace* of God, that is, the undeserved favor He bestowed upon humanity (Luke 2:40; John 1:17; 2 Thess. 1:12).

The Living Word and Written Word

How wonderful it is that God has given humanity His living Word and His written Word! But how terrible it is that people increasingly reject these and substitute the lies of the Devil (see 1 Tim. 4:1).

The living Word and the written Word are two impregnable forces, the pillars upon which Christianity stands or falls. To attempt to speak about Christianity (in the truest sense of that term) without an absolutely divine living Word and an inspired written Word of God is sheer nonsense. These two are inseparable from one another and from biblical Christianity. They constitute the bedrock of orthodox faith. Thus when people spurn God's living and written revelation, they are renouncing the Christian faith.

Denial of the Bible as the Word of God is common in our day. Unfortunately, the denial does not stop with a rejection of Scripture as God's Word. In fact, it only begins there, as it always has. Invariably, those who reject the Bible as God's written Word also reject Jesus Christ as the living Word.

Liberal and neo-orthodox sympathizers have always rejected both the living Word and the written Word, especially as they are made known in the Bible. Unfortunately, an increasing number of evangelicals tend to believe they can reject certain portions of the Bible as being free from error and yet at the same time maintain belief in the Christ of Scripture. This, in my view, is an impossible position to hold.[3]

To accept the written Word as being less than totally inerrant logically leads to a living Word who is less than "very God, of very God," as the ancients put it. Neither source of divine revelation can be held in isolation from the other. Contrary to any approach that depreciates either the living Word or the written Word, the Bible testifies to a beautiful and perfect harmony existing between both sources of divine revelation.

Both the Living Word and the Written Word Came From God

God gave to humanity both the living Word and the written Word. They both unquestionably constitute divine revelations from Him. The same God who revealed Himself by speaking to and through the writers of Scripture has spoken with fullness and finality in His Son, the living Word (Heb. 1:1–2). Christ, the living Word, not only revealed God to people (John 1:18), but also in His own Person is the Revelation of God (Heb. 1:2).

Similar statements can be made about the Bible, God's written Word. Without doubt, Scripture reveals the Person and work of God, while at the same time it is His own divine revelation.

Repeatedly, the human penmen of Scripture testify that God spoke to them and the Spirit of God was upon them as they wrote (see, for example, 2 Peter 1:20–21). These and similar acknowledgments by the human authors of God's Word indicate that Scripture originated with Him, even though it was penned by people.

What is true of the written Word is also true of the living Word. Galatians 4:4 says that when the fullness of time had come, God the Father sent forth the Lord Jesus Christ to provide redemption for humanity. Similarly, John 3:17 says that "God did not send the Son into the world to judge the world, but that the world should be saved through Him."

From these and other verses we learn that Christ is fully divine and fully human. And He who is the exact representation of the Father (Heb. 1:3) often testified that the written Word, though penned with human hands, came from God (see, for example, Matt. 22:31–32). Together the living Word and the written Word are a testimony to God's power, love, and grace.

Both the Living Word and the Written Word Claim the Same Authority

The testimony of the Bible to its own inspiration and therefore its absolute authority is abundant. While many do not accept this clear and consistent witness that Scripture has given to its own authority, rarely is it debated or denied that such claims are made by the Bible.

A popular view is the theory that the writers of Scripture and even the Lord Jesus Himself merely accommodated themselves to the mistaken notion held by their contemporaries regarding the inspiration of the Old Testament. Such an explanation of the biblical evidence, however, only complicates the problem by making Christ and the human penmen dishonest, deceptive, and less than trustworthy.

Since God gave us the written Word, it would seem self-evident that its authority would be the same as the One who gave it. The written Word is as eternal as God and therefore as authoritative as God Himself (see Isa. 55:11; 1 Peter 1:25). Since the written Word claims to come from God, to disbelieve the same is tantamount to disbelieving God and accusing Him of falsehood.

On numerous occasions, Christ, the living Word, did not hesitate to claim for Himself the authority of God the Father. Unlike the scribes, Jesus did not need to appeal to religious tradition or any other sources of humanly derived authority (see Matt. 7:28–29). This is evident in His claim to be the fulfillment of the Law and Prophets (that is, the entire Old Testament; see 5:17).

Although Christ accepted and claimed the authority of God, He did not hesitate to subscribe and to submit to the authority of the written Word. The authority that Jesus claimed for Himself and the authority that He claimed for the Scriptures are identical. These two are so interwoven that to reject one is to reject both, and to receive one is to receive both.

To His religious critics Jesus said, "the Scripture cannot be broken" (John 10:35). Such a statement about the indissoluble, inviolable authority of a minute portion of a seemingly incidental verse in Psalm 82:6 indicates Jesus' high regard for the final authority of all Scripture. And the Savior's reference to this verse as "your Law" (v. 34), "the word of God" (v. 35), and "Scripture," testifies to His regard for the irrefutable authority of the written Word.

Both the Living Word and the Written Word Complement Each Other

The written Word bears abundant testimony to the living Word. In fact, apart from the Bible's witness to Christ, we would know little about Him, for only scant reference is made to Him in noncanonical historical sources. He is the center and circumference of the Bible. It is completely unintelligible without recognition of Him. His promised advent to the earth, miraculous birth, sinless life, sacrificial death for sin, bodily resurrection from the grave, and future literal return to earth for His own forms the sum and substance of holy Scripture.

The living Word complements the written Word just as highly as the written Word complements the living Word. There can be no question about it. The living Word ascribes inspiration to the whole of the written Word, its various parts, and even to the words and letters used by the human authors. No stronger evidence exists for the total inerrancy and absolute authority of all Scripture than the Savior's own testimony.[4]

For Christ, God's Word is "truth" (John 17:17). "Scripture," He said "cannot be broken" (John 10:35). According to Christ's testimony, the "smallest letter or stroke" of the Mosaic law would be fulfilled (Matt. 5:18). Jesus embraced all the inspired books of the Old Testament Canon, and only those books, as the Word of God, not only before His critics (Matt. 23:35) but also to His own disciples after His resurrection (Luke 24:44). Moreover, the living Word promised to send the Holy Spirit, who would superintend the revelatory process so that the New Testament Canon would bear the same level of inspiration, infallibility, and inerrancy as the Old Testament Canon (John 14:26; 15:26–27; 16:13–14).

Both the Living Word and the Written Word Include the Human Element

Herein lies the miracle! It is this miraculous, supernatural aspect of both the living Word and the written Word that has accounted for the widespread rejection of both. "How," modern people in the scientific space age ask, "is it possible for a woman with a sin nature to give birth to one who is sinless?" Likewise, how is it possible for sinful human beings to write a Book that is God-breathed and without error?

The answer to both these queries is that neither is possible apart from divine intervention, and that is precisely what God did. He intervened supernaturally through the Person of the Holy Spirit and protected both the living Word and the Written Word from human corruption. This kind of supernaturalism is what the unbelieving mind rejects and what the philosophies of the world do not allow for in their closed systems.

That the living Word is fully divine is clearly taught in Scripture (see John 1:1). That to His fully divine nature was joined a perfect human nature is also abundantly taught in the Bible. The living Word "became flesh" (John 1:14). He was born, grew to adulthood, and experienced the privations common to humanity, yet without sin. There thus can be no doubt about the biblical testimony concerning the full divinity and humanity of Christ. To deny either one of these biblical doctrines is to discredit the written Word.

It was through the agency of the Holy Spirit, not the union of Mary and Joseph, that the Christ-child was conceived in the womb of Mary. Nevertheless, she was just as depraved as Joseph, and apart from divine intervention, would have passed the sin nature on to Christ. Through the miraculous work of the Spirit in Mary's womb, the Lord Jesus—though fully human—was kept from inheriting any taint of sin. Only of Him could it be said that "in Him there is no sin" (1 John 3:5). Scripture likewise teaches that Jesus was "without sin" (Heb. 4:15), "knew no sin" (2 Cor. 5:21), and was "undefiled" (Heb. 7:26).

Just as surely as the living Word has a human element to His existence, so too the written Word has a human element to its production. The penmen of the Bible were human. But they were not sinless. The same Holy Spirit who prevented the Christ-child from inheriting Mary's sin nature also kept the human writers of Scripture from including error in what they wrote.

Peter described this divine control by saying that "men moved by the Holy Spirit spoke from God" (2 Peter 1:21). In other words, they were carried along, guided, and protected by the Spirit. Without excluding their human intelligence, their individuality, their literary style, their personal feelings, or any other human factor, the Spirit protected them from all error and omission in the production of the written Word.

The previous observations underscore the inconsistency of trying to differentiate in Scripture what pertains to making people "wise to salvation" from what does not. Today, a frightening number of evangelicals are attempting to separate in Scripture what they feel is central from what they wish to call "peripheral." They wish to allow for the possibility of error in those matters that do not pertain to salvation (namely, scientific, historic, and geographic data). But is it not true that fallible human authors wrote the whole of Scripture? If the Holy Spirit kept the writers from error sometimes, why couldn't He do so at all times?

By the same token, if the presence of a human element presumes fallibility, then the Lord Jesus Christ had to be fallible, for He is human. There can be no mistake about the logic behind this incorrect reasoning. Both the living Word and the written Word were touched in some way by sinful humanity. What is insisted, therefore, about the effects of that sinful humanity upon the one must, it would seem, also be said about its effect upon the other.

How and on what basis can the student of Scripture determine when the words recorded on the original autographs of the Bible were free from error and when they were not? What precisely constitutes a truth that may be classified as central to the witness of the Bible, and what may be said to be peripheral? On what basis are questions such as these to be answered, if it is not on the basis of humanity's subjective determination? Those who disclaim inerrancy for some parts of Holy Scripture or who even allow for the possibility of error in any part of Scripture have set aside the Bible's own testimony to itself, as well as the testimony of the living Word, and have made themselves the final judge of truth.

Admittedly, there are some difficulties in the Bible.[5] Yet these are answerable. In fact, many years ago satisfactory answers were given to them. No new evidence has been discovered that would cause Christians to lose their faith in the Bible, nor have any new problems been presented. One's view of the Bible must be based on the witness of Scripture to itself, not on difficulties contained in it.

The issue is what the Bible teaches about itself, not how its difficulties can be answered. We do not wait until there has been a satisfactory solution to every problem before we believe our Lord's view and the witness of Scripture to its own inerrancy. It is an insult to God to hold His professed truth in abeyance. Christians should accept the testimony of the living Word and the written Word, believing that every difficulty does have an accurate explanation that can be harmonized with these testimonies, even though some of those explanations have not yet been found.

Those who do not believe in the inerrancy of the Bible are often ready to admit that those who first received the Scriptures, and the Christians of later centuries, did believe in the Bible's total and unique authority. But today, these evangelicals argue that we live in a "world come of age"; thus, we no longer need to hold such a rigid, antiquated view. Although these people insist on the possibility of the Bible being wrong on "peripheral" matters, they do not think this line of reasoning destroys belief in the basic reliability of the Bible. They argue that God did not intend for the Bible to be a textbook on the "peripheral" matters it discusses; yet people can trust that God has given them an errorless Word in religious matters—namely, matters about faith and life—because this is the main purpose of the Bible.

The folly of such a division between "peripheral" and central matters in the Bible is that people—the receivers—become the deciding factor. Why and on what basis do people make such a division in the content of Scripture?

Some who believe in the possibility of error in the Bible (even though it came from God), might appeal to the church to defend their view. Did not the church come from God, and is it not imperfect? Yes, God did, through the work of His Son and the Holy Spirit, establish the church. And it is true that those who make up the true church do not lead sinless lives. Yet in the economy of God, there are no blemishes in Christ's body. Positionally, every believer is perfect.

Through the Holy Spirit, God was pleased to protect the human authors of Scripture from all error and omission as they wrote. Likewise, the Spirit overshadowed Mary as she conceived and gave birth to the Christ-child. By the same Holy Spirit, God brought the church into existence. What God thus produced is already in His reckoning without spot or wrinkle (see Eph. 5:25–27).

Since individual members of the church are left here with the same capacity to sin with which they were born, they are not perfect in their walk before others. But in the sight of God every member of His family is positionally complete and perfect, for they are clothed in the righteousness of His Son. In a day yet future those who have this perfect standing before God and who are already seated in the heavens with Christ will be changed in a moment, in the twinkling of an eye. Then their perishable earthly bodies will be transformed into heavenly bodies that will never die (see 1 Cor. 15:51–53).

Neither the Living Word nor the Written Word Contradict Each Other

In conclusion, the living Word and the written Word are never at odds with each other. To be specific, the living Word never leads people to do something contrary to the written Word. Only perfect harmony prevails between these two sources of revelation. After all, they both come from God. Furthermore, the living Word came to do the will of the Father and to fulfill the written Word.

Those who accept the Bible for what it claims to be—the Word of God—are often denounced for worshiping a book and for substituting the Bible for Christ. The Savior's view of the Scripture should dispel all such arguments. Christ made no distinction between parts of the Bible. He insisted that all of it bore witness to Him (Luke 24:25–27; John 5:39).

Therefore, those who charge the one who believes in the total inerrancy of the written Word with bibliolatry must also charge Christ, the living Word, with the same offense. Yet nowhere in Jesus' teaching did He ever give the impression that to embrace His own view of Scripture was to distract or diminish one's view of Him. Without ever relinquishing His own authority as the God-man, He consistently taught the absolute authority of Scripture, which, He insisted, spoke about Him.

Perhaps our devotion to the written Word sometimes gives people the impression that we are worshiping a book rather than a Person. But this certainly is not true, even though that book is the holy Bible. God uses the inerrant written Word to reveal His inerrant living Word so that we might worship Him (see Rev. 19:10). It is Christ whom we are to love, worship, and serve, for it is He who gave Himself for us. Moreover, it is the living Word who has charged His own to hold fast the written Word while they herald it forth to a lost world (see Jude 3).

The following diagram depicts the living Word of God and the written Word of God.

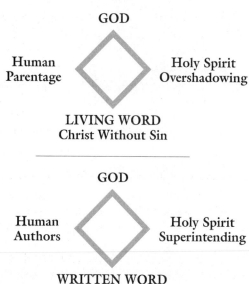

GOD

Human Parentage

Holy Spirit Overshadowing

LIVING WORD
Christ Without Sin

GOD

Human Authors

Holy Spirit Superintending

WRITTEN WORD
Bible Without Error

Notes

1. Benjamin B. Warfield, *Selected Shorter Writings of Benjamin B. Warfield-I,* ed. John E. Meeter (Nutley, N.J.: Presbyterian and Reformed, 1970), 69–70. The entire set of Warfield's works is now available: *The Works of B. B. Warfield* (Grand Rapids: Baker, 1991).

2. Ibid., 82.

3. For a complete study, see the author's *A Biblical Case for Total Inerrancy: How Jesus Viewed the Old Testament* (Grand Rapids: Kregel, 1998). For a fuller discussion of the inerrancy debate among evangelicals, see Harold Lindsell, *The Battle for the Bible* (Grand Rapids: Zondervan, 1976), and his *The Bible in the Balance* (Grand Rapids: Zondervan, 1979).

4. For a study of the whole subject of the inerrancy of Scripture, see Norman L. Geisler, ed., *Inerrancy* (Grand Rapids: Zondervan, 1980); for a concise layman oriented treatment of the same subject, see Charles C. Ryrie's *What You Should Know about Inerrancy* (Chicago: Moody, 1981).

5. One of the best sources for dealing with Bible difficulties is Gleason L. Archer's *Encyclopedia of Bible Difficulties* (Grand Rapids: Zondervan, 1982).

CHAPTER 8

How Does the God of the Bible Exist?

WHILE BEING INTERVIEWED, a Roman Catholic priest said, "I don't know if God exists."[1] The priest went on to say that he assumed God existed and that he lived as though He did, but he could not be really sure. He defended his philosophy by appealing to Christ.

> But I still believe that this was what he [Christ] felt was important—the search for God whether he exists or not . . . after death we might well find that what we have been searching for is not what we expected but at least, in the search we have, if we have gone about it properly, left the world a little better than we found it.[2]

Leaving the world a better place, the priest said, is what all religion is about and what Christianity in particular is all about "because we have the example of Jesus to follow."[3]

Those who embrace the Bible as authoritative and accept its pronouncements as final expressions of truth will not find themselves in such a spiritual quandary. Neither will sinners who have been saved by God's grace experience such a dismal outlook and have such a poor view of Jesus Christ. For the children of God the question is not: *Does* God exist? They know He does, for He is their heavenly Father.

Those who are rightly related to God through faith in Jesus Christ will find in Scripture an answer to the question: *How* does God exist? He is presented in the Bible as the supremely divine Person, the One who exists in Trinity. In other words, there is one personal God, both immanent and transcendent, who exists in three personal distinctions, known respectively as the Father, the Son, and the Holy Spirit.

The Personality of God

Definition of Personality

Personality may be defined as those set of characteristics that distinguishes someone from others. Intertwined with this definition is the concept of *personhood,* namely, the presence of self-consciousness and self-determination.

To be self-conscious means one has the ability to distinguish one's self from other entities, whether they are sentient or non-sentient. Self-consciousness is more than a mere awareness of one's existence, for even animals are able to perceive the presence of things around them. Animals, however, are not able to think objectively of their own self-existence. In contrast, humans possess both consciousness and self-consciousness.

Self-determination has to do with the ability to consider the future and prepare an intelligent course of action in light of anticipated events. Self-determination also involves the power of choice. Animals can instinctively choose to do something. But they do not have the ability to act from their own free will and thus to determine their acts volitionally.

Evidences for the Personality of God

God possesses the elements of personality. The intellect, the emotions, and the will are the three basic elements of personality. As a self-conscious being, God possesses intellect (the ability to think rationally) and emotion (the ability to respond with feelings). Scripture affirms this truth. For instance, after discussing the sovereign plan of God for national Israel, Paul wrote, "Oh, the depth of the riches both of the wisdom and knowledge of God! How unsearchable are His judgments and unfathomable His ways!" (Rom. 11:33). And John noted that "God is love" (1 John 4:8). As a self-conscious being, God possess will (the ability to act volitionally). Scripture also affirms this truth. For instance, 2 Peter 3:9 says that God is "not wishing for any to perish but for all to come to repentance."

The Bible abounds with evidence that God possesses the constituent elements of personality; therefore, we can say on biblical ground that He is a Person, and not a force, or an "it," or even the "ground of being."

The naturalistic theistic arguments for God's existence also argue for the presence of His personality. I presented these arguments in chapter 1. Despite their limitations, all the naturalistic arguments, when rightly understood, call for the existence of a personal God who is infinitely wise and powerful. Only such a supreme being could be the Creator and Sustainer of humanity and the universe.

The characteristics, or attributes, of God argue strongly for the presence of His personality. I will discuss these characteristics in chapter 10. Here I simply want to emphasize that the attributes of God are ascribed to a Person, not to an influence or power. Only a Person can be all-knowing, all-powerful, and so on. Added to this line of evidence and closely related to it is the fact that throughout Scripture God is said to speak. This would be impossible if the One speaking did not have a personality.

In Scripture, personal pronouns are used to refer to God. The use of the personal pronouns in reference to God provide further evidence for the presence of His personality.

Names ascribed to God are strong indications of the presence of His personality. In chapter 11 of this book I discuss the meaning and significance of the many names ascribed to God. Here I only want to mention that since each of the divine names describes some aspect of the character of God, these names lend strong support for the presence of His personality.

The fact that people, as God's highest creation, possess personality, is strong reason to believe that God also possesses personality. It seems highly inconceivable that a non-personal God could or would create personal beings such as humans. This is especially true since the Bible declares that God made people in His own image and likeness (Gen. 1:26–27). Surely, if this statement reveals anything at all, it discloses that there is a similarity between God and people. Of course, there are drastic differences between the two; yet there has to be a similarity, or Genesis 1:26–27 becomes meaningless.

We can be sure that the similarity does not extend to the physical body of people, for God is spirit and does not possess a physical, corruptible, and decaying body (John 4:24). There is in the immaterial part of each person a correspondence with God. Even after the fall of humanity and the cataclysmic flood, people are still said to be created in the image of God (Gen. 9:1-6). Though there may be other things to which this image of God in people relates that must be taken into account in an attempt to understand it fully, yet it cannot be denied that the reference surely relates to God's personality.[4]

There is great significance in the fact that people are made in the image of God. For believers it should serve as a reminder that they are God's representatives on earth. They are charged with the responsibility of pointing others to Christ, who is *the* image of the invisible God. The fact that all are created in the image of

God highlights the dignity of people and ought to create within them respect for all human beings (James 3:9).

While on the Hill of Ares (or Mars's Hill), Paul spoke to the Athenian leaders about the truth of the image of God in people (Acts 17:19–31). The apostle noted that since God created people in His image, they must not worship gods of their own making—namely, idols made out of gold, silver, or stone. Instead, they should worship and serve the only true God.

The moral and spiritual duties of people argue for the presence of God's personality. The moral and spiritual duties that God has given to people argue for the presence of His own personality. The Bible clearly outlines the responsibilities people have to God. For instance, every divine exhortation for people to repent, believe, pray, and obey is an argument for the presence of God's personality. After all, only a personal God could be concerned with our problems, sorrows, and joys. And only a personal Creator—God—could invite us—His creatures—to fellowship with Him. A non-personal God would and could not expect people to respond this way.

The anthropomorphic expressions used in Scripture to refer to God are indications of the presence of His personality. An anthropomorphic expression is any description of God's being, actions, and emotions in human terms. For example, God is said to have "arms" (Deut. 33:27), a "hand" (John 10:29), and a "mouth" (Isa. 58:14). Such expressions do not mean that God possesses these physical parts, for He is spirit (John 4:24). Rather, they are intended to provide information about His character and conduct. Although God is invisible, infinite, and without a body, human characteristics are frequently used to describe Him. The presence of these characteristics lends support to the contention that God is a Person.

The significance of the fact that God possesses a personality. Pantheism and atheism are two logical results of denying that God possesses a personality. Both of these ideologies are equally anti-biblical and unacceptable alternatives to the truth that God is a sentient Person, namely, someone who possesses the ability to think rationally, respond emotively, and act volitionally.

Belief in the personal God of the Bible provides both assurance and comfort for His children. Since God is a Being who possesses the three elements of personality in absolute and complete perfection, He is the One with whom believers can have fellowship. Because He is a Person, He knows and understands our deepest longings. As the song writer has so aptly expressed it, we can walk and talk with Him in sweet fellowship and prayer. Life would be hopeless and futile without the intimacy of our God. This intimacy is made possible through the Lord Jesus Christ and the ministry of the Holy Spirit.

The Trinity of God

Introduction

Holy Scripture presents God existing not only as a holy Person but also as existing in holy Trinity.[5] The doctrine is exclusively the subject of special divine revelation in the Bible. God's revelation in nature and in humanity do not contribute to our understanding of the Trinity. Much of the written revelation of God involves mystery, yet the Trinity is no doubt the greatest mystery of all revealed truth.

Though often least understood of all the doctrines of the orthodox Christian faith, the doctrine of the Trinity is one of the most basic of all areas of theology. Augustine, the church father, stated well the importance of this doctrine when he wrote, "In no other subject is error more dangerous or inquiry more laborious, or discovery of the truth more profitable."

The word *Trinity* does not occur in the Bible. Evangelical Christians believe in the doctrine of the triune God because of the teaching of Scripture as a whole and not because of one particular passage of Scripture.

There are many specific passages that present three Persons who equally and fully possess deity—God the Father, God the Son, and God the Holy Spirit. The Bible also emphasizes just as emphatically that there is but one true God with one divine essence. Geisler gives this simple working definition of essence: "What makes a thing what it is, and not something else. God's essence is what makes Him God and not anything else."[6] Taking all that Scripture has to say regarding the one and only true God and the three Persons of the Godhead, we find that the stress is upon unity and diversity in unity.

The Bible speaks about three Persons in a similar way. Scripture ascribes deity, personality, and individuality to each. And yet the Bible also reveals that there is but one God. The ancients expressed it well when they spoke about one essence, or substance, in God who existed in three Persons—Father, Son, and Holy Spirit. These are two key truths that believers should recognize and as much as possible harmonize.

Definition of the Trinity

The danger has always been to either fall into tri-theism—namely, a belief in three Gods—or to view the Son and the Holy Spirit as being less than God. Those same dangers still exist today. Also, there is an additional error that must be avoided in our understanding of the Trinity. We must not assume that the Father, Son, and Holy Spirit are merely names or varied modes of existence for the one true God.

To sum up the biblical view, which avoids both of these dangers, Christians worship one God who exists in three Persons—God the Father, God the Son, and God the Holy Spirit. The doctrine of the blessed Trinity is a reminder of the supernaturalness of biblical Christianity. The doctrine defies rationalization, yet it provides for the believer the answer to the unity and diversity in the world all around us.

How can God be one and yet exist in three distinct Persons? All illustrations fail at this point and even the best of them are inadequate. But it may be helpful to remember that in areas other than the Trinity one entity is sometimes really more than singular in its existence. For example, the human being—whom God has made in His image—is a single being, not many; yet, he is more than a single being. Each person is made up of both the *material* (a body) and the *immaterial* (a soul, spirit, heart, mind, and conscience). At the same time, it must be admitted that each individual is a single being. In this instance, one entity is more than one in its existence.

Recognizing the failure of these observations to illustrate completely or adequately the truth of God's triune existence, I might suggest water as another example of one entity being more than singular in its existence. Water is normally considered as one entity, and yet it is composed of two elements—hydrogen and oxygen.

When theologians say that God is one and that He exists in three Persons, they must be careful not to imply that each member loses His individual identity. The Father, the Son, and the Holy Spirit remain real, individual, and true Persons, even though they are one in divine essence. The members of the Godhead retain their individuality just as much as a husband remains a man and a wife remains a woman, even though they become one in marriage and are often at the same time a father and a mother as well.

In the past, theologians spoke about the economical and ontological Trinity. The latter designation was used to refer to the Trinity before creation or before time began. By economical Trinity, theologians meant the Trinity since time began. The following diagram is an illustration of the Trinity.

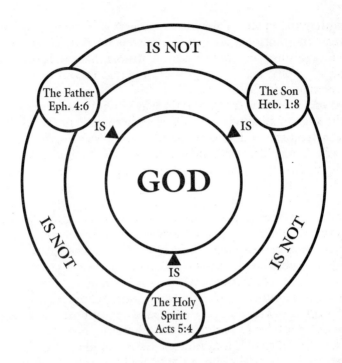

Implications of the Trinity in the Old Testament

I use the word *implication* advisedly. By it I mean there are hints, indications, or shadows of the Trinity in the Old Testament. This is in contrast to the clear and complete revelation of the Trinity in the New Testament.

God revealed His Word gradually. As the revelation of God progressed, He gave more and more truth concerning the Trinity. The truth about the Trinity in the Bible illustrates the fact that God gradually unfolded His revelation to humanity (see Heb. 1:1-2).

My comments should not be taken to mean that the earlier portions of Scripture are less inspired than the later ones, for all portions are equally God-breathed (see 2 Tim. 3:16). In the Old Testament, the emphasis is upon the unity of God, while in the New Testament the emphasis is upon the Trinity of God. This is not to say there is no teaching in the Old Testament about the Trinity of God anymore than it means to say there is no teaching in the New Testament about the unity of God.

Implications of more than one Person in the Godhead. The Hebrew word *Elohim* is a plural name used of God many times in the Old Testament (see, for example, Deut. 6:4). In fact, it is the most frequent name for God used in the Old Testament. In light of the New Testament's clear teaching on the Trinity, this name provides strong corroborative evidence for the doctrine of the Trinity.

Other plural titles are also used of God in the Old Testament. Here are two examples where the English translation obscures this truth: "your Creator" (Eccl. 12:1) is more accurately rendered "your Creators"; and "your Maker" (Isa. 54:5) is more accurately rendered "your Makers." Plural pronouns are also used in reference to God: "Let Us make man in *Our* image" (Gen. 1:26; see also Gen. 3:22; 11:7; Isa. 6:8).

In the Old Testament, Yahweh is distinguished from the Angel of Yahweh. This surely argues for more than one Person in the Godhead, especially when the Angel of Yahweh, or Angel of the Lord, is called Yahweh in one passage (Gen. 16:7–13; 22:11–18) and then in another passage is said to speak to Yahweh (Zech. 1:12–13).

In Psalm 2 the "LORD" and "His Anointed" are two separate individuals. The "Anointed" in verse 2 and the Lord's "King" in verse 6 are obviously and definitely references to Christ (God the Son), while the "LORD" in verse 2 is a reference to Yahweh (God the Father).

The deity of the Holy Spirit also supports the truth that God's existence is a plurality in unity. The Old Testament assigns attributes of God to the Spirit (see Ps. 139:7). The Hebrew Scriptures also assign the work of God (for instance, creation) to the same Spirit (see Job 26:13). Throughout the Old Testament it is clear that God the Spirit is distinct from God the Father and God the Son. Yet the Spirit possesses the full measure of deity.

Implications of three Persons in the Godhead. This section takes us one step further in our discussion. Not only are there clear statements in the Old Testament about more than one Person existing within the Godhead (indicating a plurality), but there are also definite implications of three distinct Persons in the Godhead (indicating a Trinity).

Moses instructed Aaron to bless Israel (Num. 6:24–27), and in doing so gave implication of the existence of the Trinity. There are three parts to Moses' benediction, and these parallel the ministries of the three members of the Trinity. In verse 24, the Father's love is expressed; in verse 25, the Son's redeeming and reconciling grace is underscored; and in verse 26, the Spirit's joy and peace are highlighted.

In Isaiah's vision, the response of the holy angels implies the existence of three distinct Persons in the Godhead. The threefold repetition "Holy, holy, holy" (Isa. 6:3) seems to be more than the customary Hebrew mode of emphasis, especially since the plural "Us" occurs in verse 8. The One being addressed in the passage is certainly the *Father*. When John 12:40-41 is studied along with Isaiah 6:10, it becomes apparent that Isaiah also beheld the glory of the *Son*. Moreover, when Acts 28:25-26 and Isaiah 6:9 are studied along with the record of Isaiah's vision, there is further evidence of the presence of the *Holy Spirit* in the passage.

Perhaps Isaiah 48:16 and 63:7-10 contain the clearest Old Testament presentations of the existence of three distinct Persons in the Godhead. In 48:16, the preincarnate Christ spoke, saying, "And now the Lord God has sent Me, and His Spirit." Furthermore, as Isaiah praised God for His mercy, the prophet mentioned the LORD, the "angel of His presence" (namely, the preincarnate Christ), and the Holy Spirit (Isa. 63:7-10).

Further evidence from the Old Testament for the existence of the Trinity can be found in passages that talk about the work each Person individually performs within the Godhead. My intent here is not to discuss all the various functions that each member of the Godhead performs. Rather, I have chosen two divine works to illustrate my point.

First, the creation of the material world is attributed to the Father (Ps. 102:25), to the Son (Col. 1:16), and to the Holy Spirit (Gen. 1:2; Job 26:13). Second, the work of the creation of man—whose essence is both material and immaterial in nature—is assigned to the Father (Gen. 2:7), to the Son (Col. 1:16), and to the Holy Spirit (Job 33:4).

Revelation of the Trinity in the New Testament

Though the word *Trinity* does not appear in Scripture, there is clear revelation in the New Testament that one God exists in three Persons—Father, Son, and Holy Spirit. This revelation may be categorized as follows:

Three Persons are said to possess deity. The Father is called God (John 6:27; Rom. 1:7), the Son is called God (John 1:1, 14; Heb. 1:8), and the Holy Spirit is called God (Acts 5:3-9). Each of the three Persons within the Godhead is presented as being fully equal with the other two. They are also described as being in intimate communion and cooperation with one another (Matt. 28:19; 2 Cor. 13:14). Though equal in essence and united in purpose (see John 10:30), these three Persons are distinct from one another (Matt. 3:16-17; Luke 1:35; John 12:28; 14:16; 15:26).

Each of these absolutely divine Persons possesses the attributes peculiar to deity. For example, each possesses *omnipotence* (in other words, is all-powerful). This is true of the Father (1 Peter 1:5), the Son (Matt. 28:18), and the Holy Spirit (Rom. 15:19). Each possesses *omniscience* (in other words, is all-knowing). This is true of the Father (Rom. 11:33), the Son (Rev. 2:23), and the Holy Spirit (1 Cor. 2:11). Each possesses *omnipresence* (in other words, is every where present at the same time). This is true of the Father (Acts 7:48-50), the Son (Matt. 18:20), and the Holy Spirit (Eph. 1:13-14; 2:18; 4:4; see also Ps. 139:7).

The New Testament teaches that the three Persons within the Godhead exercise divine prerogatives. For example, each receives worship from people. This is true of the Father (John 4:23), the Son (John 9:38; 20:28), and the Holy Spirit (Phil. 3:3). Furthermore, each of these Persons gives commands to the people of God. This is true of the Father (Matt. 17:5), the Son (John 15:12, 14), and the Holy Spirit (Acts 8:29; 10:19).

There is no doubt that the Father, the Son, and the Holy Spirit are coequal and coeternal. And all three Persons are equally and absolutely divine. It is also important to note that there is an order of functional priority and subordination among the three Persons within the Godhead. In other words, there is a difference in the office and role of each Person. To acknowledge this teaching of Scripture in no way denies the divine equality of the three Persons within the Godhead. I am simply making a clear and careful distinction between the divine essence that each Person equally shares and the distinct role, or function, that each member of the Trinity performs.

Let's briefly consider a few examples of what I mean. The Father sent the Son into the world (Gal. 4:4). And the Son sent the Holy Spirit into the world (John 15:26). Moreover, because of what Christ has done on the cross, believers have access to the Father through the Holy Spirit (Eph. 2:18). The subordination of the Son to the Father's will is seen nowhere more clearly than in Philippians 2:6-7: "Who, although He existed in the form of God, did not regard equality with God a thing to be grasped, but emptied Himself, taking the form of a bond-servant, and being made in the likeness of men."

Christ's upper room discourse, which is recorded in John 13:1-17:26, gives us the clearest and strongest proof found in the New Testament for the doctrine of the Trinity. As Jesus promised to send the Holy Spirit, the distinct existence of these two members of the Godhead is evident (16:7). And as Jesus prayed to the Father, the distinct existence of these two members of the Godhead is evident (17:1-3).

John 14:16 contains what is perhaps the clearest and most concise statement from Christ regarding the existence of three members in the Godhead: "I [Christ] will ask the Father, and He will give you another Helper [the Spirit], that He may be with you forever." Jesus also made it clear that each member of the Godhead is one in essence (17:11, 21-22).

The diagram below is an attempt to show in visible form what I have been seeking to set forth in the last half of this chapter.

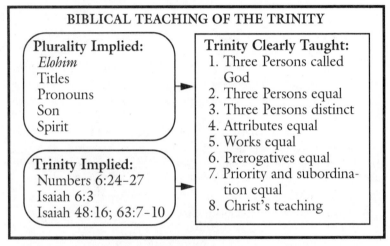

BIBLICAL TEACHING OF THE TRINITY

Plurality Implied:
Elohim
Titles
Pronouns
Son
Spirit

Trinity Implied:
Numbers 6:24–27
Isaiah 6:3
Isaiah 48:16; 63:7–10

Trinity Clearly Taught:
1. Three Persons called God
2. Three Persons equal
3. Three Persons distinct
4. Attributes equal
5. Works equal
6. Prerogatives equal
7. Priority and subordination equal
8. Christ's teaching

Notes

1. Derek Tiplen, "Portrait of a Modern Priest," *Christian Heritage,* December 1970, 6.
2. Ibid.
3. Ibid.
4. For an excellent presentation of the significance of the image of God in people, see James Oliver Buswell's *Systematic Theology* (Grand Rapids: Zondervan, 1962).
5. Classic studies on the Trinity that are perennially in print, with their usual publisher, include: Edward Bickersteth, *The Trinity* (Kregel); Lewis Sperry Chafer, *Systematic Theology,* vol. 1 (Kregel); and Charles Hodge, *Systematic Theology,* vol. 1 (Eerdmans). A more recent contribution appears in Millard J. Erickson, *Christian Theology,* vol. 1 (Baker).
6. Norman L. Geisler, *False Gods of Our Time* (Eugene, Oreg.: Harvest House, 1985), 18. *Webster's New Collegiate Dictionary* gives a similar definition: "The properties or attributes by means of which something can be placed in its proper class or identified as being what it is."

CHAPTER 9

What Is the God of the Bible Doing?

THE ANSWER TO THE ABOVE question introduces us to the doctrine of the plan of God. Theologians often call the Lord's all-inclusive plan His decree. To be sure, there are many aspects to, or ramifications of, God's all-inclusive plan. Theologians sometimes call these His decrees. Technically speaking, though, there is only one overall decree of God, though that one plan is composed of many expressions, which relate to all things.

"Calvinism," named after John Calvin (1509-1564), and "Arminianism," named after Jacobus Arminius (1560-1609), are two terms theologians use frequently in discussions about Bible doctrines. And scholars often use these terms as labels to describe their general theological positions.

Many theologians strongly believe that either Calvinism or Arminianism is totally correct and the other theological system is totally incorrect. The truth is that both these systems make assertions that are taught in Scripture and therefore should be believed. And both Calvinism and Arminianism make assertions that are not taught in Scripture and therefore should not be believed.

Not everything associated with Arminianism is erroneous, and not everything associated with Calvinism is correct. Rather than attempt to endorse or find complete agreement with any particular theological system, it is far better for us to strive to be biblicists at all costs. We never need to apologize for differing with fallible theologians. But let God's people never be guilty of differing with His infallible Word! Scripture, not a particular system of theology, provides the standard of truth.

The Sovereignty of God

If God is fully divine, He must be sovereign! In other words, He must be the supreme Ruler over all; otherwise, He cannot be truly God. This does not mean that people are not responsible for their actions. They are always responsible.

The sovereignty of God and the responsibility of people are parallel truths in Scripture. Difficulty in understanding either one of these two great doctrines comes when they are divorced from each other and when people seek to reconcile them fully with each other. The fact is, these two biblical truths are never brought together or fully reconciled with each other. It remains an inscrutable mystery how God can be altogether sovereign and yet allow for genuine human responsibility in His sovereign plan.

Both God's absolute sovereignty and humanity's genuine responsibility are taught from Genesis 1:1 to Revelation 22:21. Throughout history, people have tried to bring these two truths together, and consistently the result has been to either deny, or at best seriously weaken, the teaching about God's sovereignty or human responsibility. It is better to view these two great truths as running parallel throughout Scripture, to humbly believe both, and to live our lives according to both.

It would be wrong to assert that the doctrine of God's sovereignty and the doctrine of humanity's responsibility either contradict or conflict with each other. J. I. Packer calls the fact that these two truths are both taught in the Bible an antinomy. He offered the following explanation:

> [An antimony in the Bible] exists when a pair of principles stand side by side, seemingly irreconcilable, yet both undeniable. There are cogent reasons for believing each of them; each rests on clear and solid evidence; but it is a mystery to you how they can be squared with each other. You see that each must be true on its own, but you do not see how they can both be true together.[1]

Packer then offered an illustration from physics concerning the nature of light. He explained that light consists of both waves and particles. It is not apparent how light can be both at the same time; nevertheless, it is an undeniable fact. Just as the existence of light as both waves and particles cannot be denied, so the existence of both divine sovereignty and human responsibility cannot be denied.

Neither God's sovereignty nor humanity's responsibility must be sacrificed on the altar of our finite understanding.[2] Someday we will fully and completely understand how these two truths relate to each other. When we see God, He will make the incomprehensible plain to us. Until then, we must serve Him faithfully, trusting His sovereign wisdom and control of His world.

The shaded lines in the center of the following diagram represent the attempts of people to bring together the two truths of God's sovereignty and humanity's responsibility.

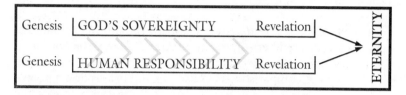

The Meaning of Divine Sovereignty

Divine sovereignty means that God is the absolute and sole Ruler in the universe. Though He uses means to accomplish His ends, He remains in complete control of His world and everything in it. Nothing escapes His notice, and nothing takes place that is beyond or outside His jurisdiction. After all, He is God!

More than the possession of absolute power and complete knowledge is meant when we say that God is sovereign. His sovereignty surely includes these attributes, but it also extends beyond them. Additionally, the sovereignty of God does not mean He is arbitrary in His dealings with humans. It is a mistake to think that He determined His plan in eternity and then carries it out in time only after some sort of trial-and-error procedure or as a blindfolded person who is seeking to find his way through a planned obstacle course. Instead, God's sovereignty includes His freedom to do whatever He deems is best.

Since God is the highest Ruler, His only limitation is Himself. All earthly rulers who are the highest in their realm are limited by themselves. So God is in a sense bound by Himself. That is to say, He can neither violate His own character nor do anything contrary to Himself or His purposes. For instance, God neither can lie nor go back on His word. Furthermore, there is no inner conflict or frustration with God, for He is always consistent with Himself.

Scriptural Evidence for Divine Sovereignty

The Bible is filled with evidence for the absolute sovereignty of God. In addition to His work in creation and providence, which surely proves His position as the most exalted and supreme Ruler, are all the attributes that He possesses. If these characteristics in Him are taken seriously, it must be recognized that they ascribe sovereignty to Him. I will say more about God's attributes, or perfections, in chapter 10.

From the multitude of passages that could be marshalled in support of God's sovereignty, I have selected the following as noteworthy examples:

- *First Samuel 2:1–10.* After Hannah, the mother of Samuel, had dedicated her son to the Lord (see 1:28), she confessed God's complete sovereignty. According to verse 2, Yahweh is beyond comparison. He raises up and brings down people as He pleases (vv. 6-8). To Him belong the pillars of the earth, and He set the world upon them (v. 8).
- *First Chronicles 29:11–12.* David was Israel's greatest and most noteworthy king, and therefore in a limited sense a sovereign. Yet he humbled himself and defended the total and sole lordship of Yahweh. After having done this, David did what all of us need to do and what we can only do in response to God's sovereignty. David thanked and praised God's glorious name.
- *John 10:29 (see also John 6:37, 44).* Christ announced that believers are eternally secure, for they are in the Father's hand and the Father is "greater than all." In other words, He is greater than everything He has made. Incidentally, this truth does not mean that the Son is subordinate in divine essence to the Father, for Christ said in verse 30: "I and my Father are one." Thus Christ, because He is equal to the Father, possesses the same measure of sovereignty. Likewise the Holy Spirit, because He is equal to the Father and the Son, also possesses the same measure of sovereignty.
- *Romans 8:28 (see also vv. 29–30).* "God causes all things to work together for good to those who love God, to those who are called according to His purpose." This verse teaches that God is in absolute control of all things.
- *Romans 9:1–11:36.* No greater treatise on the sovereignty of God has ever been penned than this. These chapters are usually explained as a parenthesis in the book of Romans. The context surrounding the passage makes it much more than that. Here Paul gave an illustration from history—the case of Israel—to demonstrate the righteousness of God in His sovereign dealings with His own people.
- *Ephesians 1:1–14.* This passage relates God's sovereignty to His salvation of the lost. This passage also clearly presents the purpose of God's sovereign dealings with humanity, namely, to bring glory to Himself. Paul repeated several similar phrases to drive home this point: "according to the

kind intention of His will" (v. 5); "to the praise of the glory of His grace" (v. 6); and, "to the praise of His glory" (v. 14).

J. I. Packer was right when he said that all Christians believe God is sovereign *in His world*. Otherwise, they would not go to Him in prayer. Furthermore, it appears that all Christians also believe that God is sovereign *in salvation,* whether or not they want to admit it. The fact that we thank God for saving us and ask Him to save others indicates our acknowledgment that sinners cannot save themselves.[3]

In the following words, Packer summarized his presentation of divine sovereignty and sounded a needed warning:

> There is a long-standing controversy in the Church as to whether God is really Lord in relation to human conduct and saving faith or not. What has been said shows us how we should regard this controversy. The situation is not what it seems to be. For it is not true that some Christians believe in divine sovereignty while others hold an opposite view. What is true is that all Christians believe in divine sovereignty, but some are not aware that they do, and mistakenly imagine and insist that they reject it. What causes this odd state of affairs? The root cause is the same as in most cases of error in the Church—the intruding of rationalistic speculations, the passion for systematic consistency, a reluctance to recognize the existence of mystery and to let God be wiser than men, and a consequent subjecting of Scripture to the supposed demands of human logic. People see that the Bible teaches man's responsibilities for his actions; they do not see (man, indeed, cannot see) how this is consistent with the sovereign Lordship of God over those actions. They are not content to let the two truths live side by side, as they do in the Scriptures, but jump to the conclusion that, in order to uphold the biblical truth of human responsibility, they are bound to reject the equally biblical and equally true doctrine of divine sovereignty, and to explain away the great number of texts that teach it. The desire to over-simplify the Bible by cutting out the mysteries is natural to our perverse minds, and it is not surprising that even good men should fall victims to it. Hence this persistent and troublesome dispute. The irony of the situation, however, is that when we ask how the two sides pray, it

becomes apparent that those who profess to deny God's sovereignty really believe in it just as strongly as those who affirm it.[4]

The Sovereign Plan of God

When the message of the Bible is accepted, there can be no doubt that God is altogether sovereign. Scripture is equally as clear in its teaching that this sovereign God has a sovereign plan for the universe and for people, a plan that He is bringing to fulfillment. Acceptance of this fact brings both comfort and conviction. It brings great assurance and consolation to know that the world is not run by chance or happenstance but by the loving and all-wise God. And conviction comes to our heart upon reflection of the truth of God's sovereign plan, for it means that He has a plan for our lives. If we genuinely love Him, we will want to know and do His will.

History, when viewed from the perspective of the truth of the sovereign plan of God, is more than just the mere recording of the events of the past. History also makes known the purposeful plan devised and executed by a personal God. Furthermore, the circumstances of the present and the happenings of the future all fit into the divine plan like pieces of a puzzle. When seen by themselves or all scattered in a box, the pieces look like odd-shaped portions of colored cardboard. But when they are fitted in their proper places by a person who knows where they go, they are a testimony to the design and plan of the puzzle maker. This is an illustration of how it is with God's plan for the universe and humanity.

The Nature of God's Sovereign Plan

Definition of the plan. Theologians have defined the decree, or plan, of God as "God's eternal purpose, according to the counsel of his will, whereby, for his own glory, he hath foreordained whatsoever comes to pass" *(Westminster Shorter Catechism)*. And Lewis Sperry Chafer defined it as "the plan by which God has proceeded in all His acts of creation and continuation."

One plan. I have been using the singular to speak about God's decree, or plan. This is as it ought to be, for there is only one divine plan. When theologians sometimes speak about "the decrees of God," they mean the many aspects of God's plan. There are many facets, or steps, in the plan of God; yet there is just one master plan that harmoniously includes all things (Acts 15:18).

Time of institution. When was the plan of God formed? His entire plan was determined at once; therefore, it is not subject to change. Like the architect who envisions the completed structure before he draws the plans, so God, the master Architect, knew the end from the beginning before He adopted His plan. According to 1 Peter 1:20, Christ's role in God's eternal plan was determined "before the foundation of the world," though He appeared in these "last times."

A wise plan. This naturally follows, for the plan comes from God and depends solely upon Him for its fulfillment (Isa. 40:12-14). The answers to the questions in these verses are so obvious that Isaiah did not give them. Instead, the prophet declared that no one ever directed or counseled the Lord. Isaiah also noted that God needed no one to teach Him and give Him understanding; therefore, He alone is responsible for the design and execution of His eternal plan. Paul praised God for the unfathomable nature of His plan and for the infinite wisdom He displayed in devising it (Rom. 11:33-36). This passage is most comforting and deserves careful study. It came from an apostle who gave us more information about the sovereign plan of God than any other writer of Scripture.

The best possible plan. Being divine, God must have been aware of other possible plans open to His choice. Since He chose the plan He did, faith must rest in the fact that it is in perfect accordance with His nature and is the best possible plan that will bring the most possible glory to God, who designed it.

The Scope of God's Sovereign Plan

Paul's declaration that God works "all things after the counsel of His will" (Eph. 1:11) makes it clear that the decree, or plan, of God includes all things. There are no areas over which He is not the supreme Ruler. All His creation is subject to Him (Isa. 46:10-11).

Though the plan of God is all-inclusive, it does not apply to His own Person. We must never think that God decreed His own existence or the mode of it in three Persons. Likewise, He did not decree to be holy and just. These attributes, and all others that concern the being of God, were not optional with Him; they were necessary by virtue of the fact that He is God.

Consequently, the plan of God relates to His acts, not to His Being. To help clarify this point, I have included a brief sampling of some of the areas that the Bible specifically states are included in God's sovereign plan: the stability of the universe (Pss. 89; 91; 119); the nations and their rulers (Acts 17:26; Rom. 13:1); the length of a person's life (Job 14:5, 14); the good deeds of the righteous (Eph. 2:10); the sinful acts of the unrighteous (Prov. 16:4; Acts 4:27-28); the death of Christ (Rev. 13:8); and the salvation of the lost (2 Thess. 2:13; 1 Peter 1:3).

There are some aspects of God's plan that He carries out directly through various means and for which He acknowledges responsibility (Job 28:26; Phil. 2:13). There are other aspects, however, such as the sinful deeds of people, that God permits without taking any responsibility for them. Instead, He always places the responsibility for the misdeeds and their results with people (James 1:13-15).

We should not conclude that the sinful acts of the wicked are either less certain or outside the plan of God. Instead, we should understand that God is free from any blame for the transgressions of people. This remains true, even though He has permitted trespasses to occur as part of His sovereign and eternally wise plan (Acts 2:23; 4:27-28).

God did not create sin, and Satan and sin did not catch God off guard. Rather, God, in His infinite wisdom, allowed the entrance of sin into the universe. Additionally, the entrance of sin was made certain by God's sovereign plan.

I have been talking about the directive will and the permissive will of God. The spiritual life is an area where Scripture makes this distinction. If there is any area where such a distinction should be made in God's will, desire, or plan, the spiritual life of the believer is the place.

Every exhortation to godly living is an evidence of God's best and highest desire for His children. Yet, honesty demands the acknowledgment of our failure to obey the injunctions of God's Word. Our acts of disobedience are not God's desire for us. Nevertheless, He is still aware of them and remains in sovereign control of them. God often permits, or allows, believers to be controlled by their sinful desires. Yet He is never pleased when His people sin, and He does not take responsibility for their transgressions.

Either there are two aspects to God's decree—the directive will and the permissive will of God—or every believer always lives a spiritual life. Surely it is His decree that we be completely controlled by the Holy Spirit, and yet many Christians are not thus controlled. Thus there must be two aspects to God's decree.

The Means of Carrying Out God's Sovereign Plan

The crucial difference between God's sovereign plan and fatalism is that God's decree, or plan, not only includes the end but also the means to accomplish that end. This is where human involvement comes in. A proper understanding of this truth—namely, the divine inclusion of the means as well as the end—moves believers from the grandstand onto the stage with God. The Lord works through His people as they pray, serve, and witness for Christ.

The beauty and marvel of the divine plan is that God has decreed to employ human beings to bring His will to fulfillment. Prayer, reading the Word, witnessing, preaching, teaching, giving, and so on are all part of God's plan to choose, call, regenerate, direct, and lead people.

In addition to human involvement, human responsibility is a part of God's sovereignty. It is not outside of His sovereignty. This is the reason why there are some things God does not do for us. For instance, He does not read the Word for us, witness for us, or live the spiritual life for us. These activities, and many others, are part of His sovereign plan and program for the victorious life. Unless we engage in them, we will not be spiritual.

The diagram below is designed to illustrate the difference between the biblical view of humanity's relation to God's plan and the view, which in theory at least and often in practice, puts human responsibilities outside God's plan and therefore minimizes the importance of human involvement and responsibility.

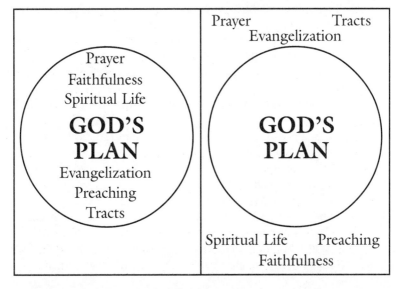

BIBLICAL APPROACH　　　NON-BIBLICAL APPROACH

Prayer　　　　Tracts
Evangelization

Prayer
Faithfulness
Spiritual Life
GOD'S PLAN
Evangelization
Preaching
Tracts

GOD'S PLAN

Spiritual Life　　Preaching
Faithfulness

The Purpose of God's Sovereign Plan

God's primary purpose in all that He does is to bring glory, praise, and honor to Himself. Benefits often come to people as God achieves His purpose, but these are secondary to God glorifying Himself (Eph. 1:12).

Yahweh's exhortation to Israel to obey was for His sake so that His name would not be profaned and His glory given to another (Isa. 48:11). The entire salvation process from beginning to end is "to the praise of the glory of His grace" (Eph. 1:6). God even designed nature to show His glory and craftsmanship (Ps. 19:1). Only He is worthy to receive glory, honor, and power, for He created all things for His glory (Rev. 4:11).

Amidst all the confusion and uncertainty in the world, it is reassuring to know that God orders our steps! Our faith should neither be in blind chance nor in random circumstances. Rather, it should be in an infinitely wise God—the God of the Bible—who does all things well, who knows the end from the beginning, and whose every desire is for our ultimate good and His glory.

The matter of God's sovereignty and His plan for the universe and mankind occupies a large part of His Word. These are family truths, and they are not understood by those outside the household of faith.

God's truth concerning Himself and His plan strengthens our faith and gives us assurance, hope, and confidence in Him. But these sublime truths should also help us see our duties within God's plan and to see them as a part of that plan. These great truths will make the children of God humble and remove any confidence we have in our weak human nature (see Phil. 3:3).

Some Usual Objections to God's Sovereign Plan

God's sovereign plan is incompatible with free will. Scripture does not say so! Rather, it teaches that humanity's responsibility and will are included in the divine plan. The amazing truth is that God remains completely sovereign even in allowing free will.

Explaining the concept of *free will* can help address the above objection. There is no such thing as an absolutely free will, not even in God, for His is not free to contradict Himself. And if people, the creatures whom God has made, possessed an *absolutely* free will, they could change the will of God and thus become gods themselves. People do possess a *relatively* free will, but God has given them boundaries beyond which they cannot go in the exercise of their will. It must also be remembered that God works upon the will of people to make them inclined to do what He has planned.

God's sovereign plan is the same as fatalism. Two truths distinguish God's sovereign plan from a fatalistic viewpoint. First, the decree of God has an intelligent personal Being behind it. Second, God's sovereignty includes both the means as well as the end to be accomplished, while fatalism does not.

God's sovereign plan makes Him the author of sin. Belief in the sovereignty of God and the reality of sin brings us to the conclusion that God permitted the presence of sin in His plan. Why He did this, we do not know. We must go back to the fact that since the Lord is God, He chose the best plan to bring the most glory to Himself, for that is the ultimate purpose of His plan.

The Bible teaches that God hates sin (Ps. 5:5). And Scripture always places the responsibility for sin squarely with people. God is the *final* cause for everything (including sin) in the sense that He has allowed everything to occur and included all things in His plan. However, He is not the *blameworthy* cause. He always holds people responsible for their sin, even though part of the fulfillment of God's plan includes their wicked deeds (see, for example, Acts 2:23; 4:27–28).

Perhaps an illustration of the difference between *final cause* and *blameworthy cause* will help. Imagine there is an investor who buys property downtown and decides to build a large office complex. He hires an architect to draw up plans for the facility, and construction corporations make several bids. Finally the investor gives the job to one of the largest companies with a sterling reputation for safety, workmanship, and reliability. The contractor hires subcontractors to do various phases of the work involving the foundation, the plumbing, the electrical wiring, the roofing, and so on. During the construction, one of the electrician's helpers, who fails to follow instructions, touches a high voltage wire and is fatally electrocuted.

The *final cause* of the accident can be traced all the way back to the investor who decided to build the office complex. If he had not made that decision, the architect would not have drawn up plans for him, and he would not have awarded the contract to the construction corporation. That company, in turn, would not have hired subcontractors, and one of them would not have hired the electrician's helper. He then would not have been killed on the job.

The *blameworthy cause* of this accident, however, cannot legitimately be placed on anyone except the man who touched the hot wire. He failed to follow instructions and is to blame for his own death.

God is the master Architect of the whole universe. He devised a plan that allowed for sin's entrance and continuance in His world. In that sense, He is the *final cause* of sin and evil, for He knew that sin would enter His world and He could have prevented it from happening. But for reasons known only to Him, He did not. This is the kind of God the Bible reveals to us.

God is fully sovereign and not the helpless victim of Satan's trickery and deceit. In no sense, however, is God to blame for the sins His creatures commit. We do the sinning. He does not. It must be said reverently and without impugning God in any way that He is the *final cause* of sin. But the sinner is always the *blameworthy cause.*

God's sovereign plan will kill missionary zeal. On the surface, this seems like a valid objection. The best response to it, however, is to remember the life and ministry of Paul. He gave us more information regarding the sovereignty and decree of God than anyone else; and yet he was perhaps the greatest missionary who ever lived. We must not forget that the means—all of them—are as much a part of the divine plan as is the end to be accomplished.

These and all other objections fade into insignificance when we remember that no matter what people think or how difficult it may be for us to reconcile seemingly contradictory facts, the Bible teaches the sovereignty of God. That is why we must believe it. It is a divine mystery! And it must always remain such.

We do not know everything about God's plan, and we do not know all that is included in His purposes. Nevertheless, we know enough to be sure of certain truths. It is far more profitable and biblical to stress what we do know than it is to spend all our time debating what we do not know and never will know in this life.

We know God will fulfill His Word. We also know that all people are sinners and must trust Christ for salvation. Further, we know that God holds sinners responsible for their unbelief and transgressions. Moreover, we know that God holds saints responsible to take to the lost the message of salvation through faith in Christ alone. Because we know these key truths, God expects us to become laborers together with Him in carrying out His plan (1 Cor. 3:9).

Paul's great anthem of praise to God for His sovereignty and His sovereign ways with people serves as a fitting conclusion to this discussion. The apostle wrote these words after he had presented an illustration of the sovereign and inscrutable ways of God with Israel (Rom. 9-11).

Under divine inspiration, Paul wrote: "Oh, the depth of the riches both of the wisdom and knowledge of God! How unsearchable are His judgments and unfathomable His ways! For WHO HAS KNOW THE MIND OF THE LORD, OR WHO BECAME HIS COUNSELOR? Or WHO HAS FIRST GIVEN TO HIM THAT IT MIGHT BE PAID BACK TO HIM AGAIN? For from Him and through Him and to Him are all things. To Him be the glory forever. Amen" (Rom. 11:33–36).

Notes

1. J. I. Packer, *Evangelism and the Sovereignty of God* (Chicago: InterVarsity, 1961), 18–19.
2. An attempt to stress both divine sovereignty and human responsibility without denying either is found in Samuel Fisk, *Divine Sovereignty and Human Freedom* (Neptune, N.J.: Loizeaux Brothers, 1973).
3. Packer, 11–12.
4. Ibid., 16–17.

CHAPTER 10

How May the God of the Bible Be Described?

No GREATER OR MORE important task could occupy the human mind than to reflect upon the nature of God. Believers and unbelievers alike would do well to consider seriously just exactly who the God of the Bible is and what He is like.

The believer's life is greatly affected by the characteristics of God. Since He is the heavenly Father of all who believe and since all who believe are members of His family, surely there ought to be a family resemblance between them and Him. This is precisely what God has commanded (Lev. 11:44; 1 Peter 1:16). In addition, those who are not the children of God by faith in Jesus Christ ought to be made aware of the fact that the God of the Bible is the One whom they must one day face as their Judge.

Too often we think of God either as a great power or influence operating in the world, or as a bearded, benevolent old grandfather. Neither of these imaginary concepts, which the minds of people have conjured up, is Scriptural. A serious study of God's propositional revelation about Himself provides the only safeguard against these erroneous ideas. And such a study involves us in the only infallible revelation about God.

Our study will be centered around two major considerations—the meaning of God's perfections and a survey of God's perfections.

The Meaning of God's Perfections

Let us begin by considering the negative side of a definition of God's perfections. We must always be sure that by our definition we are not implying that something can be added to the Person of God. The word *attribute* implies such a concept at first glance. *Perfections* is perhaps a better word for the characteristics of God, because it does not connote the idea of adding something to God.

Scripture, not human experience, is the starting point for the discovery of the real character of the true and living God. We know that God made mankind in His image. Yet we do not look to the human race and then heighten the characteristics we find in people to a level where they may be said to be true of God. Rather, we search the written Revelation, which the Creator has given to us. There, and only there, as God enlightens our minds through His Spirit, will we come to know Him as He really is.

Now let us consider the positive side of a definition of God's perfections. We begin by noting that the qualities, or perfections, of God reveal His nature. We then note that a listing of the perfections of God must never be viewed as a final or complete definition of Him. While it is true that God cannot be considered apart from the perfections that Scripture assigns to Him, yet He is more than the sum total of those perfections.

God never existed apart from His perfections, for from eternity they belonged to the divine essence. The great theologian Lewis Sperry Chafer put it this way: "The whole of the divine essence is in each attribute, and the attribute belongs to the whole essence. The attributes belong eternally to the essence."[1]

Another real danger to be avoided in thinking about God's perfections is to exalt one above another. It is true that in some contexts of Scripture, one perfection is stressed more than another. However, when we take the total testimony of Scripture, we find a harmonious presentation of the characteristics of God. It must ever be kept in mind that God always deals with people on the basis of the totality of His Being and not simply on the basis of one or even a few of His perfections.[2]

A Survey of God's Perfections

Theologians differ on how the perfections of God are to be classified. The basis for the usual twofold division is to distinguish between those attributes that are true of God alone and those that He shares in a limited sense with people. The problem with all of the standard divisions (for example, incommunicable and communicable; absolute and relative; passive and active) is that some of the perfections of God will not fit into such classifications. Therefore, it seems better not to attempt to arrange God's perfections under any particular headings but rather to deal with them individually.

Earlier in our study, I set forth the truth of God's personality and Trinity. That God possesses personality (namely, intellect, emotions, and will), that He is one in His divine essence, and that He has manifested Himself in three distinct Persons are surely descriptive of Him. Although I do not discuss here these truths about God, they should be thought of as perfections of God.

The Self-Existence of God

When considering the self-existence of God, the argument that every effect must have an adequate cause breaks down. The Bible presents God as the uncaused One. He alone possesses the ground of existence in Himself. If this were not true, He could not be God.

The Lord does not depend on anyone or anything outside Himself for His life, and He possesses life in the absolute degree. He is the source of life, and the life principle comes from Him. The Baptist theologian, Mullins, has given this definition of God's life: "The life of God is His activity of thought, feeling and will. It is the total inward movement of His Being which enables Him to form wise, holy, and loving purposes and to execute them."[3]

The life of the self-existent God is taught clearly in Scripture. For instance, Jeremiah called Him the "living God and the everlasting King" (Jer. 10:10). Paul echoed a similar thought when he told the Thessalonians that they "turned to God from idols to serve a living and true God" (1 Thess. 1:9).

According to John 5:26, God alone possesses a self-existent life: "For just as the Father has life in Himself; even so He gave to the Son also to have life in Himself." Other passages of Scripture likewise teach that God does not depend on anyone or anything for the continuance of His life. He is absolutely free with respect to His thoughts (Rom. 11:33–34), His will (Rom. 9:19; Eph. 1:5), His power (Ps. 115:3), and His counsel (Ps. 33:10–11).

Though God is not dependent upon others or powers outside of Himself for His existence and counsel, His children are to be completely dependent upon Him for everything. It is God's absolute and complete independence that becomes the basis for our dependence upon Him. God forbid that we should ever try to become independent of Him!

The Infinity of God

People correctly refer to themselves as finite creatures. By this they mean they are bound by limitations. We can only do so much, and sooner or later we reach the end of our abilities. Exactly the opposite is true of God. The infinity of God means He does not possess any limitations and is free from all limitations. He is bound only to His own nature.

When the infinity of God is related to time—that is, when we say God is not limited by time—He is called eternal. Past, present, and future are our ways of speaking about our lives. With God, however, His life is not divided by segments of time. Though God is the author of time, He is neither conditioned nor confined by it (Gen. 21:32–34; Deut. 33:27; Pss. 90:2; 102:12). This is a wonderful truth!

Equally marvelous is the exhortation of Scripture for us to make the most of our time (Eph. 5:16). We serve a God who, though not Himself limited by time, desires His children to use their time wisely and for His glory.

When the infinity of God is related to space and we say that God is not restricted by space, we are referring to the immensity of God. Berkhof, a Reformed theologian, defines the immensity of God as "that perfection of the Divine Being by which He transcends all spatial limitations, and yet is present in every point of space with His whole Being."[4] This perfection is practically synonymous with omnipresence and will be discussed later.

The Spirituality of God

Emory Bancroft rightly defined what is meant by the spirituality of God. He wrote, "God as Spirit is incorporeal, invisible, without material substance, without physical parts or passions and therefore free from all temporal limitations."[5] When used of God, "incorporeal" means He does not possess a material body. John 4:24 is the closest statement in Scripture to a definition of God: "God is spirit, and those who worship Him must worship in spirit and truth."

Earlier in chapter 8, I noted that an anthropomorphic expression is any description of God's being, actions, and emotions in human terms. These terms in no way contradict the fact that God is spirit. He is spirit in the absolute sense; therefore, He is a Being who is immaterial and invisible, and without parts or extension.

Some see a contradiction between Scripture passages that say people saw God (for instance, Exod. 24:10) and other passages that declare people have never seen Him (for instance, John 1:18). To resolve this problem, we must first note that God *is* spirit, while people only *have* spirits. We should also note that people in Bible times never observed God's invisible, glorious essence. Rather, they only saw visible manifestations of Him.

God the Holy Spirit indwells the physical body of believers (1 Cor. 6:19). The believer's body, therefore, is not to be used selfishly; rather, it is to be presented back to God as a living sacrifice (Rom. 12:1). And He is to be worshiped in spirit and in truth (John 4:24).

The Immutability of God

One privilege that some women usually want to retain—perhaps even more than some men—is that of changing their minds. And it is true of human nature that we not only change our minds, but also we change as persons. Personalities, likes, dislikes, and so on change in people. In fact, we always ought to be attempting to improve, or "change," our lives.

In contrast to people, God never changes in His essence, character, and nature. This is what theologians mean when they say that God is immutable. The inherent qualities that mark Him out distinctively as God are constant and eternal. If God were mutable, it would mean His character would be subject to change.

In Malachi 3:6 Yahweh declared, "I, the LORD, do not change" (see also Exod. 3:14; Ps. 102:26-28; James 1:7). This does not mean that God is inactive in His dealings with people. Scripture reveals that during different dispensations, God has dealt with people in various ways. The fact of God's immutability reminds us that He neither alters His purposes nor changes His nature.

Some Scriptures seem to teach that God changes His mind in the same way that people do. For example, the Lord is said to have been "sorry that He had made man" (Gen. 6:6). Also, we read that He "relented concerning the calamity which He had declared He would bring upon [the Ninevites]" (Jonah 3:10).

In explaining such statements, we first must understand what we exactly mean by immutability. The word indicates that God is changeless in His being. Second, we need to recognize that God often spoke anthropomorphically, that is, in terms of the human experience of knowledge and emotion. Third, in accordance with God's sovereign and eternal purposes, His promise of blessing or punishment was frequently conditioned upon the way people behaved (see, for example, Jonah 3:4, 10).

Great comfort comes to the believing heart that knows about God's unchanging character. And what assurance there is to know that our present lives and eternal futures rest in the care of the faithful and unchanging God! The certainty of God's Word is that even though we are unfaithful, "He remains faithful, for He cannot deny Himself" (2 Tim. 2:13).

The Holiness of God

The holiness of God means that He possesses absolute perfection in every detail. He is therefore completely separate from evil in His Person and in His dealings with mankind (Lev. 19:2; Ps. 99:9; Isa. 6:3; John 17:11; 1 John 1:5).

It is difficult for us to think about an absolutely holy Being. We are tempted to think of God arriving at His state of perfection and of maintaining that state by continued effort. Such a meager concept does not even approximate the holiness of God. The reality and nature of God's holiness is not altered by His dealings with Satan and sinful people. Holiness is an integral part of God's nature; it is operative at all times and is never diminished by circumstances.

God in His Word has told us about His hatred of sin and all evil (Hab. 1:13). The fact that God loves holiness and desires to see it in His people is proof that He Himself is holy (Prov. 15:9).

Unquestionably the greatest demonstration of God's holiness occurred at Calvary. The costly gift of His Son, who is the Substitute for sinners, reveals not only God's hatred of sin but also His willingness to deliver the lost from sin's guilt and power over their lives. God's warnings in Scripture to the wicked is another demonstration of His ineffable purity. He declares that they will be eternally separated from Him, unless they accept His provision of salvation through faith in Christ. And the promise of God's future judgment of Satan, his cohorts, and all unbelievers is further sobering evidence of the infinite perfection of our God.

To say that God is righteous and just is simply to speak about His holiness in relation to people. Righteousness implies the existence of a rule, or law, to which there must be conformity. Because there is no law above God to which He is subjected, His holy nature is His righteous standard (Neh. 9:8; Ps. 145:17; John 17:25).

The diagram below shows how God's holiness is related to mankind by His righteousness and justice.

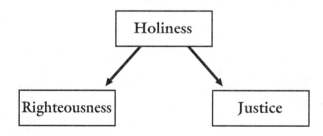

God never violates His holiness. That is why, when His creatures violate it, He requires full payment of and satisfaction for their sins. In this way God remains just (Zeph. 3:5; Rom. 3:26).

God always enforces His righteous standards justly and with equity. This means there is no partiality or unfairness in God's dealings with mankind. Christians sometimes have the mistaken notion that God is lenient and less demanding with believers than He is with unbelievers. This is not true. God meted out the just demands of His absolute, but offended, righteousness on Christ. Jesus bore all our sins at Calvary, and He completely paid the price for our transgressions. Since we are united to Him by faith, God the Father accepts, forgives, and saves us.

What responsibilities attend the members of God's family, who are vitally related to the One who is absolutely holy, righteous, and just? Scripture is crystal clear on this point: "You shall be holy, for I am holy" (1 Peter 1:16). In this verse, to be holy means to be set apart from sin and devoted to God in service. His perfect holiness is the standard. Yet, when we take into account the sinful nature of people, we understand this verse as a command for a comparative holiness in believers—as creature to that of God as Creator.

John said that "God is Light, and in Him there is no darkness at all" (1 John 1:5). The context of this passage demands that this be understood as a reference to God's holiness. But the context also emphatically connects this great truth regarding God with the responsibility of people to therefore "walk in the Light, as He Himself is in the light" (v. 7). This means to order our lives in accordance with God's holy character and will, as revealed in His holy Word.

The Love of God

The nature of God's love. Who can define love? We all understand it better when it is displayed than when it is defined. At best, our conception of love is based on human experience. It is derived from the idea that we love because of qualities and virtues we have seen in others we love.

Not so with God! His love is not so much something that He *possesses* as it is something that He *is* (1 John 4:8). He never existed apart from love. Even before He created people to be the objects of His love, He was love. Because God is perfect and holy, His love is perfect and holy. God's love of the unlovely does not alter in any way the character of His love. In fact, it is toward a sinful world and sinful people that His love finds its greatest expression (John 3:16; 1 John 4:9–10).

The objects of God's love. Scripture reveals there are three primary objects of God's love.

(1) *Jesus Christ (John 17:24).*

(2) *The world of mankind (John 3:16; 1 Tim. 2:3–4; 2 Peter 3:9).* The Bible makes no distinction between sinners in their unregenerate state. God loved and loves them all, proof of which is found in the universal provision of the death of Christ for the "ungodly" (Rom. 5:6–8). The love of God can no more be confined to a certain group (for example, only believers) than can His other perfections. And His love is not just a New Testament truth. God's choice of Israel as a nation, in which there were many rebels, was based upon His unconditional love for them (Deut. 7:7–8; Hosea 11:1). It is important to remember that God loves sinners, not their sin. This is also what we must learn to do.

(3) *The believer (John 16:27; 17:23; Rom. 5:8; 1 John 3:16–17; 4:19).* Because of the family relationship that believers have with God, they are said to be the special objects of His abundant and immeasurable love.

The relation of God's mercy and grace to His love. Closely related to the unfathomable love of God are His mercy and His grace. Mercy has to do with the patience, or long-suffering, of God. It is the basis for His pardoning disposition toward sinners and those in need (Ps. 103:8). God's mercy is shown to those who fear Him (Ps. 103:17; Luke 1:50) and to those who do not (Ezek. 18:23, 32).

The grace of God is His undeserved favor. In grace God stoops to pardon helpless sinners and transform their present and eternal futures. Grace is also the supernatural enabling or renewing power that God bestows on believers for effective Christian ministry and living (2 Cor. 12:9).

The mercy and grace of God function harmoniously in Him, and both are expressions of His love. God's mercy allows Him to withhold deserved punishment, while His grace allows Him to bestow freely His unmerited favor (Ps. 103:8; Eph. 2:8–10). Grace opened the way of redemption (Rom. 3:24). By it sinners are justified (Rom. 4:16; Titus 3:7) and blessed (2 Cor. 8:9; 2 Thess. 2:16).

The diagram below visualizes how God's mercy and grace are expressions of His love.

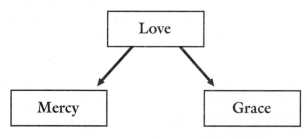

The application of God's love, mercy, and grace. Scripturally speaking, the best illustration of God's love is the love in the family (Eph. 3:15; 5:25; 1 John 4:7). It is just that simple and just that important. A proof that we have been born into God's family is our love for God and His children. In light of God's unconditional love, mercy, and grace for us, is not the following exhortation clearer, "we also ought to love one another" (1 John 4:11)?

The diagram below helps us to recognize our responsibilities in view of the perfections of our heavenly Father.

GOD'S PERFECTIONS	MAN'S PERFORMANCES
1. Self-existent life	1. Depend upon God for life.
2. Infinity	2. Rest in His greatness.
3. Spirituality	3. Worship Him always and continually in spirit and in truth.
4. Holiness, righteousness, and justice	4. Rely upon His unchanging Word to us.
5. Love, mercy, and grace	5. Exercise love, patience, and a gracious spirit toward saints and sinners.

The last three perfections that I want to deal with begin with the word *omni.* This prefix comes from the Latin word *omnes,* which means "all."

The Omniscience of God

When omniscience is applied to God, it means that He knows and comprehends all things—whether past, present, or future and whether actual or potentially possible. Such knowledge is instantaneous, simultaneous, exhaustive, universal, and absolutely correct.

Perhaps at no period in the history of humanity has there been a greater thirst and search for knowledge than today. All of our knowledge is received by the process of discovery and learning from others. This is not so with God. His knowledge is not only infinitely above humanity's but it is also virtually incomprehensible to finite creatures.

Divine omniscience is knowledge without the discovery of facts. Since God is perfect and therefore possesses perfect knowledge, He not only has no need to learn, but He has never and will never learn (Isa. 40:13–14; Rom. 11:34–36). If this were not true, the Lord would have been less than God in the past, and could conceivably become more than God at some time in the future.

People learn new things from past experiences both about themselves and about others. They add to their knowledge, line upon line and precept upon precept. But there is no such progression of knowledge with God. Past, present, and future are all brought simultaneously together in His omniscience (Acts 15:18). The outworking of God's plan and His dealings with people occur within the realm of time; yet to God the events of the past and future are as real as the here and now.

To help us understand better the omniscience of God, imagine we were viewing a parade from the roof of a high building. We would be able to see the entire procession, whereas people standing on the corner of two main streets would only be able to see a small portion of the parade. When we speak of God's omniscience, we mean that His knowledge instantaneously encompasses the whole without one fact preceding another.

Not all in evangelicalism understand God's omniscience as described above. Some are proposing what they call "free-will theism" and an "open view" of God. Robert Strimple, who is opposed to these ideas, correctly describes them as nothing short of sixteenth century Socinianism.[6]

Richard Rice and Clark Pinnock are representatives of "free-will theism" and an "open view" of God. Both have attacked the doctrines of God's omniscience and foreknowledge.[7] These men and others who hold their views affirm that they believe in God's omniscience. But for them, omniscience means knowing all that is possible to know. What God cannot know, they argue, are the free decisions of free creatures and the subsequent consequences of those decisions.

David Basinger, who holds to the "open view" of God, claims that advocates of the position believe in the "present knowledge" of God. This means "God can never know with certainty what will happen in any context involving freedom of choice."[8]

This "open view" of the God of the Bible embraces aspects of the "process theology" of Alfred North Whitehead and Charles Hartshorne. Proponents of process theology believe God cannot see or know the future and therefore constantly changes in response to human actions. Gregg Easterbrook in the *U.S. News and World Report* summarized accurately Hartshorne's view in these words: "If the future could be known supernaturally, Hartshorne reasoned, then God would already be fated to do whatever brings about the foreseen: Even the Maker would lack free choice. But if the future does not yet exist, it is a non-thing, unknowable even to a deity. Working from the second assumption, Hartshorne concluded that a changing God is involved in an ongoing process of responding to humanity. This, he felt, could explain leading puzzles of theology, such as how the wrathful God of the Old Testament became the compassionate Maker of the Bible's second half."[9]

A deity who cannot know ahead of time what His creatures are going to decide is limited indeed and is nowhere revealed in Scripture. The God of the Bible is not constantly learning and broadening His knowledge as humans make decisions and experience positive and negative consequences. Thus, the God of "free-will theism" is not the God of the Bible.

Divine omniscience is knowledge that is complete. God knows perfectly, and He knows all that there is to know about everything there is to know. Therefore, nothing surprises Him or takes Him off guard. What often appears to us to be a complete reversal of God's plan or what seems to contradict His will and plan comes as no shock to God. Likewise, despair and perplexity never come to Him.

God must not be pictured as someone who uses the trial and error method and who wrings His anthropomorphic hands in frustration when people disobey Him. God is never at a loss to know what will take place or what to do next. For example, He knew that Satan would rebel against Him. And God knew that the first Adam would sin and plunge the whole human race in guilt. Further, God knew that people would crucify His Son, the last Adam. Clearly, the God of the Bible is not learning with the passing of time.

Divine omniscience is knowledge that is all-inclusive. God not only knows perfectly the past, present, and the future; He also knows the actual (what has come to pass or will come to pass) and the potentially possible (what could have taken place or might take place but will never occur). Furthermore, God knows every possible variation of everything, all the contingent elements of everything, and the relation that all things have to each other.

Every exhortation in Scripture to the believer to live a dedicated, Spirit-filled life is proof of the fact that God knows and has warned about the results of failure to do His will. This certainly involves knowledge about things that are possible but, in the lives of some, never become actual. Such knowledge is also true in relation to the unbeliever. God knows what will happen if and when the unregenerate turn to Him in faith. He also knows what will be true if they refuse to believe (Matt. 11:21-23; see also 1 Sam. 23:5-14; 2 Kings 13:19).

Does it not follow that since God is the great divine Architect who designed the plan, He would know everything about it and everything that relates to it? God is in complete control of His world; and since that is true, He must know all things. Otherwise, there could be no divine control.

That God thus knows the free actions of humans and therefore all conditional events does not in any way remove from them either their responsibilities or culpability for their actions. We must never deny God's complete knowledge or our duties and accountability. The fact of God's omniscience does not mean He coerces or forces us against our own will. It does mean that God knows what the choices for each person will be and brings one to the place where His will freely comes to pass.

Divine omniscience and divine wisdom are different. Though closely related, knowledge and wisdom are not the same. And they do not always accompany each other. No doubt we have all known those who had acquired a great deal of facts but who lacked the ability to use them wisely. Both knowledge and wisdom are imperfect in humans but perfect and perfectly related to each other in God. Only He knows how to use His infinite knowledge to the best possible end.

Through His wisdom, God applies His knowledge to the fulfillment of His own purposes in ways that will bring the most glory to Him. The Lord is said to be the *only* "wise God" (Rom. 16:27). And Scripture relates the wisdom of God to many things including creation (Pss. 19:1-7; 104:1-34), providence (Ps. 33:10; Rom. 8:28), and redemption (Rom. 11:33; 1 Cor. 2:7).

Scripture declares that God knows from eternity past what will be in eternity future (Isa. 46:9-10; Acts 15:18). He knows everything in nature (Ps. 147:4; Matt. 10:29), He knows all the ways of all people (Ps. 139:2-4; Prov. 5:21; Amos 9:2-4), and He knows us in a special sense as His own (2 Tim. 2:19). The believer's sorrows (Exod. 3:7), needs (Matt. 6:8, 32), and details of life (Matt. 10:30) are all known by our God.

Recognition and acceptance of the fact that God knows everything produces heart-searching on the part of the child of God. Sins covered from the sight and knowledge of people are naked and open to God's view. On the one hand, this should bring conviction to the child of

God. On the other hand, how wonderful it is to know that pure motives and holy ambitions, though often misunderstood by many, are understood and eternally rewarded by God.

The diagram below summarizes the crucial aspects of God's omniscience.

OMNISCIENCE–ALL KNOWLEDGE
Psalm 139:1-6

1. Without discovery of facts
2. Complete
3. All-inclusive
4. Incentive to dedicated Christian service

The Omnipresence of God

By the omnipresence of God, we mean that since God is infinite, transcending all spatial limitations, He is present everywhere with His whole Being at the same time. Difficult as it may be for us to understand, the Bible presents God as being present everywhere at the same time. This follows naturally from the infinity of God. Although God is simultaneously and instantaneously present everywhere in His creation, He is not limited by it in any way.

In the unmistakably clear words of Psalm 139:7-16, David expressed the biblical concept of God's omnipresence:

> Where can I go from Your Spirit? Or where can I flee from Your presence? If I ascend to heaven, You are there; if I make my bed in Sheol, behold, You are there. If I take the wings of the dawn, if I dwell in the remotest part of the sea, even there Your hand will lead me, and Your right hand will lay hold of me. If I say, "Surely the darkness will overwhelm me, and the light around me will be night," even the darkness is not dark to You, and the night is as bright as the day. Darkness and light are alike to You. For You formed my inward parts; You wove me in my mother's womb. I will give thanks to You, for I am fearfully and wonderfully made; wonderful are Your works, and my soul knows it very well. My frame was not hidden from You, when I was made in secret, and skillfully wrought in the depths of the earth; Your eyes have seen my unformed substance; and in Your book were written the days that were ordained for me, when as yet there was not one of them.

There are three serious errors to avoid in our understanding of God's omnipresence. First, some erroneously think that God is diffused through space so that parts of Him are present everywhere. God is one in divine essence and thus cannot be divided into parts. He is wholly present in every place. Perhaps the best illustration of this is the biblical doctrine of the Lord manifesting His presence in each and every believer. Each child of God does not have a part, or portion, of Him. Rather, God is present in His entire Being with every saint (John 14:23).

Second, some erroneously think that God manifests His presence in the same way everywhere, or they think of His presence in a bodily or material sense. We must remember that God is Spirit and therefore invisible to our eyes. The special dwelling place of God is in heaven, where His throne is (Isa. 66:1; Matt. 6:9). The way He manifests His presence there is surely different from the way He manifests His presence through the Holy Spirit in every believer (1 Cor. 3:16-17; 6:19-20). Different still from these is the way He manifests His presence through His righteous judgment in hell (compare Ps. 139:8 with 2 Thess. 1:9).

Third, some erroneously hold to the view of pantheism. Pantheists say that God is everything and everything is God. It is the problem of confusing the Creator with the created. Genesis 1:1, as well as many other Scripture passages, is diametrically opposed to such thinking. The Creator and the created are always set apart in the Bible. God's presence with or in whatever He has created does not mean the loss of identity for either God or the created entity.

Three theological terms are closely related to omnipresence and should be explained here.

Immensity. This is a classic theological term that is sometimes used synonymously with omnipresence. Immensity means that God is not restricted by space. Obviously, this is similar to saying that God is omnipresent.

Immanence. When applied to God, this means He is within the world, acting within and through His creation, rather than from without and upon it. Theological liberals have been famous for their overemphasis of God's immanence. They have taken the truth to extremes by identifying God so closely with the world that He is not far above people. God has been humanized and people have been deified.

Transcendence. This is the counterpart of immanence. In reference to the God of the Bible, transcendence refers to the wholly otherness of God. It speaks of His position above and beyond the creation. In contrast to liberalism, neo-orthodoxy supposedly holds to the transcendence of God.

The biblical viewpoint accepts both the immanence and the transcendence of God. He is immanent in the sense that He is present and working in the world (Pss. 19; 139:1–10; Rom. 1:20). And God is transcendent, for He is the great Designer and Fulfiller of His plan for the universe and for people. Moreover, God is eternal and infinitely superior to the temporal and finite (Isa. 55:8–9).

Below is a diagram that highlights the way in which the omnipresence of the God of the Bible relates to other perfections of His Being.

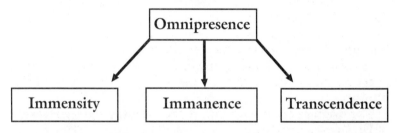

No person can hide from God (Jer. 23:23–24). Because Adam and Eve had sinned, they wanted to get away from the Lord's presence (Gen. 3:8). But He still found them and gave them the message of redemption. Jonah also tried to hide from God, but he did not succeed either. Although Jonah went in the exact opposite direction from where God had told him to go, the Lord still spoke to him there in the belly of the great fish (Jonah 1:3ff.).

The message of the Bible is the inspired record. It does not teach that people are searching for God as they grope in the darkness of their sin. Rather, Scripture teaches that God is ever reaching out to the lost with the probing question, "Where are you?"

Humanity's inability to hide from God applies to both the unsaved and the saved. No matter how much sinners try to get away from God and all that is holy, righteous, and good, they are still under God's all-seeing eye. So it is with the saved. All the veneer of hypocrisy and superficiality is removed by the Lord's gaze. Not only does God know and see our every motive and action now, but at the judgment seat of Christ we will be evaluated according to the life we really lived.

In relation to the unsaved, the truth of God's continual presence means they can never escape His constant observation and also the certainty of judgment to follow. For the saved, God's presence becomes a real source of protection and blessing as well as an incentive for holy living.

The believer who is living for God and who therefore attempts to do great things for God may be assured of the special presence of the Lord. At least the spiritual Christian will be more aware and especially cognizant of God's indwelling presence. God's presence should not be viewed as simply a theological truth to be memorized. Rather, there are attendant blessings afforded the children of God who embrace the truth of God's presence with them. Here are three of those blessings:

(1) *Direction.* God's presence with the Israelites was evident from the pillar of cloud by day and the pillar of fire by night (Exod. 13:21). His presence today in believers through the indwelling Spirit will also provide guidance for them.

(2) *Joy.* An understanding of the truth of God's presence should bring delight and encouragement to the trusting heart (Ps. 16:11).

(3) *Protection.* All the assaults of the wicked one must first penetrate the protective presence of the Lord before they ever can harm us.

The diagram below summarizes the meaning and significance of God's omnipresence.

OMNIPRESENCE—PRESENT EVERYWHERE AT THE SAME TIME
Psalm 139:7-16

1. Immensity
2. Immanence
3. Transendence
4. Incentive to dedicated Christian service

The Omnipotence of God

The infinite power of God is called His omnipotence (Matt. 19:26; Rev. 19:6). The word "almighty," which is a synonym for omnipotence, is used fifty-six times in our English Bibles and never refers to anyone but God. From both terms we learn that God has unlimited power to do anything that does not contradict His nature.

God's omnipotence must be understood in relation to the other divine perfections. For instance, the omnipotence of God gives life and action to all His other perfections. And without the exercise of God's power, we would not know about His love, grace, mercy, and so on. Further, in keeping with God's holy Person, there are some things He cannot do. For example, He cannot lie, change, deny Himself, or do anything in opposition to His nature or His Word.

God's power is potential as well as actual. In other words, there are things He could do that He does not do simply because He has chosen not to include them in His plan. This truth indicates that God's omnipotence does not depend upon His action.

There is no effort involved in the display of God's power. For instance, when God created the world, He spoke, and it was done; likewise, He commanded, and it stood fast (Ps. 33:9). And God both controls His universe with ease and sustains it without any loss of divine power.

We often think of a large army as a symbol of power and might. Yet consider how quickly such things as intense heat, burning desert sandstorms, or cold winter frostbite can diminish the power of such armies. In contrast, the power of our God is measureless and boundless.

The unbelieving mind cannot grasp the truth of God's creative power: "And God said, 'Let there be' . . . and it was so" (Genesis 1). The little that people can do must always be accomplished with tools and materials. It is not this way with God! By the mere word of His power countless worlds instantly and simultaneously came into being. When we acknowledge God's power in the creation of the universe and in the creation of humanity, it is easy to recognize and accept that His power exists in all other areas (Jer. 10:12).

God brought the universe into existence and holds it together by the word of His power (Ps. 36:6; Heb. 1:3). Just as no creature has the power to create itself, so none has the power to preserve itself (Job 8:11). God alone can begin and sustain life. What awesome power He has!

Several outstanding examples of God's judgment upon sin will serve to illustrate His power. The judgment upon Adam, Eve, the serpent, and the earth because of humanity's fall reminds us of God's power. The universal flood in Noah's day, the destruction of Sodom and Gomorrah, and the drowning of Pharaoh's army are all reminders of God's limitless power.

God is not through displaying His power in judgment upon sin. According to Revelation 20:11–15, in a day yet future all who have rejected God's offer of mercy in Jesus Christ will be cast alive into the lake of fire, where they will be tormented forever and ever.

No greater display of power has ever been given than when God raised Christ from the dead (2 Cor. 13:4). There will be an equal demonstration of the same divine power when God raises deceased believers from their graves (1 Cor. 6:14; 15:1-58).

The salvation of the lost is certainly an illustration of the display of God's infinite power. Even the angels, who belong to a higher order of creation than people, want to know more about God's work of saving the lost and to learn more about His power evident there (1 Peter 1:12).

God's great power is not only evident in the salvation of notorious sinners—down-and-outers—but also in the salvation of people who were reared in a Christian home. It took just as much of the power and grace of God to save even the "best" sinner as it did to save the "worst" one. Deliverance from the wrath of God and the condemnation of hell (John 3:18-19) and the impartation of divine life (2 Peter 1:4) are further evidences of God's power. And these are true of every sinner saved by grace.

One of the most amazing truths of Scripture is that God's measureless power is available to every child of His. The bestowal of God's power upon His people does not depend upon their educational abilities, cultural background, or status in society. Rather, it depends upon their yieldedness and surrender of their meager abilities to His almighty power. The power of God to transform us morally and spiritually is beyond our comprehension (1 Peter 2:9).

Power in prayer and in the whole Christian life comes from God. Part of Isaiah's encouragement to the faint and weak included a reminder of this power (Isa. 40:2-31). Paul spoke about the power of prayer as being available to every believer (Eph. 1:19-20). The Lord Jesus, having received power and authority from the Father, said to His weak and humanly powerless disciples: "All authority has been given to Me in heaven and on earth. Go therefore and make disciples of all the nations" (Matt. 28:18-19). "Authority" here refers to the infinite power of God.

All of God's children need to draw upon His limitless power. Too much activity in the church is done in the power and strength of our weak, sinful human nature. Without the Lord's power we can do nothing (John 15:5); but with His power we can do all things that God desires (Phil. 4:13).

These truths may be illustrated by the father who deposits in the bank enough money for all the needs and desires of his son. The only stipulation made is that the son must write a check for each need. All the money is available to the son, but he must draw it out in a sequential fashion. Our God possesses all power, and He has made that power available to us, His children. But if we are to benefit from His power, we must first draw upon it by faith.

Notes

1. Lewis Sperry Chafer, *Systematic Theology,* vol. 1 (Grand Rapids: Kregel, 1993), 191.
2. Further discussions about the perfections of God can be found in J. I. Packer's *Knowing God* (Downers Grove, Ill.: InterVarsity, 1973).
3. Taken from Emery H. Bancroft, *Elemental Theology* (Hayward, Calif.: J. F. May Press, 1948), 22.
4. L. Berkof, *Systematic Theology* (Grand Rapids: Eerdmans, 1968), 60.
5. Bancroft, *Elemental Theology,* 23.
6. John H. Armstrong, gen. ed., "What Does God Know?" in *The Coming Evangelical Crisis* (Chicago: Moody, 1996), 140–41.
7. See Richard Rice, *God's Foreknowledge and Man's Free Will* (Minneapolis: Bethany, 1985); "Divine Foreknowledge and Free-Will Theism," *The Grace of God and the Will of Man: A Case for Arminianism,* ed. Clark H. Pinnock (Grand Rapids: Zondervan, 1989); and Clark H. Pinnock, "God Limits His Knowledge," in *Predestination and Free Will,* edited by David Basinger and Randall Basinger (Downers Grove, Ill.: InterVarsity, 1986).
8. David Basinger, "Practical Implications," *The Openness of God* (Downers Grove, Ill.: InterVarsity, 1994), 163.
9. Gregg Easterbrook, "A Hundred Years of Thinking About God," *U.S. News and World Report,* 23 February 1998, 61, 65.

CHAPTER 11

Why Are There So Many Names for the God of the Bible?

IN THE LAST CHAPTER WE learned that God's perfections are revelations of His Person. The names that God chose for Himself and that are ascribed to Him are also revelations of His Person. Furthermore, these names disclose key truths about God's character and His relation to humanity. It should be clear that the information appearing in this chapter will build on what I presented in the previous chapter.[1]

The divine names are not meaningless titles that people used to refer to God. Rather, each of these names reflects an unfolding, or a development, in the divine revelation to humanity. They individually make known something new and unique about the nature and character of our great God. For example, the names of God tell us many truths about His care and concern for His own. And His names tell us that He has been active in the affairs of people.

It must always be remembered that the many names of God are not mere ascriptions that people have assigned to the Lord. Rather, they are in most cases God's descriptions of Himself. It also would be incorrect to think that these names are descriptions of different gods. Rather, they are descriptions of the true and living God—the God of the Bible.

As we learn about the different names of God, we will examine the various circumstances that brought forth each name. We will also consider the practical and spiritual circumstances in which God made known His character-revealing names. This will prove to be a fascinating study of Scripture!

The Name of God in General

The Meaning in the Old Testament

I want to begin by commenting on the phrase "the name of God," and its equivalents, that appear throughout the Old

Testament. The writers of Scripture used these as broad labels to refer to the total revelation concerning the Person and character of God.

There are many instances where no specific name of God is employed, but *the name* of God is used. For example, Abraham called on *the name* of the Lord (Gen. 12:8; 13:4). The Lord proclaimed His own *name* before Moses (Exod. 33:19; 34:6). Israel was warned against profaning the *name* of the Lord (Lev. 22:32). The *name* of the Lord God was not to be taken in vain (Exod. 20:7; Deut. 5:11). The priests of Israel were to minister in *the name* of the Lord (Deut. 18:5; 21:5).

We learn something about the meaning and intent of the phrase, *the name of the Lord*, when we realize that to refuse to obey injunctions such as those cited above meant to refuse God and to depart from Him. In contrast, to call on the *name* of the Lord was to worship Him as God (Gen. 21:33; 26:25).

We must conclude, therefore, that such phrases as "the name of the LORD" or "the name of God" referred to His whole character. These were summary statements that embodied the entire Person of God. These phrases surely spoke about God's covenant relationship to His people. And the divine name became a token, or pledge, of all that God had promised to do and be (1 Sam. 12:22; Ps. 25:11). Furthermore, the honor and integrity of Yahweh were at stake whenever His *name* was involved.

The Meaning in the New Testament

We do not have to read far in the New Testament to discover that the name of Jesus is used there in a similar way to the name of God in the Old Testament. Salvation is through belief in Jesus' *name* (John 1:12). Christians are to gather together in His *name* (Matt. 18:20). Prayer is to be in Jesus' *name* (John 14:13-14). The servant of the Lord who bears the *name* of Christ will be hated (Matt. 10:22).

Just as the *name* of God in the Old Testament spoke about the holy character of God the Father, so the name of Jesus in the New Testament speaks about the holy character of God the Son. The Book of Acts makes frequent mention of worship, service, and suffering in the *name* of Jesus Christ (see, for example, Acts 4:18; 5:28, 41; 10:43; 19:17). And it is in the *name* of Jesus that every knee will one day bow and every tongue confess that Christ is Lord to the glory of God the Father (Phil. 2:10-11).

The Primary Names of God in the Old Testament

There are three prominent names for God that appear in the Old Testament. The first is *Elohim,* which is translated *God;* the second is *Adonai,* which is translated *Lord,* and the third is *Yahweh,* which is translated LORD. Two of these names, *Elohim* and *Yahweh,* are used frequently in combinations with other words to form compound names.

God (Elohim)

Genesis 1:1 is the first place in the Bible where *Elohim* occurs. Though this name for God appears 2,550 times, its meaning is set forth clearly in its first usage. By associating *Elohim* with the creative activity of God, it is clear that His eternal power and might are to be understood. The reader also realizes that God is the absolute and supreme Source of all things.

Genesis 1:1 is most striking in that, at a time when humans believed in many gods, Scripture set forth the one and only true God with unmistakable clarity. It was not long, however, until the worship of the one Creator—God—became corrupted (see Rom. 1:18-23).

As the nations scattered and the people intermarried, they carried with them the name of *Elohim;* but they no longer used it to refer only to the true God. They also applied it to parts of God's creation and to the gods of their own making. For example, Scripture speaks of the *Elohim,* or "gods," of Egypt (Exod. 12:12; Num. 33:4). Also consider God's command to Jacob to go to Bethel and Jacob's subsequent command to the people to put away the strange *Elohim,* or "gods" (Gen. 35:1-4).

These passages indicate three facts. First, the name *Elohim* was retained and used by people. Second, people began to forget the true meaning of the name. Third, *Elohim* thus became a meaningless term to them. This is a fitting illustration of the believer who retains the name *Christian* but whose life contradicts the real meaning of that name!

There is a twofold significance to the fact that *Elohim* is a plural Hebrew word. First, the Israelites sometimes used the plural form as a way of expressing a special meaning that could not be conveyed by using the singular form of the same word. For example, they used the plural *Elohim* to speak of God's greatness, incomprehensibleness, majesty, and power. Second, this plural form is in perfect harmony and consistency with the doctrine of the Trinity. For example, *Elohim* (the triune God) said, "Let Us make man in Our image" (Gen. 1:26).

God Almighty (El Shaddai). The prefix *El* is a shortened form of Elohim. In Genesis 17:1, where "El Shaddai" first occurs, and in the many other instances where the term appears in Scripture, it is rendered "God Almighty." However, in view of the contexts in which *El Shaddai* is found, this rendering does not seem to do complete justice to the name.

Elohim—or in this case *El*—refers to God as the mighty One or the strong One. But when "Shaddai" is added to that, something more must be meant than what "Elohim" by itself conveys. Some think *Shaddai* is derived from a root word that refers to a mother's breast,[2] while others think the term originated "from a related word that means 'mountain,' thus picturing God as the overpowering Almighty One, standing on a mountain."[3]

God is not only the Almighty One, but at the same time He is full of grace and mercy. And He is always ready to give out of His infinite resources. Thus *El Shaddai* is a most tender name for God, and it is used to refer to His relationship to His children. The great Creator is to His child what a loving mother is to her dependent infant. God sustains, succors, and satisfies His own.

Two outstanding characteristics seem to be associated with the name *El Shaddai*. First, God comforts His own and makes them fruitful. The account of Isaac's blessing upon Jacob and Jacob's subsequent fleeing from his brother Esau is a good illustration of this characteristic.

Jacob was lonely and afraid as he made the dangerous trip to Mesopotamia. Isaac beseeched *El Shaddai's* blessing upon his son, even though Jacob had cheated and connived to get what he wanted. Of course, God's blessing did not rest upon Jacob because of his sin but in spite of it and because he was the one through whom God would one day bless Israel.

Isaac's prayer of blessing displays the tender and compassionate nature of *El Shaddai*: "May God Almighty bless you and make you fruitful and multiply you, that you may become a company of peoples. May He also give you the blessing of Abraham, to you and to your descendants with you" (Gen. 28:3-4). If anyone ever needed mother-like comfort, it was Jacob, and *El Shaddai* provided it for him. Likewise, it was *El Shaddai* who made him fruitful by blessing him and his descendants.

Another illustration of God as the One who comforts, protects, and makes fruitful is found in Psalm 91:1-2. The promise is that those who dwell in the "shelter of the Most High will abide in the shadow of the Almighty." Notice that in these two verses four names are used to refer to God. Evidently the psalmist was seeking to show that the God of strength and power is the same One who is able to comfort the weary and protect the weak. Additionally, *El Shaddai* is the One who will deliver His own from the enemy and will give them refuge under His wing (v. 4).

The second outstanding characteristic is that *El Shaddai* often chastens His own to make them more fruitful. A careful distinction must be made between punishment or judgment because of sin, and chastisement or correction. God does judge and punish sin, but in the Old Testament the name of *Yahweh* occurs when references are made to His punishment. In contrast, the name *El Shaddai* is used when child training or correction is in view.

The losses and blessings that Naomi and Ruth endured is evidence of *El Shaddai* chastening His people in order to make them more fruitful (see Ruth 1–4). No better illustration of this truth is to be found than in the book of Job. Thirty-one times *El Shaddai* occurs in this book. There was no punishment involved in God's dealing with Job. He was blameless and upright. He trusted God, and had done nothing wrong (Job 1:6–22). God took away everything from Job; yet He was not punishing him. God is not always punishing His own when He takes things away from them. He may, as in the case of Job, be seeking to make us more fruitful by chastening us. Certainly, Job was made more fruitful, for God gave him more than he had before his trials occurred (42:10–17).

The Most High God (El Elyon). According to the English translation, this name for God seems to mean the same as *El Shaddai.* Of course, all the names we are considering refer to the same God. Nevertheless, each name reveals a different aspect of the character of our God.

We have seen that *El Shaddai* refers more to God's grace than to His power or might. We now learn that the translation of *El Elyon* as "The Most High God" is more accurate than the translation of *El Shaddai* as "The Almighty." The two names are linked beautifully in Psalm 91:1: "He who dwells in the shelter of the Most High *[El Elyon]* will abide in the shadow of the Almighty *[El Shaddai].*" How wonderful it is to know that the God who is Most High is also the God of mercy and grace!

The name *El Elyon* occurs first in the Bible in the account of Melchizedek's blessing of Abram (Abraham) after he had delivered his nephew Lot by defeating a coalition of five kings (Gen. 14:17). Verse 18 introduces us to Melchizedek, the king of Salem and a priest of "God Most High" *(El Elyon).* In verse 19, Melchizedek blessed Abram by referring to "God Most High *[El Elyon]*, Possessor of heaven and earth."

What a revelation of God there is in this name! Though He is superior to all things, this does not prevent Him from being concerned with the needs of His creatures. In fact, His sovereignty and greatness enables Him to take interest in the minutest details of His universe.

Satan sought to usurp the throne and supreme rule of God when he said, "I will make myself like the Most High" (that is, *El Elyon;* Isa. 14:14). However, the Devil did not succeed, and God thrust him down to Sheol (namely, the realm of the dead; v. 15).

Our *El Elyon* is still on His throne and rules in the affairs of all people. And yet, He is so interested in us that He "causes all things to work together for good to those who love God, to those who are called according to His purpose" (Rom. 8:28). The strong God, *El,* is also the most high God, *El Elyon,* who is interested in our personal situations.

The Everlasting God (El Olam). By itself the word *olam* means something that is secret, hidden, concealed, or unknown. When the Israelites wanted to refer to an unknown time, an uncalculated time, or an indefinite time, they used the word *olam* (for example, "a *permanent* right" in Lev. 25:32; and "from *ancient* times" in Josh. 24:2). From the idea of secret or hidden, the Israelites soon attached the concept of "eternity," which of course indicates the incalculable past and the incalculable future. Thus *olam* came to mean "everlasting," and is so translated in our Bibles (for example, "the *Everlasting* God" in Gen. 21:33).

The idea of God's unchangeableness is involved in most of the passages where *El Olam* occurs. He is all His people have need of from generation to generation (Pss. 100:5; 103:17). Times change, needs change, and people change; but *El Olam* never changes. This idea is expressed clearly in Isaiah 40:28: "Do you not know? Have you not heard? The Everlasting God, the LORD, the Creator of the ends of the earth does not become weary or tired. His understanding is inscrutable."

Two outstanding characteristics of *El Olam* are evident from Isaiah 40:28. First, God is inexhaustible. The seventh day—the day of rest in Genesis 2—was not designed to allow God to recuperate from His six days of creative activity, for He does not faint or grow weary. He rested because His work of creation was finished, or completed.

Second, there is no point to try to search the depth of God's understanding, for His ways are past finding out. Remember that *Olam* means "secret" or "hidden," and that root meaning is present in Isaiah 40:28. Thus, from this verse we learn that the secret things belong to God alone.

The message of the New Testament is the same as the message of the Old Testament concerning the immutability, or unchangeableness, of God. Paul referred to Him as the "eternal God" (Rom. 16:26). Through all the vicissitudes of life and the waywardness and instability of His people, there is with God "no variation or shifting shadow" (James 1:17). Blessed is the promise that though all else perishes, God remains the same (Heb. 1:10–12).

You Are a God Who Sees (El Roi). This outstanding and tender name for God occurs only once in the Bible, and that one instance comes from the lips of Hagar, the Egyptian handmaid, or slave, of Sarai (Sarah; Gen. 16:13).

Years after God had given Abram (Abraham) the promise to make a great nation from his descendants, Sarai, his wife, still remained childless. In ancient times a married woman who could not have children was shamed by her peers. In accordance with the customs of the time, Sarai gave her slave Hagar to Abram to bear him a child. When Hagar knew she was pregnant, she began to treat Sarai with contempt (Gen. 16:4). Sarai, in turn, treated Hagar harshly, and the slave girl ran away (v. 6).

Hagar suddenly found herself friendless, homeless, and alone in the wilderness. In her moment of need, the Angel of the Lord— the preincarnate Christ—visited her (Gen. 16:9–12).

Hagar undoubtedly knew much about the gods of Egypt. The idols people made of them had eyes and ears; yet these powerless and lifeless objects could not see or hear. But now the true God, *El Roi,* came to the rescue of the pregnant slave girl. Though forsaken by everyone else, Hagar found herself being not only observed by the God of Abraham but also cared for by Him as well. To commemorate the incident, Hagar referred to the Lord, who had spoken to her, as "You are a God who sees" (*El Roi;* Gen. 16:13).

Though this divine name is not attested elsewhere, the characteristics that *El Roi* reveals are everywhere evident in Scripture. For example, God revealed to Jacob in a dream that He was fully aware of the lying and cheating of Laban (Gen. 31:10–12). God saw all the affliction and persecution of His people in Egypt (Exod. 3:7–8). No doubt many of those praying Israelites often wondered whether God really knew and cared about them and remembered His covenant with them. He did! He always sees the affliction of His own, and He cares about their circumstances.

God also saw the sham and hypocrisy of Israel (Jer. 7:11). The Lord knew then what He knows now—that all too often the lives of His people contradict what they claim to believe. If God could see the need of a seemingly insignificant Egyptian slave girl named Hagar, He can also see the hypocritical and shameful deeds of His people.

The diagram below relates the names of God studied thus far to the perfections of God studied earlier.

NAMES OF GOD	PERFECTIONS OF GOD
1. *Elohim*	1. Omnipotence
2. *El Shaddai*	2. Love and grace
3. *El Elyon*	3. Omniscience/sovereignty
4. *El Olam*	4. Eternity/immutability
5. *El Roi*	5. Omnipresence/omniscience

Lord *(Adonai)*

Like the name *Elohim* (God), the Hebrew word rendered "Lord" in our English Bibles occurs most frequently in the plural form *Adonai*. When so used, it always refers to God. The singular form does occur, however, and is used to refer to people. The context makes it clear to whom the word is referring.

When used to refer to individuals, the word speaks of an intimate and personal relationship. For instance, the word is used to refer to the master of a slave and the husband of a wife, thus connoting the idea of authority, love, and faithfulness. Two truths are evident from the use of the word in the master-slave relationship.

The Master has a right to expect obedience. In Old Testament times, slaves were the absolute possession of their master and had no rights of their own. Their main objective was to fulfill the wishes of their master. Slaves had a relationship and responsibilities that were different from that of hired servants. For example, hired servants could quit if they did not like the orders of their master. In contrast, slaves had no other option but to obey their master (see, for example, Gen. 24:1-12).

The call of Moses serves as another illustration. His hesitation to obey the call of God eventually ended when he acknowledged God as *Adonai*, or Lord (Exod. 4:10-18). When Moses admitted his position as a slave and God's position as the Lord—the Master—

there was only one viable option—to obey. When Moses called God *Adonai,* he acknowledged that it was not his place as the slave to choose his work; he had to heed his Master's directives.

The commission of Isaiah gives us another illustration of the right of *Adonai,* the Lord, to expect absolute obedience from His servants (Isa. 6:1-8). Though the closing years of Uzziah's reign were filled with disobedience to God, this Judean monarch, in comparison with many other kings, was still considered godly, for "he did right in the sight of the LORD" (2 Kings 15:3). It's possible that Isaiah had been encouraged by Uzziah's reign. And at times the prophet may have been tempted to look to Judah's king, rather than to Yahweh, for the continued prosperity of the nation.

All that changed, however, when Uzziah died. In that year (740 B.C.), Isaiah had a vision of "the Lord *[Adonai]* sitting on His throne, lofty and exalted" (Isa. 6:1). This revelation of God as the absolute Lord ruling over the affairs of people caused the prophet to lament over his own sinfulness. God then took the initiative to spiritually cleanse Isaiah. Then, when the prophet heard "the voice of the Lord *[Adonai]*" (v. 8), he said, "Here am I. Send me!" Isaiah was ready and willing to do the bidding of his Master.

In the New Testament, *Kurios* (translated "Lord") is frequently used to refer to Christ. In fact, Jesus even uses this word to refer to Himself. For instance, John 13:1-12 relates that the disciples had gathered together in the upper room and that each one had refused to wash one another's feet. Note Jesus' words in verses 13 and 14. Here was the Lord *(Kurios)* taking the place of the servant in order to teach His followers the need of having the attitude of a servant. The disciples had forgotten that they were servants of Christ, their Master. As their Lord *(Kurios),* He reminded them of the importance of being humble and sacrificial in their service.

The slave may expect provision. Slaves usually did not worry about their daily affairs. This is because it was the master's business to provide food, shelter, and the other necessities of life. Since slaves were the possession of their master, their needs became the responsibility of the master to fulfill. Obedience was the only condition for this provision.

This truth is marvelously displayed in the life of Paul, who considered himself a bondslave of Christ. The apostle reflected a true servant's heart when he assured the Philippians that God, their Master, would supply all their needs (Phil. 4:19). Only obedient slaves can expect such provisions from their master.

The master is also responsible to manage the affairs of his slaves, for their work is the master's bidding. So it is with God as our Adonai, or Lord. When we are willing to be His obedient servants, He will give us direction in our service for Him. Consider, for example, Moses. At one point in his life he tried to serve God in his own strength and in his own way, and he failed miserably. Forty years later when Moses admitted that he could not serve God in his own power, the Lord saw fit to use him as the leader and liberator of His people.

Romans 12:1–2 teaches the importance of believers being holy living sacrifices to God. They should not copy the behavior and customs of the world, but rather allow God to transform their thinking. It is only when this renewal process has taken place that believers will be able to "prove what the will of God is, that which is good and acceptable and perfect."

LORD *(Yahweh)*

The Hebrew word *Yahweh*, which is translated "LORD" in our English Bibles, appears 6,823 times in the Old Testament. Most scholars agree that it should be pronounced *Yahweh*.

The ancient Israelites considered the name *Yahweh* too sacred to be pronounced. When the Masoretes added vowel sounds to the Hebrew text, they attached vowel signs to the four consonants YHWH to indicate that in its place one should read the Hebrew word *Adonai*, which means "Lord." Ancient Greek translators used the word *Kurios* ("Lord") for the name *Yahweh*. The Hebrew word *Adonai* is translated as "Lord" in small letters in our English Bibles to distinguish it from *Yahweh*, which is translated "LORD" in large and small capital letters.

Yahweh seems best explained as coming from the Hebrew verb for "to be." Thus, *Yahweh* speaks of God as the self-existing One. Exodus 3:14 is a key passage to consider when discussing the meaning of *Yahweh*. Moses had asked God what he should say to the Israelites when he went to see them (v. 13). God responded by saying, " 'I AM WHO I AM'; and He said, 'Thus you shall say to the sons of Israel, "I AM has sent me to you." ' "

Though the exact derivation and meaning of this divine name remain uncertain, we know that it means "I AM," for this is the way God used it in His response to Moses. Exodus 3:15–22 indicates that *Yahweh* is not only the self-existent One but also the unchangeable One. He would be to the Israelites of Moses' day what He had always been to the patriarchs Abraham, Isaac, and Jacob.

The word *Yahweh* does not occur in the Bible until after God's creation of humanity (see Gen. 2:4). Up until that point the word *Elohim* appears. This suggests that *Yahweh* is the name of God that denotes His relationship with His people. In contrast, *Elohim* is the name of God that refers to His power and might. Whereas *Elohim* identifies God as the Creator and moral Governor of the universe, *Yahweh* reveals Him as the faithful God of the covenant. In fact, the covenants were made in the name of *Yahweh* (see Exod. 19:1–3; 20:2; Jer. 31:31).

Some outstanding characteristics of *Yahweh* are revealed in the biblical passages that use this title, and His name is associated with each of these virtues: (1) God's absolute holiness (Lev. 11:44–45; 19:1–2; 20:26); (2) God's hatred and judgment of sin (Gen. 6:3–7; Exod. 34:6–7; Deut. 32:35–42; Ps. 11:5–6); and, (3) God's love for sinners and His provision of salvation and redemption for them (Gen. 3:8, 21; Exod. 3:1–10; Isa. 53:1, 5, 6, 10).

God designed the tabernacle, its furnishings, and the worship conducted in the sanctuary to teach His people about His ineffable purity and absolute holiness. Likewise, His hatred and punishment of sin were evidences of His own holiness. Furthermore, His demand for separateness from sin on the part of His people is another evidence of His holiness.

Yahweh's reaching out to sinful humanity in love demonstrates His desire to redeem sinners. This truth also flatly contradicts the modern notion that fallen people make any effort to search for God. The good news of salvation is not that people try to reach God (Rom. 3:10–11). It's the other way around. God reaches out to the lost through the provision of His Son (vv. 21–31).

The Lord Jesus claimed the title of *Yahweh* for Himself, thus substantiating His assertion of being fully divine (John 8:58). The Jewish leaders had been boasting about their relationship to Abraham, and Christ reminded them that Abraham rejoiced to see His day (v. 56). The authorities could not understand what Jesus meant, for they noted that He was not yet fifty years old (v. 57). They considered His claim to absolute eternal existence to be blasphemous, and thus took up stones to throw at Him (vv. 58–59).

It's clear that the Jewish leaders got Christ's message. He was claiming to be *Yahweh* of the Old Testament. This meant He was equal with the self-existent, unchanging, covenant God of Israel.

As God unfolded His person and purposes to His people, the name *Yahweh* took on fresh new meanings for them. To express these additional meanings, the Israelites attached other names to *Yahweh*.

The LORD *will provide.* Here the name *Yahweh,* with all that is implied in that title, is joined with *yireh* which means "to see to it" or "to provide." Technically, this name is used to refer to a place that served as a reminder of a truth concerning God (Gen. 22:14). *Yahweh yireh* occurs only once in the Old Testament, though the characteristic of God that it reveals is emphasized throughout Scripture.

For example, when Abram (Abraham) was old and Sarai (Sarah) was past the age of childbearing, God promised them a posterity (Gen. 17:1-8). Isaac was born after much rebellion and unbelief on the part of both Abraham and Sarah (Gen. 21:1-8).

God challenged Abraham's faith when He told the patriarch to offer his son, Isaac—the promised heir and the one through whom the covenant was to be fulfilled—on the altar of sacrifice (Gen. 22:1-14). Abraham's neighbors were accustomed to offering human sacrifices in their pagan practices. Now the true God was testing Abraham. Was his love for God as great as the love the pagans had for their false gods?

It is noteworthy that until verse 14 Moses used the word *Elohim* to refer to God. For example, Abraham told his son Isaac that *Elohim,* the God of power and might, would provide the burnt offering for the altar (Gen. 22:8). And He did, but He did so as *Yahweh yireh.* The Lord truly provided in the hour of need!

All of us need to be willing to surrender to the Lord what is most precious to us. We need to make the trek to that special place where we can demonstrate to God our complete love, utmost devotion, and total surrender to Him. When that is done, we will come to understand God more fully as *Yahweh yireh,* the LORD who provides.

The LORD *of Hosts.* The word *sabaoth* means "to assemble," and when coupled with *Yahweh,* it is translated "LORD of hosts." The underlying thought seems to involve warfare and the warrior. This title for God first appears in 1 Samuel 1:3, and it is used repeatedly thereafter in the writings of the prophets. Usually, however, this title for God occurs in connection with some great need or national crisis on the part of Israel. There is definitely a relationship of God with His own expressed in this title.

Prior to 1 Samuel 1:3, when *sabaoth* was first used to refer to God, the title was used to refer to Israel (Exod. 12:41). Later on the title was also used to refer to angels (Pss. 103:21; 148:2). From the combination of *Yahweh* and *sabaoth,* we learn that God is the Lord of both heaven and earth. He marshals the hosts of heaven to the aid of His people on earth. He truly is the LORD of hosts, and the Guardian, the Leader, and the Protector of His own.

The LORD our Banner. Exodus 17:8–16 provides the historical context for this divine name. The Israelites were only a few days' journey from Egypt when the Amalekites attacked them from the rear (see Deut. 25:17–18). The Amalekites were a pagan and immoral people who were opposed to God and His people (Exod. 17:16; Num. 14:44–45; Deut. 25:17; 1 Samuel 15).

God's people were unprepared for battle; yet Moses ordered Joshua to lead the fight against Amalek. Moses took the staff of God and went to the top of the hill. As long as Moses held up the staff with his hands (perhaps as a sign of dependence on God), the Israelites prevailed in battle. Eventually Joshua and his troops were able to crush the army of Amalek (Exod. 17:9–13).

In accordance with the Lord's command, Moses wrote on a scroll that the Israelites had prevailed over the Amalekites. This would serve as a memorial to Joshua and the rest of God's people that He would "utterly blot the memory of Amalek from under heaven" (Exod. 17:14). Why did God think Joshua needed such a keepsake? The memorial would remind him and the rest of the Israelites that the victory was not due to their cunning and might but because of God's power operating in their lives.

Moses also built an altar and named it *Yahweh-nissi*, which means "The LORD is My Banner" (Exod. 17:15). The Hebrew term rendered "banner" underlies "staff" in verse 9. In ancient times a staff was used as a standard in battle and also marked the rallying point for troops. Moses declared that God Himself is the Standard of His people.

Yahweh-nissi associates God with warfare on behalf of His people. Through all the conflicts that Israel was to have, *Yahweh* wanted His people to know that He would fight their battles. The Israelites could not defeat their enemies in their own strength. Rather, they had to depend on God's power for the victory.

Amalek is a reminder of the flesh, or the old sin nature, which constantly wars against the Spirit and the new nature. Paul taught that this is a spiritual conflict that every child of God must endure (Rom. 7:14–25; Gal. 5:16–18). Victory in these battles comes by equipping ourselves with the "full armor of God" (Eph. 5:11) and by allowing God to be our *Yahweh-nissi*, that is, our source of victory.

In the battle against the Amalekites, the victory belonged to *Yahweh*. Nevertheless, Joshua and his troops still had to fight and

Moses had to hold up his hands. From this we see that there were some things that *the people* had to do; God would not do these things for them. So it is with us. While spiritual warfare is waged in God's strength and in His name, it is still *we* who must fight and pray.

The LORD who sanctifies. This is no doubt the least familiar of all God's names; yet it is one of the most important. Unlike many of the other names for God appearing in the Old Testament, the Hebrew word *m'qaddishkhem* is not transliterated in our English versions. The name, which first appears in Exodus 31:13 in connection with the keeping of the Sabbath, means "The LORD who sanctifies"; in other words, *Yahweh* is the One who sets apart His people as being holy.

Long before *Yahweh* made Himself known as the One who consecrates His people, He had been busy sanctifying them. For instance, He set apart Abraham as His servant (Gen. 12). He consecrated the Israelites as a people who were to be separate from the nations around them (Exod. 19:4-6, 10, 14). God set apart the Aaronic priesthood and the rituals they performed (Exod. 28:1-3). And He set apart the tabernacle as a sacred place of worship (Exod. 25:8-9; 29:42-44).

Having done all this, *Yahweh* next reminded His people that He was the One who had set them apart for His own glory (Exod. 31:13). They were to be consecrated for holy living because they served a holy God. Just as the tabernacle and all the items and ceremonies associated with it were sanctified for holy use, so God commanded His people to be set apart for holy living.

God is still our *LORD who sanctifies.* He is still setting apart a people for His name (John 17:17, 19; Heb. 10:10; 1 Peter 1:15), to function as a royal priesthood (1 Peter 2:9; Rev. 1:6), and to be a sacred dwelling place for the Spirit (1 Cor. 6:19; Eph. 2:20-22). What a challenge for holy living exists for every child of God!

Herbert Stevenson in his helpful book, *The Titles of the Triune God,* lists eight descriptive titles of God. These are not quite the same as the proper names we have been discussing, but they certainly spotlight important aspects of the character of God worth considering. Six of the eight titles that Stevenson includes are especially descriptive and are listed here:

(1) *Rock* (Deut. 32:4, 15, 18, 30, 31). The granite strength of rocks is an appropriate symbol of the strength and unchangeableness of God.

(2) *Fortress* (2 Sam. 22:2; see also Pss. 18:2; 31:3; 91:2). This

title speaks of the protection provided by God.

(3) *Shield* (Gen. 15:1) and *buckler* (Pss. 3:3; 28:7). God's defense of His own is made known in these titles.

(4) *Mighty One* (Gen. 49:24; Ps. 132:2, 5). In addition to the strength of God, this title speaks of His forbearance and faithfulness.

(5) *Strength* or *Glory* (1 Sam. 15:29). As used in this reference by Samuel in his rebuke of Saul for his disobedience, the changelessness of God is in view.

(6) *Jealous* (Exod. 20:5; 34:14). Every usage of this title with God is in connection with His desire for the exclusive worship of His people.

The diagram below shows the believer's responsibilities in relation to the names of God.

NAMES OF GOD	RESPONSIBILITIES OF MAN
1. Lord *(Adonai)*	1. Obedience
2. LORD *(Yahweh)*	2. Dependence

Notes

1. I am indebted for this summary to Herbert F. Stevenson, *Titles of the Triune God* (Westwood, N.J.: Revell, 1956), and to J. Dwight Pentecost for his treatment of the subject in unpublished mimeographed class notes at Dallas Theological Seminary.
2. *The Scofield Reference Bible,* footnote, p. 26.
3. *The Ryrie Study Bible, Expanded Edition,* footnote on Gen. 17:1, p. 28.

CHAPTER 12

The Work of the God of the Bible in Salvation

SALVATION IS THE WORK OF God from beginning to end—from the moment of regeneration to the time of glorification. This means the new birth is not mostly the work of God and partly the work of people. A weak and unscriptural view of the salvation of the sinner is inevitably the result of and is accompanied by an equally weak and unscriptural view of the total lostness and helplessness of the sinner. When humanity's separation from God and their absolute inability to please God are acknowledged, it naturally follows that if ever sinners are to be made right with God, *He* must make the first move; *He* must do the saving.

Through all the ages of time, God has had but one *basis* for the salvation of the lost—the atoning sacrifice of Christ. It was God who initiated the reconciliation of the lost to Himself. And it was God who, even before He created people, designed a plan for their redemption. Before the death of Christ, the Israelites related to God on the basis that, in the divine plan, Christ's death was absolutely certain. The sacrifices and rituals recorded in the Old Testament were ultimately symbols that anticipated Jesus' coming death (see Heb. 9:8-10; 10:1-3).

Likewise through all the ages of time, God has had but one *means* of appropriating salvation. That means has always been by faith. God has always saved people in the same way, though their knowledge of the Redeemer has come gradually, as God has been pleased to reveal it to them.

Thus, the *object* of faith was not always as clear as it is now to us, who have the completed Canon of Scripture. For example, the people of Old Testament times did not understand all that we now know about Christ's atoning work on the cross. This is because God had not given them all the revelation we have about Him. Yet the Israelites were responsible to believe God's promises to them. When the people of the Old Testament believed those

144

promises and demonstrated their faith through obedience to the law and the offering of sacrifices, God applied the benefits of Calvary to them in view of the future death of Christ (Rom. 3:25; 4:3).

What a marvelous condescension it is that God would provide salvation for sinful humanity! All that has been said about God to this point amplifies the marvel of God's concern for people—the Creator moving to save His erring creatures.

The Work of God in Eternity Past

From humanity's perspective it may appear that everything about the salvation of the lost began at the moment they trusted in Christ. Often, people think it was *their* decision—and *their* decision alone—that initiated their salvation and will consummate it when they finally reach heaven.

Many place so much emphasis upon what *they* have done to receive this "so great salvation" that God's work in eternity past and in eternity future is virtually forgotten. In this way of thinking, salvation is a humanly initiated and completed work, not the sole work of God. Believers will only come to appreciate their salvation fully when they realize that long before they trusted in Christ, *God* chose a plan of salvation and a people for that plan.

The Demand for the Plan of Salvation

The divine problem. Humanity's sin had a great affect upon God. In fact, sin always affects God in some way. Surely sin made its mark upon Adam and Eve and upon the whole human race. God, in His holiness and righteousness, inflicted severe penalties upon Adam and Eve, upon the serpent, and even upon the ground because of humanity's sin (see Gen. 3:14-19). But what relationship did Adam's sin, and our sin in him (see Rom. 5:12), have with God?

The answer to this question is not difficult, if we remember that sin—all sin—is an offense against God. He is the Norm, the Standard, and the Criterion of judging right from wrong. Therefore, sin is an offense against His holy character. We should not think that sin surprised God or that it intruded into His universe unnoticed. This is not the case. Such a scenario could not possibly be true if God is truly and fully divine.

The divine problem can be expressed as a question: How can God remain holy and just and at the same time forgive sinners and allow them into His presence? We know God's ineffable purity cannot tolerate sin in any form. He is so holy that He cannot look with favor upon evil. How, then, can people ever come before

Him in worship, love, and fellowship? Asked another way, how can God legitimately "be just and the justifier" (Rom. 3:26)?

Paul's question spotlights the tension that must be resolved. God, who is absolutely righteous and holy, has to exact justice for the transgressions of sinners. Yet, in His unconditional love, He also wants to deliver them from the eternal judgment that His righteousness demands He must impose on them.

The divine solution. God has solved the problem that humanity's sin presented to Him. And He is the only One who could solve the problem. After humanity's fall, God the Father began in time the plan of salvation that He had ordained in eternity past. This divine plan centered in His divine Son.

Notice what Scripture reveals about God's plan of salvation: The Lord "gave His only begotten Son" because He "so loved the world" (John 3:16). "We know love by this, that He laid down His life for us" (1 John 3:16). "By this the love of God was manifested in us, that God has sent His only begotten Son into the world so that we might live through Him" (1 John 4:9). From these and other verses, the relationship between God's love and His action toward sinners is clearly presented (see also Rom. 5:8 and Gal. 2:20).

From the time God clothed Adam and Eve with the skins of the slain animals, the great program of redemption through substitution was begun. Genesis 3:15 in particular anticipates the coming of the Seed of the woman who was to inflict a fatal wound upon Satan. This Seed was none other than Jesus Christ, the Messiah. The sacrifices of the Old Testament were ultimately types of Him who was to come. The Bible reveals that God clothed in human flesh would be the sacrificial Substitute for every member of Adam's lost race.

In the divine solution, Christ was the righteous One who alone could satisfy every demand of the offended righteousness of God. The cross of Christ is presented in holy Scripture as the declaration of the righteousness of God (Rom. 3:25). Through that cross, God was in Christ reconciling the world to Himself (2 Cor. 5:19). That is to say, the relationship of the world to God and God to the world was changed through Christ's sacrifice. The world of lost humanity—namely, all of those who sinned in Adam—are now savable. They may all be saved, if they trust in Christ. Since Calvary, the question before lost humanity is not primarily one concerned with their original sin. Rather, it is now a question of what they will do with Christ, the Son of God, who died for them.

This is all a part of the divine solution. But there is still another factor that, to our minds, seems hard to reconcile with God's love. The divine plan of salvation, which God formulated in eternity past, allowed for the entrance and continuance of sin until that day appointed by God when sin and the author of it shall be forever banished.

We know that God allowed for the entrance and continuance of sin, for Scripture speaks forthrightly on the matter. In Peter's sermon at Pentecost, he said the following concerning Christ: "This Man, delivered over by the predetermined plan and foreknowledge of God, you nailed to a cross by the hands of godless men and put Him to death" (Acts 2:23). On another occasion, after the authorities had released Peter and John, the two reported to the disciples what had happened (4:23). The disciples concluded that the crucifiers of Christ were doing "whatever Your hand and Your purpose predestined to occur" (v. 28).

It goes without saying that if the historic death of Christ was a part of the divine plan as the solution to the sin question, the entrance of sin that made Jesus' death necessary was also known and permitted by God. This statement is confirmed in 1 Peter 1:20, "For He [Christ] was foreknown before the foundation of the world, but has appeared in these last times for the sake of you."

The Designer of the Plan of Salvation

What I have been saying about our great God and His infinite ability and wisdom underscores that He is the Designer of the plan of salvation. My purpose here is not to deal with all the specifics related to God's sovereign plan, but only to demonstrate that He chose a perfect plan of redemption that included the death of His Son. God's selection of this plan in eternity past made it absolutely certain of accomplishment long before He created earth and humanity.

Let us remember that God has not been and is not now operating His universe on a contingency basis. According to His sovereign plan and eternal purpose, He is in the process of moving history to a predetermined end. He has designed this end and the process associated with it to bring maximum glory to His name. The most crucial aspect of God's plan and program—the one that determines the eternal future of all people—is the death of Jesus Christ and humanity's relationship to His death.

Scripture clearly reveals that lost people did not initiate their salvation. Rather, God did by selecting a plan for the salvation of humanity that included the death of His Son. Here are several of the crucial passages bearing upon this point:

- "This Man, delivered over by the predetermined plan and foreknowledge of God, you nailed to a cross by the hands of godless men and put Him to death" (Acts 2:23). The point here is that, even though people arrested Christ and crucified Him, the determinate counsel and foreknowledge of God consigned Him to death on the cross. Those who executed Christ were not upsetting God's plan, though they were fully responsible for their crime.
- "For truly in this city there were gathered together against Your holy servant Jesus, whom You appointed, both Herod and Pontius Pilate, along with the Gentiles and the peoples of Israel, to do whatever Your hand and Your purpose predestined to occur" (Acts 4:27-28). Much the same truth as above is expressed here. All people are guilty of Christ's death. And yet those who literally took part in that dastardly act were doing what God had planned to be done.
- "For He was foreknown before the foundation of the world, but has appeared in these last times for the sake of you" (1 Peter 1:20). Here again, Christ, as the Lamb slain for the remission of sins, was foreknown and predetermined "before the foundation of the world."
- "All who dwell on the earth will worship him [namely, the beast], everyone whose name has not been written from the foundation of the world in the book of life of the Lamb who has been slain" (Rev. 13:8). In words similar to those of Peter, John spoke about Christ's sacrifice as being a certain event even before God's creation of the world.

The complex miracle of physical birth requires a divine plan and Planner. This is even more true of the miracle of spiritual birth into the family of God. The Author of the plan of redemption is none other than God Himself. The Creator of the universe and of humanity—the One who spoke and by His command brought all things into existence—sovereignly chose to devise a plan of salvation for His disobedient and fallen creatures.

John declared that those who trust in Christ have the right to become children of God; and, in fact, their spiritual rebirth comes from God (John 1:12-13). Paul wrote that Christ, the Savior, is the "wisdom of God" (1 Cor. 1:30). The apostle also revealed that it was God the Father who "displayed publicly" Christ to be the "propitiation," or full satisfaction, for our sins. This was the Father's way of remaining just and at the same time the One who could justify all who believe in Christ as Savior (Rom. 3:25-26).

We must never view salvation as an afterthought or as the only possible way that God could get Himself out of a hopeless dilemma. Rather, the plan of salvation is as eternal as God. The Lord was not shocked when Satan rebelled and Adam and Eve fell into sin, for God is eternal, and His sovereign plan extends from eternity past to eternity future.

The Lord's wisdom is unsearchable, and His ways are past finding out (Rom. 11:33). He eliminated every possible human instrument in the plan of salvation. That is why John said spiritual rebirth is not the result of natural descent, of human decision, or of human achievement. Rather, it is all of God (John 1:13). It is His plan from start to finish. Salvation is of the Lord!

The Basis of the Plan of Salvation

We have noted above the relationship between God's love and the sending of His Son. It's undeniable that the Father was motivated by His own divine love. It is equally as scriptural to say that His grace is the basis for His plan of redemption.

God is both merciful and gracious. His grace has to do with His display of undeserved favor toward sinners. And His mercy prompts Him to withhold merited judgment. Therefore, God's grace is His giving of undeserved blessings, and His mercy is His withholding of deserved judgments.

The plan of salvation makes known more than just the fact that God is gracious. It also discloses that He is the God of grace. Because He is characterized by grace and because grace is a part of His essential nature, He can be gracious in His dealings with people.

From the human viewpoint, believers often think that everything about their salvation began when they decided to trust in Christ. The fact is that God was at work on our behalf long before the moment we believed. We did not and could not initiate the salvation we enjoy in Christ.

Scripture declares that we were chosen in Christ "before the foundation of the world" (Eph. 1:3-4). And the Bible tells us we were "chosen according to the foreknowledge of God the Father" (1 Peter 1:1-2). Paul put it this way: "For those whom He foreknew, He also predestined to become conformed to the image of His Son" (Rom. 8:29).

The Purpose of the Plan of Salvation

God's highest motive in His plan of salvation is that redeemed sinners might bring glory to Him. In fact, the entire work is to "the praise of His glory" (Eph. 1:12, 14).

Numerous questions come to our minds about many issues related to the divine plan of salvation. For instance, we do not understand why God has been pleased to do the things He has, and we will never know the answers to many of our queries until we see the Lord face to face (see 1 Cor. 13:12; 1 John 3:2). One truth we do know, however, is that God's plan is the best one possible to bring the most possible glory to His name. And His Word tells us that He does all things well (see Mark 7:37).

For some reason the human mind delights to ponder the inscrutable mysteries of God. This is not wrong, unless such thoughts keep us from carrying out the many human responsibilities outlined for us in Scripture. The precious truth that God chose to save us will not make us proud and unconcerned for the salvation of the lost, if we correctly understand this truth and balance it with God's commands for us to love, trust, and obey Him. Believers too often view God's plan as the result of His arbitrary declarations and decisions. This is not true, for God knows the end from the beginning (see Isa. 46:10). His plan is the result of His infinite wisdom and love, and it is in keeping with His absolute holiness and justice.

The Human Agents in the Plan of Salvation

It is not a contradiction to say that God is the supreme and absolute Ruler of the universe and everything in it, and, at the same time, to say that people are responsible for their actions. The marvelous thing about God's wonderful plan of salvation is that it includes human instrumentality and responsibility.

It is a part of God's sovereignty that believers take the good news of the Gospel to the lost. Of course, the Holy Spirit brings sinners under conviction and draws them to the Savior. And the Spirit does His saving work only through the ministry of the Word. No one was ever saved apart from a knowledge of Scripture.

How wonderful it is to realize that we are colaborers with God in the Gospel ministry (1 Cor. 3:5-9). It is not His plan that angels be ambassadors for Him. He has left that noble position for believers to fill. This is what Paul meant when he said: "For we are His workmanship, created in Christ Jesus for good works, which God prepared beforehand so that we would walk in them" (Eph. 2:10).

The fact that we are workers together with God and that God expects good works from us after our salvation does not detract from the highest motive of God in saving us. Rather, the one complements the other. We bring glory to God's name through our labors of love for Him and in His power (2 Cor. 12:9-10).

The Bible views every believer as an ambassador for Christ: "Therefore, we are ambassadors for Christ, as though God were making an appeal through us; we beg you on behalf of Christ, be reconciled to God" (2 Cor. 5:20). There is no room for choice here. We are *His* representatives! The question is this: How well are we representing Him and His cause?

The eternal plan of salvation includes not only the *end*—namely, a redeemed company in glory—but also the *means* to the end. The plan likewise includes a holy, loving, and intelligent Being behind it. These truths distinguish this plan from fatalism, which does not include the means. And fatalism also does not have an intelligent Being behind it.

Scripture does not present God's plan of salvation as being incompatible with the will of people. Rather, the sovereign plan includes the actions and responsibilities of people. They are both part of the divine plan. This fact harmonizes well with two other biblical truths. The first is that God hates sin, and therefore is not the Author of it. The second is that God always holds people responsible for their actions and judges them for their sin.

Paul associated his call to salvation with his responsibility to serve Christ (Gal. 1:15-16). Likewise, God's choice of us for salvation should be the motivating force behind our service to Him. These truths concerning God's plan of salvation ought to humble us. And when we correctly understand and appreciate them, we will be humble in our attitude. It behooves us to remain humble, and also to recognize that God's ways in choosing us for salvation are inscrutable.

A proper understanding of these glorious truths will bring us to the same conclusion that Paul had concerning the absolute sovereignty of God. The apostle's hymn of praise should be made our own: "Oh, the depth of the riches both of the wisdom and knowledge of God! How unsearchable are His judgments and unfathomable His ways! For who has know the mind of the Lord, or who became His counselor? Or who has first given to Him that it might be paid back to Him again? For from Him and through Him and to Him are all things. To Him be the glory forever. Amen" (Rom. 11:33-36).

The People God Chose for the Plan of Salvation

Left to their own choice and apart from the movement of God in their life, no person would ever choose to trust in Him for salvation. That is what Scripture clearly teaches (note, for example, Ps. 51:5; Jer. 17:9-10; Rom. 3:10-11, 23). The Bible also reveals that people are living in rebellion against God (Rom. 5:8, 10).

They are spiritually dead in trespasses and sins, and they can do nothing to please God (Eph. 2:1–3). The unregenerate do not need medication. They need new life!

The sincere student of Scripture cannot avoid the truth of God's choice of individuals from among the sinful race of people. No one comes to faith in Christ on their own; instead, God makes the first move. We may not fully understand this clear biblical truth, but we must never deny it, for it permeates the teaching of Scripture. It is not an isolated doctrine of the Word. Here are several basic passages that are crucial to this matter:

(1) *John 6:37, 39, 43–44.* To the multitude gathered on the shore of the Sea of Galilee at Capernaum, Jesus said: "All that the Father gives Me will come to Me, and the one who comes to Me I will certainly not cast out" (v. 37). Again to the same group He said: "This is the will of Him who sent Me, that of all that He has given Me I lose nothing" (v. 39). These teachings brought grumbling from the Jewish authorities, for Christ taught that He is the Bread of life (vv. 35, 41). In response, the Savior said: "Do not grumble among yourselves. No one can come to Me unless the Father who sent Me draws Him" (vv. 43–44).

These passages are clear and forthright. No one comes to faith in Christ as Savior unless the God of the Bible, whom Jesus called His Father, draws that person to Him.

(2) *Romans 8:28–30.* "And we know that God causes all things to work together for good to those who love God, to those who are called according to His purpose. For whom He foreknew, He also predestined to become conformed to the image of His Son, so that He might be the firstborn among many brethren; and these whom He predestined, He also called; and these who He called, He also justified; and these whom He justified, He also glorified."

The certainty of God's election of the believer is the grand truth in this passage. Nothing could be clearer than the fact that those whom God foreknows (v. 29) He will also glorify (v. 30). The foreknowledge spoken of here does not mean simply that God possesses foresight. Based on what is said here and in other passages, it is clear that a relationship eternally exists between the One who knows His own beforehand and those who are thus known by Him (see Acts 2:23; Rom. 11:2; 1 Peter 1:2, 20).

Foreknowledge does involve prior knowledge, but it also involves an eternal and intimate relationship with the one so known by God. Scripture does not tell us what—if anything—there is in the foreknowledge of God that causes Him to choose us for salvation. But we do know it is not our inherent goodness, for we have none.

(3) *Romans 9–11.* No other passage in Scripture reveals more clearly that God's election of some is not based on either their physical ancestry (9:6-9) or on their human merit (vv. 10-13). Rather, His choosing is solely based on the exercise of His mercy (vv. 14-24). As Paul contemplated the greatness of God and His plan of redemption, the apostle determined that an anthem of praise was the only fitting conclusion (11:33-36).

(4) *Ephesians 1:1–12.* That God chose a people for His name is here clearly set forth. God made His choice before the foundation of the world (v. 4). And the good pleasure of God is the only basis for His sovereign election (vv. 5, 11). God chose sinners to be saved so that He might be glorified (v. 12).

Some might object to this teaching by asking, Why bother to evangelize the lost, if God has already sovereignly chosen some to be saved (see Rom. 9:19-24)? Perhaps the best answer is to remind the scoffer of God's clear commands to proclaim the Gospel. The great evangelistic and missionary fervor of Paul also serves as an example of our responsibility in this regard. More than any other New Testament writer, this apostle was used by God to give us information about election, predestination, and so on. And yet Paul was also perhaps the greatest missionary the world has ever known (that is, after Christ).

Sovereignty and election are God's business, not ours. Our responsibility is not to question God's plan, but to accept it and allow it to motivate us to proclaim the good news of salvation by grace through faith in the finished work of Christ. God has not only chosen a plan of redemption and a people for that plan but also the means to the end whereby lost sinners can be saved.

If we could get half as concerned about our responsibility as we do about philosophical problems surrounding the doctrine of God's sovereignty, we would see many more people come to faith in Christ. Let us acknowledge that God has chosen the lost to be saved. Thank God that He has, for if He had not, no one would be saved. Why not allow God to do as He pleases? He will anyway. So then, having acknowledged this clear and undeniable truth, let us get on with our part in His plan—namely, proclaiming the good news that Christ died for all sinners (see 1 John 2:2).

It is clear from Scripture that God has given a universal offer of the Gospel. Whoever desires may be saved. God will not reject anyone who wants to be His child and who actually comes to Him in faith. To put it another way, all who want to be saved can be saved (see 1 Tim. 2:4; 2 Peter 3:9).

The Work of God in Time

The Coming of God the Son

"But when the fullness of the time came, God sent forth His Son, born of a woman, born under the Law, so that He might redeem those who were under the Law, that we might receive the adoption as sons" (Gal. 4:4-5). Here is clear evidence of God bringing to pass in time what He had planned in eternity past. Christ was virginally conceived and born, lived a holy and sinless life, and then died on the cross as the substitutionary sacrifice for sinners.

Christ's life of absolute holiness made it possible for Him to be the only acceptable Sacrifice to atone for the iniquity of sinners. And Christ's holy life and life of suffering proved Him to be the qualified One to make such a propitiation. Through Jesus' death upon the cross, full substitution was made for the root of sin (John 1:29; Rom. 6:10) and the fruit of sin (Col. 2:14; 1 Peter 2:24).

It is clear from Scripture that Christ's great completed work on the cross provided full redemption for humanity. As the last Adam, His sacrifice extends to the entire human race, who were plunged into sin and death by the transgression of the first Adam (Rom. 5:12-21).

Second Peter 2:1 tells us that Christ redeemed, or paid the purchase price, even for those who will never trust in Him. And 1 John 2:2 reveals that Jesus' work of propitiation is good not only for the sins of those who believe but also for the sins of the whole world. Furthermore, 2 Corinthians 5:18-19 says that the death of Christ changed the relation of all people (not only the elect) from being enemies to being savable. (Of course, people must first believe in Christ in order for salvation to become a reality for them.)

In light of these truths we can better understand what Jesus meant when He announced from the cross, "It is finished!" (John 19:30). Christ had completed the saving work the Father had planned for Him to accomplish before the foundation of the world.

The Work of God the Holy Spirit

In salvation. Before the Savior went to the cross, He promised to send another Helper to His disciples (John 14:16), the Spirit of truth (16:13). The Spirit has come to convict the world of sin, righteousness, and judgment (vv. 8-11). He performs this convicting ministry upon all, even though all will not respond favorably to His work in their lives. The Spirit has also come to continue the work of sanctification that Jesus began in the lives of believers.

Since people are spiritually dead, there must be a work of God on their behalf that enables them to see their need to trust in Christ for salvation. God the Holy Spirit is the One who enlivens the sin-darkened mind of the unregenerate so that they will respond in faith to the Gospel. (For more information, see the biblical passages that speak about the divine call resulting in salvation; for example, Rom. 1:1, 6; 8:28, 30; Eph. 1:18).

According to John 6:36 and 40, the Father's work of bringing sinners to repentance and faith is absolutely essential to salvation. He uses the Spirit to convince sinners of their need for redemption and to enable them to trust in Christ. Of course, it is the sinner's responsibility to accept Jesus' gift of salvation (see Eph. 1:13).

What a wonderful salvation is ours in Christ! God designed it in eternity past and made it a reality in time through the Savior's death. Clearly, salvation is completely the work of the Lord, so that "no man may boast before God" (1 Cor. 1:29).

In service. God sent His Son to die on the cross for humanity's sin. And the Son, in turn, sent the Holy Spirit to convict the lost, bring them to faith, and give them new life. But this is not all the Spirit came to do. He also sets apart believers for Christian service.[1] As Ephesians 2:10 makes clear, the salvation we received by faith alone is supposed to issue in good works.

Paul always maintained a scriptural balance between the doctrines of God's sovereignty and the believer's responsibility. For example, the apostle never sidestepped the subject of human responsibility to emphasize the sovereignty of God. And Paul never allowed human responsibility to nullify the concept of God's sovereignty. The fine balance between these two biblical truths was evident in the apostle's life (see Gal. 1:15-16) and in his teaching (see 2 Thess. 2:13).

Salvation—A Work of the Triune God

Many verses of Scripture could be cited to show the work that each member of the Godhead performs in our salvation. No clearer passage can be found, however, than Ephesians 1:4-14. Here the Father is seen as the One who *plans* our salvation; the Son is seen as the One who *provides* our salvation; and the Holy Spirit is seen as the One who *protects* (guarantees) our salvation.

The Work of the Father in Planning Salvation (Eph. 1:4–6)

First Peter 1:20 and Revelation 13:8 both teach that before the foundation of the world, the Father foreordained the death of

Christ to be the means of redeeming the lost. In Ephesians 1:4-6, we also read that the Father chose us in Christ before the foundation of the world.

The *basis* for God's choice rests in Him, not in the ones He chose. His election is "according to the kind intention of His will" (v. 5). The *purposes* of God in choosing sinners to be saved were "that we should be holy and blameless before Him" (v. 4) and "to the praise of the glory of His grace" (v. 6). This latter phrase occurs at the close of each of the sections in this passage (namely, vv. 6, 12, 14). Here is where faith must rest—in the wisdom and goodness of God.

The Work of the Son in Providing Salvation (Eph. 1:7–12)

Ephesians 1:6 concludes by making reference to the "Beloved," who is Christ. It is He who provided, through the shedding of His blood, this great salvation. This was "according to the riches of His grace" (v. 7).

Here's an important distinction worth considering. It is not "out of" the abundance and riches of Christ's grace that we have redemption and forgiveness of sin. Rather, it is "according to," or in keeping with, the limitless reservoir of His grace that we are saved. When a wealthy person makes a donation "out of his riches," it may involve a small amount of money. But when the same person makes a donation "according to his riches," this means it will be commensurate with his vast wealth.

The basis of Christ's atoning work was "His kind intention" (v. 9) and "His purpose who works all things after the counsel of His will" (v. 11). Verse 12 makes it clear that the Son's purpose is identical to that of the Father.

The Work of the Holy Spirit in Protecting Salvation (Eph. 1:13–14)

Even though the Father planned the salvation of the lost and the Son provided it, people must still trust in Christ before they are actually saved. When Jesus' atoning sacrifice is received by faith, the believer is "sealed in Him with the Holy Spirit of promise" (v. 13). The Spirit becomes the guarantee of the believer's salvation. What God planned in eternity past, what the Son provided at Calvary, and what the sinner receives by faith, the Spirit safeguards by His own presence forever (see 1 Peter 1:4-5).

The Holy Spirit is the "pledge of our inheritance" (Eph. 1:14). That is, He is the deposit or down payment, ensuring that the redeemed will one day be raised from the dead and receive glorified bodies. Thus, the presence of the Spirit in believers is God's assurance to them that He will fulfill all the promised blessings of salvation. This, of course, is "to the praise of His glory" (v. 14). Surely salvation is entirely the work of God from beginning to end!

We know that in eternity past the Father planned the work of redemption. We also know that He is solely responsible for beginning that great work in our lives. We can rest assured that what He started He will bring to completion at the divinely appointed time (see Phil. 1:6).

Knowing these truths can give us the confidence we need as we witness for Christ. It is His work to save; we are simply ambassadors for Him. We are responsible to proclaim the Gospel, for "it is the power of God for salvation to everyone who believes" (Rom. 1:16).

The necessity of trusting in Christ for salvation is emphasized throughout the Bible. In fact, Scripture teaches that faith is the one and only condition for salvation. This great gift from God must be received and appropriated by sinners before it can be of any benefit to them. Faith is not a work that people perform, and it is not a contribution they make to their otherwise free salvation (Rom. 4:4–5). Rather, faith is simply receiving what someone else has already provided. Salvation is and always has been by grace alone through faith alone in Christ alone (Eph. 2:10).[2]

Notes

1. Three outstanding monographs on the work of God the Father, God the Son, and God the Holy Spirit in salvation are: Zane C. Hodges, *Absolutely Free: A Biblical Reply to Lordship Salvation* (Grand Rapids: Zondervan, 1989); Anthony A. Hoekema, *Saved By Grace* (Grand Rapids: Eerdmans, 1989); and Charles C. Ryrie, *So Great Salvation* (Wheaton, Ill.: Victor, 1989).

2. A most helpful little volume on this whole issue of the sovereignty of God, salvation, and human responsibility is J. I. Packer's *Evangelism and the Sovereignty of God* (Downers Grove, Ill.: InterVarsity, 1961). See also the author's *Sin, the Saviour and Salvation* (Grand Rapids: Kregel, 1991).

CHAPTER 13

Christ's Teaching About God the Father

GOD THE SON'S TEACHING concerning God the Father touches upon all the areas we have studied up to this point. What the Lord Jesus Christ said about the Father is not found in any single passage of Scripture. Rather, it is found in many passages, and it is sometimes quite unexpectedly introduced and informally given.

It is not my intent to merely present Christ's teachings concerning the doctrine of God. After all, the words of Jesus recorded in Scripture are not more inspired than any other words of Scripture.[1] My desire is to use the Savior's teaching as a means of reviewing the entire biblical teaching concerning the God of the Bible.

Christ's deity makes what He said about the Father especially important. Since He is God the Son, what He said about God the Father becomes doubly significant. Furthermore, to understand Christ's teaching about the Father is to more clearly understand what He said about Himself and everything else.

The Person of the Father

The Father's Existence

The Old Testament Scriptures, which the Jews at the time of Christ had in their possession, assume the existence of God throughout. The Hebrew writings make no attempt to prove His existence. The faith of the Jews rested firmly on the fact that their God is real. They never questioned this truth, and in spite of the prevailing polytheism (namely, belief in many gods) around them, they held strongly to their belief in the one and only true God: "Hear, O Israel! The LORD is our God, the LORD is one!" (Deut. 6:4).

Thus when our Lord came, He lived among those who believed in God. And He Himself confessed faith in the same God of Abraham, Isaac, and Jacob. Christ never questioned the belief of the Jews on this point. He also never argued for the existence of God; He simply assumed God's existence. It is thus evident that Christ's teaching about the Father operates on the same unquestioned truth about God's existence to which the Jews of the day held.

The atheist denies the existence of God, and the agnostic denies the possibility of knowing with certainty that there is a God. The teaching of Jesus contradicts both of these philosophies. Though He never sought to prove the existence of God, Christ nevertheless based His teaching on the reality of God's existence.

Numerous passages could be used to illustrate Christ's acceptance of God's existence. A few will suffice, however, to establish my point. When Mary, Jesus' mother, noted that she and Joseph had been anxiously looking for Jesus, He replied, "Did you not know that I had to be in my Father's house?" (Luke 2:49). In response to the assaults and temptations of Satan, the Savior repeatedly appealed to God and His written Word (Matt. 4:1–11). Without any attempt to argue for the existence of God, Christ simply claimed before the religious critics of His day to have been sent by the Father (John 5:37). Christ's faith in God the Father was just as evident when He dealt with His disciples as when He responded to His detractors (Mark 11:22).

Beginning with the Old Testament concept of God, Jesus brought to people a new revelation of the Father. In the Old Testament, the Lord is depicted for the most part as the God of the nation, who is rather removed from the individual. In the Savior's teaching, He brought God near to people (see, for example, Matt. 6:8; 10:29–30). Jesus presented God as being interested in people and their everyday lives.

The Father's Names

In His teaching concerning the Father, Jesus referred to God by the use of several personal titles. These titles were God, Father, Lord, and King. Of these, the two most outstanding names were God and Father. The most frequent in occurrence was Father. Each of these titles conveys some aspect of God's character. Note that this was also true of the names used for God in the Old Testament (which we discussed earlier).

God. By His use of this title, Christ was revealing the strength of the Father. On many of the occasions in which Christ used this name, He had a need for special strength to endure the trial at hand (Matt. 4:1–11; 27:46).

Father. This is the most frequent name that Christ used to refer to God. The first recorded words that fell from Jesus' lips include this name (Luke 2:49). The name expresses what is characteristic and fundamental in the being of God.

In the Old Testament, *Yahweh* is sometimes called "Father" (for example, in Pss. 68:5; 89:26; Isa. 64:8; Mal. 1:6). The main difference between the Old Testament usage and Christ's is that He used the title in an individual sense rather than in a national sense. With the exception of His prayer on the cross, Christ used this intimate name for God in all His prayers (see Matt. 6:4, 9; 11:25; Mark 11:25; 14:36; Luke 11:2).

Lord. It was only when Jesus quoted from the Old Testament that He used this title. The word *Lord* was very familiar to the people of Christ's day. When He used it of God, He elevated the Father in their eyes. In addition, each time Jesus used the title, He revealed God as the Governor, Ruler, and Master of all. The people may have had many lords over them, but God was Lord over all—slaves and earthly rulers alike.

King. Like the title *Lord,* this title also speaks about the authority and lordship of God. Christ seldom used this title to refer to God, though Jesus often spoke about the kingdom of God. The Savior did use the title in His teaching about oaths (Matt. 5:34–35) and in connection with two parables, where the king is clearly intended to represent God (Matt. 18:23; 22:2).

The Father's Perfections (Attributes)

As in the case of God's existence and His names, so in the matter of God's attributes, Christ based His teaching on the Old Testament revelation. Christ's acceptance of and dependence upon the Old Testament Scripture as the Word of God is apparent throughout His teaching.

Numerous passages of Scripture could be cited to illustrate Christ's reference to each of the Father's perfections. The verses I have selected to present seem to be central, but the list is by no means exhaustive. Meanings of these perfections are elsewhere in this book.

1. The life and self-existence of God (John 5:26)
2. The unity of God (Mark 12:29)
3. The spirituality of God (John 4:24)
4. The love of God. Christ emphasized this perfection more than any other. God loved the world (John 3:16). He loved

the Son "before the foundation of the world" (17:24). And God loves the believer (16:27). Jesus taught His disciples to love all people, including their enemies. In so doing, they would show themselves to be like their gracious heavenly Father (Matt. 5:44–45).

Jesus also taught about the wrath of God. This is not opposed to the love of God; rather, the Father's wrath becomes intensified by the presence of His love. God is just and perfect; therefore, He must be wrathful against sin, for His holy character demands it. Christ's own attitude and action toward sin reveal His Father's wrath better than any specific statement He made (see, for example, Matt. 24:13–36; 24:1–51; Luke 12:46; 14:21).

5. The holiness of God (John 17:11)
6. The righteousness of God (John 17:25). Holiness in God is related to His conduct toward sin, while righteousness is related to His conduct toward redeemed people.
7. The goodness of God (Matt. 19:16–17; Mark 10:17–18; Luke 18:18–19)
8. The mercy of God (Matt. 5:45–48; 20:1–16; Luke 6:36)
9. The truth of God (John 17:3)
10. The eternity of God (John 17:5, 24)
11. The omniscience of God (Matt. 6:6, 32; 11:27)
12. The omnipotence of God (Matt. 19:26; Mark 14:36; Luke 18:27)
13. The omnipresence of God (Matt. 6:4, 6, 18)

The Work of the Father

The Father's Work in Creation

Jesus made only a few direct statements concerning the work of God in creation. There are other lines of proof that can be advanced, however, to show that Christ believed the world and the things in it were created by the God of the Bible.

For example, Jesus' use of the titles *Father, God, Lord,* and *King* provide proof that God eternally existed before all things and above all things. Also, Christ's ascription of the perfection of omnipotence to God teaches the same truth. Furthermore, since Christ taught that the Father existed "before the world was" (John 17:5, 24), it is reasonable to conclude that He must have created all things.

There are two areas of creation to which Jesus alluded in His teaching—nature and human life.

In the realm of nature (Mark 13:19). The context of this verse includes the mention of such objects as the sun, moon, stars, and the fig tree. In other passages, Christ spoke about God clothing "the grass of the field" (Matt. 6:30), feeding "the birds of the air" (v. 26), and knowing where a sparrow will "fall to the ground" (Matt. 10:29).

In the realm of human life (Matt. 19:4; Mark 10:6). God's care for mankind argues for His creation of people (see also Matt. 5:45; 10:28-30; Luke 6:35). Christ indirectly taught that God created people when He said: "For just as the Father raises the dead and gives them life, even so the Son also gives life to whom He wishes" (John 5:21). If God can raise the dead and give them life, it is reasonable to conclude that He gave them life in the first place.

The Father's Work in Redemption

The national redemption, or deliverance, of Israel was the major emphasis of God's work in the Old Testament. Building on that concept, the Savior taught that God the Father's plan also involved the redemption of the individual. In other words, Jesus personalized God's work of redemption (John 6:37, 44).

Christ's teaching concerning the Father's work in redemption centers in mankind and in Himself, the Redeemer.

The Father's work for mankind. According to Christ's testimony, God originated the plan of redemption that He, the Son, brought to fruition (Matt. 26:36-46). The three references to the Father's will in Jesus' prayer provide evidence that what Christ's death was about to accomplish was the climax to God's eternal plan of redemption.

The Savior taught that God the Father gave people to the Son for their redemption (John 6:37, 44; 10:29; 17:2, 6, 9, 12). And according to Christ's teaching, it was the Father's will to save those whom He had sovereignly chosen to receive eternal life (Matt. 18:14; John 6:39-40).

In Christ's teaching, God possessed and exercised the power to secure the salvation of those who are genuine disciples of Christ (John 10:29). In the high priestly prayer recorded in John 17, Christ taught His own that God the Father secures the salvation of all who believe on the Savior (John 17:21, 24-25). Jesus not only taught that the Father worked in the redemption of people, but Jesus also taught that His Father loves and cares for them after He redeems them (Matt. 6:32; 7:11; Luke 15:1-32; John 14:21, 23; 16:27).

The Father's work for the Redeemer. Since Christ is the sinless Redeemer (1 Peter 2:22), God's work for Him was vastly different from His work in carrying out the eternal plan of redemption. Jesus lived in the awareness of the Father being present with Him (14:10). It was the Father who directed the activities of the Son (5:19; 14:31). Often as the Lord prayed, He did so audibly so that His disciples could learn from Him. And as He prayed, He revealed the sustaining work of His Father upon Him as He carried out the Father's will (11:41; 17:20-24). The Father's love for the Son was the basis for Christ loving believers (John 15:9). Even in the most trying moments, Christ never questioned the Father's love, care, and concern for Him (18:11).

The Fatherhood of the Father

God's Fatherhood in Relation to the Son

Christ's teaching about the fatherhood of God is diametrically opposed to the teaching of liberal theology on the subject. Jesus never ascribed God's fatherhood to all people in a redemptive sense. That God sends rain on the just and the unjust and that He created all people does not mean He is the Father of all in the sense that all are part of His redemptive family.

In spite of that, Christ did teach that God was His Father. At least twenty-nine times in the Gospels, Jesus referred to God as "my Father" (see, for example, Matt. 7:21; Mark 8:38; Luke 2:49). Frequently when Christ claimed God as His Father, He did so to support His own authority. In an absolutely unique sense, God was the Father of our Lord Jesus Christ.

God's Fatherhood in Relation to the Disciples

In all the many instances when Christ addressed those who did not accept His claims, He never once said that God was their Father. Yet in many passages, He said that God is the Father of His own (see, for example, Matt. 5:1-7:29). Jesus often used the possessive "our Father" to stress that His disciples are spiritual children of the heavenly Father.

God's Fatherhood in Relation to the Unsaved

Christ taught that God is the Father of all people in the sense that He created all people and allows certain natural blessings to come upon them all. Yet, Jesus never taught that this creative aspect to the fatherhood of God was sufficient to save the lost. Quite to the contrary, Christ taught (for example) that even the religious leaders of His day, who refused to believe Him, were children of the Devil (John. 8:40-44).

God's attribute of love is the basis of His fatherhood over all as their Creator. But the basis of His fatherhood over the redeemed is their individual relationships to Christ, the Son. Jesus unmistakably limited God's fatherhood in the sense of salvation to the redeemed.

The Father, Son, and Holy Spirit

Christ had a considerable amount to say about the relation of the members of the Godhead to each other. Though Jesus' teaching, without question, embraced the unity or oneness of God, it did so with a recognition of the personal distinctions that exist within the Godhead.

The Father's Relationship to the Son

The Son's equality with the Father. Sixty-five times in the Gospels, Christ called God His Father, thus establishing His own Sonship. Jesus claimed equality with the Father by associating His work with the Father's work (John 5:17) and by requesting the same faith in Himself that people had placed in God (14:1). Christ also claimed equality with the Father by His direct statements (8:24; 10:30). In His high priestly prayer, Christ spoke about the eternal relationship He had with the Father (17:5, 24). Jesus' relationship of equality with the Father always existed, for He has always been the Son.[2]

The Son's subordination and dependence upon the Father. Though equal in deity with the Father, yet in coming to earth to accomplish the plan of redemption, Christ occupied an office of subordination to the Father. The Savior recognized that the Father had sent Him (John 8:42). And throughout Jesus' ministry on earth, He recognized His dependence upon the Father (4:34). No clearer evidence of Jesus' complete reliance upon the will of the Father can be found than in His Gethsemane experience (Matt. 26:39, 42, 44). As in life, so in death Christ surrendered to the will of God the Father (Luke 23:46).

The Father's Relationship to the Holy Spirit

The Holy Spirit's eternal relationship with the Father. Just as the Son was always with the Father, so the Holy Spirit had an eternal relationship with Him (John 15:26). He proceeds from the Father; thus He must have been eternally with the Father.

The Holy Spirit given by the Father. In two passages Jesus clearly stated that the Holy Spirit was a gift from the Father (Luke 11:13; John 14:16-17). The gift of the Holy Spirit, like the gift of the Son, originated with the Father. The word translated "another" in John 14:16 comes from a term that means "another of the same kind," not "another of a different kind." This reinforces the truth that the Holy Spirit is equal with the Son and the Father as God.

What has come to be known as the "Great Commission" (Matt. 28:18-20) serves as a fitting conclusion to Christ's teaching concerning God the Father. These verses, which were given by Christ, confirm the truth that there are three Persons within the Godhead (in other words, a Trinity). These verses also substantiate that each member of the Godhead is fully divine, and coequal and coeternal with the other two.

Summary

The purpose of this section of the study has been to acquaint the reader with the God of the Bible. I have surveyed what holy Scripture has to say about God, and I have arranged and organized the information in an orderly fashion.

Many have tried to come up with a definition for God. But since He is divine, no attempt can succeed in fully defining Him. The finite cannot confine the infinite! The best we can do is provide descriptions of God that set Him apart from all others and all else.

Nothing is of greater importance than for people—the creatures—to be rightly related to God, the Creator and Redeemer. Communion with the God of the Bible comes through faith in Christ. Those who trust in Him are reconciled in their relationship with the Father and become members of His spiritual family. Communion with God is nurtured through a knowledge and understanding of Him, as revealed in the Bible, which is His holy inerrant Word. The most basic and important of all Christian doctrines are those about God and the Bible, for upon these the entire superstructure of Christian theology either stands or falls.

Beyond the rational arguments for the existence of God, there is the presentation of Him in the Bible. Though Holy Scripture does not set out to prove God's existence, it is assumed throughout its pages. While the naturalistic theistic arguments for the existence of God provide substantial evidence that He exists, only special revelation in the Bible makes known what He has done through His Son to save people.

In recent times so-called "experts" have proclaimed the death of God. Despite all the attempts of His critics, whether ancient or modern, the only true and living God of the Bible is still alive and active in His world. Ironically, the "God" of the "God-is-dead" theologians has indeed died. The fact is, this deity never existed in the first place and has no identity with or relationship to the God of the Bible.

Nature contains a clear revelation of the God of the Bible. Humanity's lostness and their need of salvation in Christ alone are not made known in natural revelation. But the heavens do declare the glory of God, and the skies display His marvelous craftsmanship (Ps. 19:1). Though people distort and reject this revelation of God's existence, it is nevertheless real. This revelation also leaves people without an excuse before their Maker for rejecting the truth of His existence.

Humanity's sin made God's revelation in His written Word necessary. The Bible, God's written Word, and Christ, God's living Word, are in perfect harmony. The Savior accepted the full and final authority of the Scriptures. Therefore, people cannot really have the Savior unless they also accept the Savior's Scripture. Likewise, people cannot rightly claim Christ, the living Word, unless they also embrace the Bible, the written Word.

The God of the Bible does not exist as "being," "ultimate being," "reality," or "ultimate reality." Rather, as a divine Person, He possesses intellect, emotions, and will. Though one in His divine essence, He exists as the Father, the Son, and the Holy Spirit. Each member of the Godhead possesses personality and is fully God. With the God of the Bible there is unity in Trinity and Trinity in unity.

With infinite power and precision the God of the Bible is bringing His sovereign plan to fulfillment. Not only has this sovereign God chosen a plan for humanity and for the world, but He has also chosen a people for that plan.

God's perfections, or attributes, describe Him. In other words, they tell us what He is like. These are not characteristics that are true of people and merely possessed by God in perfection. And the divine perfections are not just an assorted collection of virtues that belong to God. Rather, God's attributes are an essential part of His nature. He cannot be separated from them, and they cannot be separated from Him. He is what each of these say about Him (for instance, He is love, holiness, truth, and so on); and yet, He is more than the sum total of all His attributes.

The names of God, like His perfections, reveal truth about Him.

In other words, they describe Him. In fact, God's names parallel His perfections in meaning and significance. Each of the perfections and names of God reveal an attendant responsibility for those who have the God of the Bible as their own heavenly Father.

The God of the Bible is not only the great Revealer and Creator, He is also the great Redeemer. In infinite love, He sent His only begotten Son into the world to provide redemption for the lost. God also sent His Holy Spirit to convict people, to show them their need for salvation, and to bring them to faith in Christ. Through the Holy Spirit, God secures for believing sinners their salvation.

The Lord Jesus Christ gave us a complete teaching regarding His Father, the God of the Bible. For example, in the three short years of the Savior's public ministry, He revealed that God the Father is characterized by love, holiness, and truth (to mention just a few virtues).

All religions and their devotees have their deity or pantheon of deities. None of these, however, in any way compares with the God of the Bible. Unfortunately, even those who believe in the God of the Bible and who are members of His spiritual family often put other gods before Him. These are not limited to graven images but also include such idols as fame, pleasure, and success (to name a few). Whatever people live for, whatever they are enslaved to, and whatever they are controlled by is their god. For believers, whatever comes between them and the God of the Bible is an idol.

The God of the Bible is in a real sense incomprehensible. Peter Krey summarized God's incomprehensibleness in this way:

> The true God who reveals Himself to us in nature and in the Bible is not a god no more than a super human being as the gods of pagan Rome and Greece, nor is He the sum total of all things as some philosophical systems have taught, nor the mind or spirit of the Cosmos as some believe; He is a far more wonderful Being than all that. He is incomprehensible in His Being. For what does He say of Himself in Holy Scripture? How does the Bible portray Him to us? The picture or idea that the Bible gives us of God is so grand and overwhelming that our reason cannot grasp it, but only repeat, believe, and adore what the Bible says about God.[3]

Revelation concerning the God of the Bible is clear and extensive. On the basis of that inspired revelation and the contrast of the God of the Bible with all other gods, people must make a decision. The words of Joshua to the ancient Israelites are still pertinent today: "Choose for yourselves today whom you will serve: whether the gods which your fathers served which were beyond the River, or the gods of the Amorites in whose land you are living; but as for me and my house, we will serve the LORD" (Josh. 24:15).

Notes

1. Christ's view of the Scriptures is set forth in the author's *A Biblical Case for Total Inerrancy: How Jesus Viewed the Old Testament* (Grand Rapids: Kregel, 1998).
2. For a discussion by evangelicals (who embrace Christ's deity) of the current denial of Christ's eternal Sonship, see the author's *Sin, the Savior and Salvation* (Grand Rapids: Kregel, 1996), 52-57, and George W. Zeller and Renald E. Showers, *The Eternal Sonship of Christ* (Neptune, N.J.: Loizeaux Brothers, 1993).
3. Peter Krey, "God Is Incomprehensible in His Being," *Christian News* 5 (May 22, 1972): 1.

PART 3

OTHER "GODS"

CHAPTER 14

The God of the Bible and Other "Gods"

Introduction

HOW TRUE IS THE STATEMENT that people the world over are incurably religious. No matter what the race, language, culture, education, or the lack of it, people everywhere have always worshiped and will continue to worship. It is not always formal worship. Sometimes it is elemental and crude by comparison to worship in a highly liturgical church. People everywhere, however, acknowledge a higher power, whether personal or impersonal, and bow before it. No matter what or how it is done, there is worship nonetheless.

What is worshiped ranges from the true and living God of the Bible to the individual self. The method of worship varies, as do the means of worship. Even the most ardent self-described atheists give devotion and deep respect to their own ideas. In reality, they adore their minds and laud their abilities to affirm that there is no God.

In contrast, agnostics assert they are too finite to have the ability to explore all conceivable "evidences" for God's existence. They thus maintain that they do not know and will never be able to know whether God exists. In doing so, however, agnostics also bow before the conclusions their minds have formed. Whether it is the true and living God, or sticks, stones, the elements of nature, something a person's hands have formed, an imaginary being, or self, people engage in worship, and they bow in reverence to something.

At the end of this chapter, you will find a chart depicting the god or gods of major Western cults and world religions. On this chart these pagan deities are contrasted with the God of the Bible. The chart also includes key personalities, with dates for each of the cults and religions. Furthermore, the chart displays how each belief system views the Lord Jesus Christ and the Holy Spirit. Moreover, the "Bible," or source of authority for each belief system, is included.

"Have No Other Gods Before Me"

Many students of world religions work on the assumption that all
people everywhere seek the one true God and that all of humanity's
efforts indeed lead, sooner or later, to this God. David G. Bradley
of Duke University, a student of world religions, summarized this
prevalent philosophy, though he disagrees with it:

> The affirmation of the poet mystic, William Blake, that "all
> religions are one," is often quoted and is the working
> hypothesis of many interpreters of religion. The proposition
> presented by such persons usually has a double aspect. The
> first part states that there actually is only one true God for
> all men. To this statement is added the claim that all
> mankind, whether consciously or unknowingly, is seeking
> this one true God, though in many different ways. These
> various ways to the one God comprise the various religions
> of man. A corollary to this twofold proposition is that
> although there are many ways to this God, since each road
> shares this common god—all roads lead to the same God—
> there is no final difference between the religions of men.[1]

The Bible flatly contradicts the philosophy expressed above. For
example, in response to Moses' questions and hesitations to do
God's bidding, God told him that he had to go in the name of
"the LORD." This was none other than Yahweh, the God known
to Abraham, Isaac, and Jacob, and the God who was distinct from
all other gods (Exod. 4:1-15).

In the generation following Moses, Joshua, writing under the
guidance of the Spirit, warned the people of God against confusing
Yahweh, the God of the Bible, with other gods (Josh. 24:14-15).
In this declaration, Joshua made it clear that not only was it possible
to serve other gods but also that the true worship and service of
the God of the Bible required the renunciation of all other gods.

This same emphasis runs through the major and minor prophets
of the Old Testament. The prophets all soundly condemned the
Israelites for turning aside from Yahweh to worship other gods (see,
for example, 1 Kings 17-18; Isaiah 42-45; Hosea; Amos 2-4).

The New Testament continues to emphasize the importance
of worshiping the one true God and to abandon all other gods.
For example, early on in Jesus' earthly ministry He said, "No one
can serve two masters; for either he will hate the one and love the
other, or he will be devoted to one and despise the other. You
cannot serve God and wealth" (Matt. 6:24). And toward the end

of Jesus' ministry, a scribe asked Him which commandment was foremost of all (Mark 12:28). Our Lord responded by quoting Moses' words recorded in Deuteronomy 6:4 (see Mark 12:29-30).

Paul told the carnal Corinthian Christians that though there were many so-called gods, yet for the believer "there is but one God, the Father, from whom are all things and we exist for Him; and one Lord, Jesus Christ, by whom are all things, and we exist through Him" (1 Cor. 8:6).

The God of the Bible is altogether unique and separate from all other gods. As the one true and only God, His divine essence is undivided. And as the triune God, He has manifested Himself in three separate and distinct divine Persons. The God of the Bible is infinite and eternal. He is the Creator and the Sustainer of humanity and all things. His knowledge and power are limitless, and His love is boundless and measureless. The goodness, glory, and grace of the God of the Bible are fathomless; these virtues are beyond description or comparison.

Only the God of the Bible has revealed Himself in His world and in His Word, the Bible. The one and only true God is not mute; He has spoken! In the Scriptures, He has made known His will for humanity. Not only has God spoken, but He has also acted. He sent His Son into the world not to condemn the lost but to save the lost through faith in Him.

Those who do not know the God of the Bible as their heavenly Father through faith in His Son are not the only ones who have other gods. Even those who believe in the God of the Bible and who are in His spiritual family are often guilty of some form of polytheism. Like the Israelites of old, they too must be reminded, "You shall have no other gods before Me" (Exod. 20:3).

This is the first commandment of the Decalogue. Before giving it, God reminded the Israelites how He had delivered them from Egypt, brought them through the Red Sea, and provided for them in their wilderness journey. The first four of the Ten Commandments have to do with humanity's relation to the God of the Bible. The remaining six are concerned with humanity's relation to things and other people.

The first commandment is calculated to take the attention of people away from themselves and all else and to focus it on God alone. People cannot be truly happy unless they worship the only true God. By placing the commandment to refrain from idolatry first, God was establishing the basis for humanity's true happiness and obedience to all the other divine commands.

Bowing Before False Gods

Death was the penalty for violating the first commandment (Exod. 22:20; Deut. 6:14-15). This reveals the importance and seriousness of this decree from God's standpoint. The New Testament has no record of this first commandment; yet the principle involved in it appears often (Acts 14:15; 1 Tim. 2:5; James 2:19), though physical death as a penalty for its infraction is never stated or even implied.

Believing merely in the existence of the God of the Bible does not mean one will automatically go to heaven. Eternal life is the gift of the God of the Bible given to all who trust in His only begotten Son, the Lord Jesus Christ, as personal Savior from sin.

There are many people who believe in the existence of God, either because of their home training, contact with a church, or contact with others who believe in His existence. Yet many of these same people do not worship God. They really bow before the false gods of this age. However, these idols are not always, and perhaps even seldom, recognized as gods.

Earthly possessions, ambitions, and accomplishments are usually the most important things in life for those who have not been born again. Spiritual goals and values are of little importance to them, even though they would quickly affirm belief in God and would even seek Him in prayer, at least when all else fails.

A fitting conclusion to this study comes from the words of Ravi Zacharias: "Apart from God, chaos is the norm; with God, the hungers of the mind and heart find their fulfillment."[2]

Notes

1. David G. Bradley, *Circles of Faith* (Nashville: Abingdon, 1966), 32. See Aldous Huxley, *The Perennial Philosophy* (New York: Harper & Row, 1945), and Joseph Campbell, *The Hero With a Thousand Faces* (New York: Pantheon, 1949).
2. Ravi Zacharias, *Can Man Live Without God?* (Dallas: Word, 1994).

Christianity vs. Major Cults and Religions

	GOD OF THE BIBLE	NEW AGE	WAY INTERNATIONAL	CHRISTIAN SCIENCE
KEY PERSONS	God the Father God the Son God the Holy Spirit	Alice Bailey Benjamin Creme Shirley Maclaine David Spangler	Victor Paul Wierville	Mary Baker Eddy
LIFE SPAN	Eternity to Eternity		1917–	1821–1910
GOD	There is one God and He has manifested Himself in three Persons— God the Father God the Son God the Spirit	God is all and all is God He is the sum total of all that exists Pantheistic	Rejects Trinity God only one Person called Father because He created Christ Called Holy Spirit when viewed as Giver of the Holy Spirit Variety of Unitarianism	Denies personal God God is impersonal principle of love Pantheistic Denies Trinity God viewed as Father-Mother Christ is the spiritual idea of sonship The Spirit is divine science
CHRIST	He is, always has been, and always will be very God of very God Conceived by work of Holy Spirit Lived a sinless life Died a substitutionary death Ever lives to make intercession for His own	Denies deity of Christ Separates human Jesus from divine Christ Christ is divine in the same sense we are divine Christ is one of many appearances of God to awaken in man his innate divinity	Not God Before Mary's conception by God He existed only in foreknowledge of God Only a man	Christ is divine idea Denies deity Christ is the idea of sonship Jesus is the human man and Christ is the divine idea
HOLY SPIRIT	He is, always has been and always will be fully God He is a divine Person, the third Member of the holy Trinity	Denies deity of the Holy Spirit	"Impersonal power from on high" Another name for God Not a Person of Godhead	An accommodation to mortal thinking Divine science
AUTHORITY	The inspired Word of God in the Old and the New Testaments "Sola Scriptura"	Special and continuous personal revelations Denies inspiration of Bible	Wierville claims special revelation from God Bible accepted after corrected by him	*Science and Health with Key to the Scriptures*

	GOD OF THE BIBLE	ISLAM	JEHOVAH'S WITNESSES	MORMONISM
KEY PERSONS	God the Father God the Son God the Holy Spirit	Muhammad	Charles Taz Russell Joseph Franklin Rutherford Nathan Homer Knorr	Joseph Smith, Jr. Brigham Young
LIFE SPAN	Eternity to Eternity	571–632	Russell 1852–1916 Rutherford 1870–1942 Knorr 1905–1977	Smith 1805–1844 Young 1801–1877
GOD	There is one God and He has manifested Himself in three Persons— God the Father God the Son God the Spirit	Allah Denies the Trinity Monotheism	Denies Trinity A solidarity being always existing, unrevealed, and therefore unknown No one exists as his equal to make him known	God is exalted man Adam is the only God The Mormon priesthood is the kingdom of God To disobey this priesthood is to disobey God Polytheism
CHRIST	He is, always has been, and always will be very God of very God Conceived by work of Holy Spirit Lived a sinless life Died a substitutionary death Ever lives to make intercession for His own	Denies the deity of Christ Denies Jesus was crucified An angel was responsible for Mary's conception of Christ	Denies the deity of Christ He is *a* God, the chief of God's creatures He is the archangel He is forever dead He is a perfect human being Denies Christ's resurrection	Jesus is the son of Adam, God, and Mary Joseph Smith is a descendant of Christ who was a descendant of David through Bathsheba Denies the virgin birth of Christ Denies Christ's eternal pre-existence
HOLY SPIRIT	He is, always has been, and always will be fully God He is a divine Person, the third Member of the holy Trinity	Denies the deity of the Holy Spirit	Denies the deity of the Holy Spirit "He is not an intelligent person" He is an "invisible force" He is a divine influence	An immaterial substance spread through space It is the purest substance Received through laying on of hands by members of the Mormon priesthood
AUTHORITY	The inspired Word of God in the Old and the New Testaments "Sola Scriptura"	The Qur'an or Koran The Hadith—Muslim tradition The Sunnah—customs of Muslim life	The Watchtower, etc. The New World translation of the Holy Scriptures	*The Book of Mormon* and Bible insofar as it is correctly translated according to them

	GOD OF THE BIBLE	HINDUISM	BUDDHISM	BAHA'I FAITH
KEY PERSONS	God the Father God the Son God the Holy Spirit	Aryans invaded India (1800–1500 B.C.) No definite founder Pre-Aryan artifacts date to 2500 B.C.	Buddha with the personal name of Siddhartha and the family name of Guatama	Mirza 'Ali Muhammad—"Bab" Mirza 'Husayn 'Ali—"Baha'u'llah"
LIFE SPAN	Eternity to Eternity		563–483 B.C.	Bab 1819–1850 Baha'u'llah 1892
GOD	There is one God and He has manifested Himself in three Persons— God the Father God the Son God the Spirit	Polytheism—holds to hundreds of gods with none everlasting to be the King of gods and men. These grow together and lose their identities. New deities emerge resulting in pantheistic monism	Pantheistic—all gods finite and subject to death No eternal infinite being Atheistic	Denies Trinity Worships the glory of God manifest through Baha'u'llah Monotheistic
CHRIST	He is, always has been, and always will be very God of very God Conceived by work of Holy Spirit Live a sinless life Died a substitutionary death Ever lives to make intercession for His own	Christ and others such as Muhammad may be prophets added to hundreds of others	Denies the Christ of the Bible	Denies deity of Christ One of nine manifestations of the divine being He was the way, the truth, and the life for his time but not for all times Denies resurrection
HOLY SPIRIT	He is, always has been, and always will be fully God He is a divine Person, the third Member of the holy Trinity	Denies the Holy Spirit of the Bible	Denies the Holy Spirit of the Bible	Denies the personality of the Spirit Denies the deity of the Spirit Baha'u'llah is the comforter Christ promised
AUTHORITY	The inspired Word of God in the Old and the New Testaments "Solo Scriptura"	Vedas, 1500–800 B.C.E. Brahmanas, 850 B.C.E. Upanishads, 500 B.C.E. Bhagavad Gita, an epic	The teachings of Buddha Walpola Rahula, *What the Buddha Taught* Visuddhimagga, Samyutta Nikaya, Digha Nikaya, Sutta Pitaka, Anguttagata Nikaya Only absolute truth is that there is no absolute truth	Teaching of Mirza 'Ali Muhammad and Mirza 'Husayn 'Ali

A Synopsis of Major Cults and Religions

ONE REASON FOR THE GROWTH of cults and religions in the West is that positive images engendered by public relations have replaced real understanding of who these groups represent and what they teach. The previous chart compared the God of the Bible with the gods of these other faiths, along with references to key founders and sources of authority. This appendix expands on that information, presenting sketches of the history, major doctrinal views, and strength of these movements at the end of the twentieth century.

Included, where possible, is an estimation of the number of adherents at the time of this writing.

Baha'i

History and Background

The Baha'i faith is a movement that emerged out of Islam. As a despised stepchild, it has been persecuted greatly by followers of Islam, especially in Iran. A reign of terror was inflicted on Iranian adherents to Baha'i after the strict Shi'ite Ayatollah Ruhollah Khomeini rose to power in 1979.

Muslims generally view Baha'is as apostates, primarily because Baha'is insist that two true prophets came after Muhammad— Mirza Ali Muhammad, referred to as the Bab ("Gate"), and Mirza Hoseyn Ali Nuri, who declared himself Baha'u'llah ("The Splendor of Allah"). Baha'u'llah styled himself as the long-expected Messiah. Expectation of the Messiah was tailored to Islamic theology from Judaism as a tenet of the Shi'ite sect. The Bab is generally viewed as a forerunner preparing the way for a greater one to come. Yet the Bab viewed himself as the manifestation of God and was compared to and compared himself with the Christ of Christian Scripture. From its founding in 1844, members of the sect first

178

called themselves "Babists." Within a decade, the Turks had martyred the Bab and tried to exterminate his followers, but under Baha'u'llah, who was tortured, imprisoned, and exiled but allowed to live, the faith was reborn in the 1860s.

The Baha'is do not have professional clergy. Some lay leaders become full-time teachers. In contrast to Islam, the Baha'i faith stresses individual rather than group prayer. Both religions emphasize fasting. Baha'is fast nineteen days each year.

Major Theological Beliefs

Many doctrinal differences have arisen between the Baha'i faith and its parent, Islam. Some Baha'i tenets sound superficially like Christianity, but their meanings are decidedly *not* Christian.

God. According to Baha'i, there is no trinity in a godhead, but God is known through manifestations. As might be expected, Baha'u'llah is the latest manifestation. Since he "manifests" God, he is equal to God. Other manifestations, also called prophets, include Adam, Noah, Abraham, Moses, Jesus, Zoroaster, Siddhartha Gautama (the Buddha), and Muhammad. The way these prophets or manifestations are recognized or identified is by the power and effectiveness of their word. Through these prophet-manifestations God makes His will known.

Sin. Humans are slaves or servants, rather than children, in relation to God. This relationship does not denote lowliness or baseness. Baha'u'llah taught that humankind is basically good so long as the proper ethical teachings are available.[1] Abdu'l-Baha did not believe in the existence of sin. There are only good human qualities sometimes used wrongly.

Humanitarianism. Despite their rejection of sin, Baha'is are activistic in ethics and society and take great pride in their humanitarian work. Texts from the Christian Bible are sometimes used to support their work and word.

Other Distinctives. Baha'is are very careful to speak no evil of others. This practice is based, they claim, on the teaching of Jesus in the Sermon on the Mount. They stress humility, honesty, and self-realization. Scientific knowledge is honored; truth never contradicts truth, they argue. Baha'is work hard at repudiating nationalism and prejudices in general. Gender equality is preached fervently.

Current Status

In the late 1800s, Ibrahim George Kheiralla was the first missionary for the Baha'i faith sent to North America. Only after some time did he openly incorporate Baha'i teachings in his work. Eventually he stirred up much interest in Baha'i teachings, though his teachings came to contradict what Baha'is believed. By 1920 Baha'is had more followers on the North American continent than in any other region.

Since Kheiralla's departure, the Baha'i religion has grown steadily all over the world, especially in the West. As of 1994 there were more than five million adherents.[2] The Baha'is continue to proclaim peace and unity.

Buddhism

History and Background

Buddhism was founded by Siddhartha Gautama as a reform movement within Hinduism. Guatama was born about 560 B.C. to a high caste Hindu family. His parents sheltered him from the world's suffering. When he finally learned about suffering from others, he set out to renounce it and to seek a cure for it. Gautama was twenty-nine years old when he deserted his family, including his wife and son, to search for enlightenment.

At first, Gautama practiced strict asceticism but almost died as a result. Next, he tried to strike a balance between self-denial and indulgence that led to meditation. During a time of deep meditation while sitting under a tree, he finally reached the "state of enlightenment" or Nirvana. This release from suffering and the finite self is not to be confused with the Bible's heaven or God. Nirvana is attained strictly through self-effort. It was at this time, too, that Gautama became the *Buddha*, which means "the enlightened one." In the end, his religion was very different from the Hinduism Gautama had initially practiced.

For almost fifty years, the Buddha gained a large following as he heralded his message throughout northern India. In 480 B.C., at the age of eighty, the Buddha died from food poisoning.

Buddhism has enormous influence internationally. There are many varieties of Buddhism in the United States. These groups are transplants from abroad which developed especially after World War II.

There are two basic forms of Buddhism. *Theravada* ("the way of the elders" or "southern Buddhism") thrives in places like Burma, Thailand, Cambodia, and Laos. It is conservative and still reveres Buddha.[3] *Mahayana* ("the great vehicle") Buddhism developed in China, Tibet, Japan, and Korea. This "northern" Buddhism is much more open and flexible, paying little serious attention to the religion's historical roots.[4]

Major Theological Beliefs

Buddhism rejects the God of the Bible—Father, Son, and Holy Spirit—and most other Christian tenets. Needless to say, there are major differences between Buddhism and biblical Christianity. Buddhist teachings center on what Buddhists refer to as four basic truths and an eightfold path:

1. All existence involves suffering.
2. The cause of suffering is desire.
3. The way to escape suffering is to get rid of desire.
4. To be delivered from desire, one must follow the eightfold path: (1) right knowledge, (2) right aspirations, (3) right speech, (4) right conduct, (5) right livelihood, (6) right effort, (7) right mindfulness, and (8) right meditation involving the techniques of Raja Yoga.[5]

Current Status

Since there are many varieties of Buddhism, generalities can be misleading. However, there are core beliefs and all Buddhists reject even the essentials of Christianity.

In 1998, there were about 356.9 million Buddhists.[6]

Church of Christ, Scientist

History and Background

The founder of Christian Science, Mary Ann Morse Baker Glover Patterson Eddy, is more commonly known as Mary Baker Eddy. She was born in 1821 to staunch Congregationalists. She suffered a number of physical illnesses from birth, and as a young woman rejected her church's doctrines.

Mary married George Washington Glover in 1843, but he soon died. In 1853, she embarked on a tumultuous twenty-year marriage to Daniel M. Patterson. During this time she traveled to Portland, Maine, where "the healer," Phineas Parkhurst Quimby, developed and practiced a system he called "The Science of Health" or "Christian Science." She said Quimby healed her of a spinal disorder. Later she plagiarized much of Quimby's writings in her 1875 book *Science and Health with Key to the Scriptures*. She claimed to have received this book's contents directly from God.

In 1877, Mary Glover Patterson married Asa Gilbert Eddy. She continued to teach her beliefs in Lynn, Massachusetts, and later in Boston. The Church of Christ, Scientist, grew dramatically and claimed more than twenty thousand members by 1900. It is reported that Eddy was worth over three million dollars at the time of her death from a heart attack in 1882.[7]

Major Theological Beliefs

The Bible. The fact that Mary Baker Eddy claimed her writings were divine revelations on a par with the Bible shows her weak view of the Scriptures. While she claimed the Bible to be her only authority, she pointed out its many "errors" and even labeled some portions "lies." A study of her *Science and Health* alongside the Bible quickly reveals that she accepted what she thought agreed with her revelations and rejected the rest.

God. Christian Science rejects the God of the Bible—Father, Son, and Holy Spirit.

Sin. Pantheism—God is all and all is God—characterizes Christian Science. This belief leads to a complete denial of evil. People cannot sin, and sickness and death are not real. Sin is likened to degrees of insanity. Kenneth Boa describes Christian Science as "a form of absolute idealism which claims that matter as such does not exist."[8] Human beings cannot sin because they derive their essence from God and have no original or underived power to rebel. As long as we believe that a soul can sin, we will never understand the science of being. Sin, sickness, and death are illusions.

Salvation. Because humankind is not in a fallen state, there is no need of salvation. Jesus was not God, though He was human. So there is not only no sin; there is no Savior. Mary Baker Eddy believed she was the successor to and equal of Christ. Those who are described as "spirit people" all know there is no hell, devil, resurrection, or judgment.

Current Status

Though still a nationally recognized movement, Christian Science is in numerical decline. One reason is that the denial of the reality of sin, sickness, and death does not fit postmodern culture and flies in the face of reality. What Christian Science believes and advocates goes far beyond what most can take seriously. Yet Christian Science will likely be around for a long time. Its *Science and Health* still enjoys a large readership, and *The Christian Science Monitor*, a well-respected newspaper, has a large circulation.

Church of Jesus Christ of Latter-Day Saints (Mormonism)

History and Background

The founder of Mormonism, Joseph Smith Jr. (1805–44), grew up poor in Palmyra, New York. In 1820 he claimed that God the Father and God the Son both told him in a vision that he was to restore the true gospel. In 1823 the angel Moroni appeared to him, telling him about a number of golden plates he would uncover and translate. These plates were discovered in a hill called Cumorah near Palmyra in 1827. Smith then received the Aaronic priesthood from John the Baptist in a vision in 1829. Smith founded the Church of Jesus Christ of Latter-Day Saints shortly thereafter. He led his followers to various places in Ohio, Missouri, and Illinois. In Carthage, Illinois, he and his brother were shot and killed by a mob who hated and feared the new sect for both real and imagined reasons. Not all the animosity Mormons encountered wherever they went was mindless intolerance and xenophobia, as historians usually color the persecution. The group quickly showed a tendency to become violent with any who opposed them.

After the Smith brothers' deaths, the movement split between those who tempered the teachings of Joseph Smith with a more biblically based faith, and the majority who looked to the more radical Brigham Young for leadership. Young became the new First President and prophet and led thousands of Mormons southwest to the Salt Lake Valley of Utah in 1847. Young continued as leader until his death in 1877. During his time of leadership, Young encouraged the practice of polygamy and married twenty-five women. He ruled the church with an iron hand and resisted the government and its laws—on occasion, by armed confrontation.

The Church of Jesus Christ of Latter-Day Saints maintains its headquarters in Salt Lake City, Utah, where the most revered "temple" is located, along with a ruling hierarchy of First President, Twelve Apostles, and the Council of Seventy, plus other teachers and counselors. Mormonism has undergone many splits and factions. The original "reorganized" split-off church still exists with some members of the Smith family in leadership. Its beliefs are heretical but a little closer to those of historic Christianity. In all there are six major different sects within Mormonism today. There is general agreement by most groups regarding beliefs. Differences tend to be over qualifications for leadership, polygamy, and Smith's *Inspired Version of the Bible.*

Major Theological Beliefs

Sources of Authority

Mormons claim the Bible, *The Book of Mormon* (the translation of the golden plates found by Smith), *Doctrines and Covenants,* and *The Pearl of Great Price* as sources of authority. Strangely, though the plates on which *The Book of Mormon* was based were supposedly buried in the year 428, about twenty-five thousand words in it were taken verbatim from the 1611 King James Version of the Bible.

Mormons do not believe the Bible is very trustworthy; however, from childhood they memorize large portions of the King James Version, especially texts that seem to support Mormon doctrine.

Mankind. Humans have the potential to become gods, for as humans are, God once was.

Salvation. Salvation is the process of achieving godhood. The biblical doctrine of sin is denied by Mormons. Humans are born innately good; children, however, are said to sin (i.e., make wrong judgments) and become accountable for their sins.

Baptism by immersion into the Mormon Church is absolutely essential for salvation. But this baptism need not be done by the individual personally. Someone else may be baptized for a person who has been long dead—thus the Mormon passion for genealogy. Genealogies of the candidates are determined, and "Gentile" ancestors are baptized by proxy to assure their salvation. In Mormonism, Christ's death removes guilt for past sins. The person must begin at that point to earn salvation through good works.

The doctrine of hell is minimized. All people go to one of three heavens at death. Those who do not believe go to the telestial heaven, while those who are not Mormons but religious go to terrestrial heaven. Only Mormons go to the celestial heaven.

Polygamy. Until 1890, when polygamy was outlawed by the government, it was an important doctrine. In its place the church has substituted what is known as "celestial marriage." This means a man can make certain he will have a number of wives for eternity.

These marriages must be sealed in the secret temples. This practice, it is said, is also a benefit for women. Apart from a celestial marriage, they cannot reach the highest glory. Procreation in life after death is necessary to attain this.

Current Status

Mormonism continues to grow; in 1995, a membership of nine million was reported.[9] An aggressive proselytizing program recruits seekers by stressing a strong family orientation and high moral standards. Young men can ensure a future of leadership in their local assemblies by working as missionaries. Many spend two years working full-time for the church. At any one time, approximately twenty thousand missionaries are going door to door. They are trained in Mormon doctrine and are especially active in college towns.

The Mormon Church sponsors Brigham Young University and other schools. The church is a part of a large corporation with vast holdings.

Hinduism

History and Background

Hinduism is an ancient religion with highly complex beliefs. Throughout its history, so many sects have formed within its womb that it is not a single religion, in one sense, but a family of religions. A Hindu finds no difficulty living in this diverse family, for Hinduism is tolerant of religions that differ widely from it. It sees similarities and shared vision in them all.

There are three stages of development in the history of Hinduism: the Pre-Vedic, the Vedic, and the Upanishadic. The Pre-Vedic period began with a series of intertribal invasions and assimilations more than three thousand years before Christ and produced an advanced culture in northern India. In about 1500 B.C., people called Aryans invaded and imposed their religion on northern India. This began the Vedic period. These Aryans did not worship things made by human hands as had the Indians. Instead, they worshiped the powers of nature. Following the Vedic period in about 600 B.C., the Upanishadic period arose when divisions erupted among the masses. Upanishads were sacred books that gave new interpretations of the beliefs of the Vedic period. At the center of this new system was belief in one single principle or universal soul.

Upanishad belief was based in a pantheistic monism. During the

Upanishadic period, life was viewed with great pessimism. Much corruption and legalism prevailed. Reform efforts arose within Hinduism, among them Buddhism. There was even a movement toward worship of a personal God. This was not a monotheistic Hinduism, however. Instead, a triad of Hindu gods was often used to represent the impersonal and absolute *Brahman*. *Brahma* (the masculine form of the word *Brahman*) was regarded as the Creator, *Vishnu* as the Preserver, and *Shiva* as the Destroyer.

Major Theological Beliefs

Authority. Boa has compiled a list of the major books of Hindu scripture. These may be broken down into a revealed canon, the *Sruti*, and a semicanonical body of tradition writings, the Smriti.
The Sruti include:
- Vedas *(Rig-Veda, Sama Veda, Yajur-Veda, Atharva-Veda)*
- Brahmanas
- Aranyakas
- Upanishads
- *Bhagavad Gita* (the last part of the *Mahabharata*)

The semicanonical Smriti literature includes:
- Sutras
- Codes of Law
- Agamas
- *Mahabharata*
- *Ramayana*
- Darshanas
- Puranas[10]

Salvation. Salvation is acquired in three different ways. (1) *Jnana Yoga* is salvation by knowledge. This involves listening to many readings and practicing meditation. (2) *Bhakti Yoga* is salvation by devotion. In this popular approach, a manifestation of God is selected by the individual, who then hopes to be united with God. (3) *Karma Yoga* involves salvation by works such as sacrifices, pilgrimages, and good behavior and actions.

Hinduism teaches that each person lives a succession of lives in which it is possible to gain salvation. The "saved" person is one who has broken out of the cycle of reincarnations. In such a works-oriented salvation, there is a weak view of sin. In fact, in Hinduism there is no sin against God. Wrong actions are simply the result of ignorance, not violations of God's laws.

The caste system. Caste is central to Hindu belief. From *Manu*, who was the first man created by *Brahma*, came four different types of people. From Manu's head the best and most holy people came, the *Brahmins.* The *Kshatriyas* came from Manu's hands. These were the rulers and warriors. From his thighs came the *Vaisyas*, the craftsmen. All others came from Manu's feet and were named *Sundras.* This structure in the caste system is said to be divinely inspired.[11]

The Sacred Cow. Very early in the history of the Hindu religion the cow was revered and believed to possess great power. The cow is identified with the universe itself. The following is from the *Atharva-Veda:*

> Worship to thee, springing to life, and worship to thee
>   when born!
> Worship, O Cow, to thy tail-hair, and to thy hooves, and
>   to thy form!
> Hitherward we invite with prayer the Cow who pours a
>   thousand streams,
> By whom the heaven, by whom the earth, by whom these
>   waters are preserved. . . .
> Forth from thy mouth the songs came, from thy neck's
>   nape sprang strength, O Cow.
> Sacrifice from thy flanks was born, and rays of sunlight
>   from thy teats.
> From thy fore-quarters and thy thighs motion was
>   generated, Cow!
> Food from thine entrails was produced, and from thy belly
>   came the plants. . . .
> They call the Cow immortal life, pay homage to the Cow
>   as Death. . . .
> The Cow is Heaven, the Cow is Earth, the Cow is Vishnu,
>   Lord of Life. . . .
> He who hath given a Cow unto the Brahmans winneth
>   all the worlds.
> For Right is firmly set in her, devotion, and religious zeal.
> Both Gods and mortal men depend for life and being on
>   the Cow.
> She hath become this universe: all that the Sun surveys is
>   she (*Atharva Veda*, 10.10).[12]

Current Status

Hinduism enjoys great influence in the West through such movements as Hare Krishna, New Ageism, and transcendental meditation. These all have affinity to and embrace essentials of Hinduism.
In the late 1990s, there were more than 767.4 million Hindus.[13]

Islam

History and Background

The history and contemporary thinking of Islam revolve around
Muhammad, who was born around A.D. 570 in Mecca, Arabia.
As a young man, he soon became dissatisfied with the polytheism
and crude superstitions around him. Muhammad came to believe
in only one God, Allah. At forty years of age he began having
visions that he attributed to God. These visions continued until
his death twenty-two years later in 632.

Muhammad was not well received in Mecca. He took his teachings to Medina, Arabia. Islamic calendars show 16 July 622 as the
birthdate of the religion. Medina did not accept Muhammad's
teachings well either, and he soon returned to Mecca and tri-
umphed over those who opposed him. From that point until his
death, Islam spread throughout the region.

Muhammad died without naming a successor, so a tremendous
power struggle erupted among his followers. Ali, Muhammad's
son-in-law, eventually became the Caliph (successor), but he was
murdered by another who believed himself to be the true successor.
Followers of Ali are known as the Shi'ites. Islam consists of many
sects and divergent groups.

Major Theological Views

Authority. The basis for all belief and behavior in Islam lies in
the *Qur'an,* the *Hadith,* or Muslim body of recorded folk
traditions, and the *Sunnah,* or customs of Muslim life.

Muslims hold the *Qur'an* in a high level of regard, as Christians
do the Bible, though their conception is somewhat different from
that of evangelical Protestants. The Bible is the Word of God as
revealed through the writers of the Old and New Testaments. The
thought content is what God gave. Muslims believe that
Muhammad recorded by dictation the exact wording of an eternal
document that exists in heaven. Thus only the Arabic is the true
Qur'an, for it alone records the words Muhammad received from
the angels. An English *Qur'an* for example, is merely an
interpretation that has no standing.

Five articles of faith. Five articles form the major platform of belief for Islam.

1. *God:* The only true god is Allah. He alone is all-knowing and all-powerful. He is the sovereign judge. Muslims call Allah a god of grace, but in the works-righteousness of Islam, he acts most clearly as a god of judgment. All good or evil proceeds from Allah's will.

2. *Angels:* Muslims believe the angel Gabriel dictated the revelation to Muhammad. There is a devil in Islamic belief and spirit beings (neither angels nor humans) that can be good or evil.

3. *Scripture:* The *Qur'an* supersedes the biblical Torah of Moses, the Psalms, and the Gospels.

4. *Prophets:* God has spoken through prophets in the past, including Adam, Noah, Abraham, Moses, Jesus, and Muhammad. Muhammad, however, is the greatest of all.

5. *Last days:* "The last day will be a time of resurrection and judgment. Those who follow and obey Allah and Muhammad will go to the Islamic Paradise, a place of pleasure. Those who oppose them will be tormented in hell."[14]

Five pillars of faith. The five pillars are observances that are basic to Islam and therefore are duties every Muslim is bound to observe.

1. *The creed:* "There is no God but Allah, and Muhammad is the Prophet of Allah."

2. *Prayer:* There are daily rituals at set times during which Muslims pray as one with all other Muslims everywhere.

3. *Almsgiving:* Muslims are required to give one-fortieth of their income for the destitute.

4. *Fasting:* During the holy month of Ramadan, faithful Muslims fast all day.

5. *Pilgrimage:* At least once in their lifetime, all Muslims, particularly men, must make a pilgrimage to Mecca. This is vital to gaining salvation.

Current Status

Because of all the turmoil in the Middle East, Islam has gotten much attention in recent years. In many nations of the Middle East, West Asia, and North Africa, Islam is the driving force. It continues to grow; in fact, some view it as the fastest-growing religion in the world. In mid-1998, there were about 1.18 billion followers of Islam.[15]

Jehovah's Witnesses

History and Background

Charles Taze Russell (1852–1916) founded the organization that came to be known as Jehovah's Witnesses. He was in the Congregational Church until he became exposed to and involved in Seventh-Day Adventism. He turned away from his earlier belief in the eternal torment of the unregenerate in hell. Before long, Russell began to disagree with the Adventists and began publishing his magazine, *Zion's Watchtower and Herald of Christ's Presence.*

Several years later he began the Zion's Watchtower Tract Society, which was incorporated as a religious organization. In 1896, the Society was renamed the Watchtower Bible and Tract Society. Russell wrote and published many pamphlets. His most famous volume was *Studies in the Scriptures.* Present-day Jehovah's Witnesses usually distance themselves from Russell because of his egotism and the charges of fraudulent activity and adultery that were made against him.

Joseph Franklin Rutherford became the second president of the Watchtower Bible and Tract Society in 1872 and held the office until his death in 1942. His authority was seldom challenged. He was ruthless in his criticisms of other religions, churches, and institutions. He wrote much but was not seen in public as often as Russell had been. Doctrinally, Rutherford held to the same views as Russell.

Nathan Homer Knorr was the third president of the Society. He took over in 1942 and remained president until his death in 1977. Membership in the Society grew steadily under Knorr's presidency—from 115,000 to more than two million. While Knorr was president, the Society produced *The New World Translation of Holy Scriptures.* Knorr also stressed the training of both leaders and laypeople. Frederick W. France is the current president of the Society.

Major Theological Views

Authority. The source of authority for Jehovah's Witnesses comes from their various publications rather than a formal doctrinal statement. They claim the Bible as their ultimate source of authority.

The Trinity. The biblical doctrine of the Trinity is denied and is believed to be a satanic effort to distract the lost from the truth about Jehovah and His Son Christ Jesus. Christ was a "god," but not the Almighty God who is Jehovah. Christ the man is forever dead. He was a perfect human being.

The Holy Spirit is not a part of the godhead. Both the personality and deity of the Holy Spirit are denied.

Salvation. Salvation is by works. Sinners not only have to show their worthiness to have everlasting life, but they must also live a life of obedience. Jehovah's Witnesses deny conscious eternal punishment for the unregenerate, but believe in a painless extinction for those not qualified for heaven.

The Return of Christ. According to Jehovah's Witnesses, Christ (as a spiritual being) returned in 1914. It was then that God's kingdom was fully set up in heaven. They believe "the times of the Gentiles" extended to 1914, when Christ returned.

Other Distinctives. Jehovah's Witnesses do not believe in blood transfusions or in human government as normally understood. They believe it is an act of idolatry to salute the flag of any nation. They claim to show allegiance to Jehovah alone.

Current Status

The Jehovah's Witnesses movement continues to grow. This is evidenced by the increased number of kingdom halls and the widespread distribution of their literature, especially by their itinerant missionaries.

New Age Pantheism

History and Background

The New Age philosophy of life is a contemporary expression of ancient humanism, Eastern mysticism, and, in particular, Hinduism. It is generally pantheistic in orientation, believing God is all and all is God. Postmodern thinking marks New Ageism: There is no objective reality. Human consciousness creates whatever reality there is. Absolute truth is nonexistent. Everything is relative. In his thorough analysis of the New Age movement, Norman L. Geisler sets forth a working definition of the movement: "The New Age movement is a broad coalition of various networking organizations that (a) believe in a new world religion (pantheism), (b) are working for a new world order, and (c) expect a new age Christ. Of course, not all who participate in the New Age Movement are necessarily conscious of all these aspects."[16]

Major Theological Views

The Bible. New Age enthusiasts refer frequently to the Bible. However, they do not accept the Bible as the inspired Word of God, but read their own ideas into the text.

Special and continual revelations are a vital part of New Age thinking. Many key figures in the movement claim to have had special and continuous revelations from God and various paranormal entities. These revelations become authoritative for their own disciples at least and influential among others.

David Spangler, a religious New Age movement leader, had this to say about the revelations he received:

> No other revelation to equal it has been offered to humanity, but all revelations of the past have led up to it. Jesus gave the great bridge through proclaiming our kinship with God, our sonship with him. Buddha gave the great bridge in enabling us to find the balance of our own being so that the energies we receive are expressed in harmony with the whole. Through knowing wisdom and through knowing love we now should be at a point, and we are at a point, where God can reasonably say to us, "All right, I have given you the keys. I have given you the tools. Now build with me."[17]

Humankind. New Age followers do not believe in good and evil and right and wrong as traditionally understood. To be consistent they should have no moral values. Each person is viewed as spirit and therefore good. If each human being is infinite and omnipotent, the main task is to discover personal divinity.[18] Wrote Marilyn Ferguson, "One of the major teachings of the Christ [is] the fact of God immanent, immanent in all creation, in mankind and all creation, that there is nothing else but God; that we are all part of a great Being."[19] According to Geisler, Ferguson illustrates this worldview in her story of a man watching his sister drink milk: "All of a sudden I saw that she was God and the milk was God. I mean, all she was doing was pouring God into God."[20]

In New Age thinking humankind is in reality a thought of God. After all, God is said to be immanent in all creation. The movement is strictly pantheistic—God is all and all is God.

Sin. It can easily be seen from the New Age view of nonabsolutes that there is no place for sin. Since there is no personal God, there is also no moral law. Individuals choose what moral values to believe. None have been revealed by God. There is no good or evil, no right or wrong. There is only the cosmic force of love, which is universal and all-inclusive.

If there is no sin, the only salvation needed is reunification with God. Geisler describes it as "overcoming the inexorable law of karma, which condemns one to suffer in the next life for things done in this one."[21]

Current Status

It is impossible to know how many adherents there are to the New Age movement because it is not a movement as such, but a "diversified stream of coalitions, organizations, and individuals all striving to induce a new age of enlightenment and harmony in our society."[22] New Age philosophy is making the most damaging inroads in education. Textbooks, especially in history, are rewritten to eliminate chief cornerstones of civilization. One of the new terms is *Global Education*, which is a means for setting forth New Age philosophy.

Students are taught a one-world view rather than a national view. Patriotism is even discouraged. New Age doctrines, we are told, must be advanced in public schools and brought to bear on politics. Planetary Citizens is an organization with the specific purpose of setting forth the New Age political agenda. World Goodwill is another society with the same goals.[23] New Ageism is a strong religion, even without a defined organization.

The Way International

History and Background

The founder of The Way, Victor Paul Wierwille (1916–85), was an Ohio pastor who became disillusioned with his denomination and its orthodox interpretation of Scripture. Even before Wierwille left his church in 1953, he began teaching a course of study called "Power for Abundant Living" (PFAL). It was a very successful endeavor and spread his teachings. The Way International was organized in 1958. Wierwille claims that an encounter with God gave rise to The Way's founding: "God spoke to me audibly, just like I'm talking to you now. He said he would teach me the word as it had not been known since the first century if I would teach it to others."[24] Wierwille thus made a clear claim to superior knowledge; all before him were inaccurate in their understanding of what God's Word says.

In an official publication, *This Is the Way*, a more definitive statement about what The Way International is and what it claims is set forth: "The Way International is a biblical research and teaching organization concerned with setting before men and women of all ages the inherent accuracy of the word of God [the Bible] so that everyone who so desires may know the power of God in his life. The Way is not a church, nor is it a denomination or a religious sect of any sort."[25]

Major Theological Views

The Bible. Followers of The Way affirm that the Bible is their source of authority. In reality, however, only the Bible as interpreted by the organization is authoritative. Wierwille was the true and only accurate interpreter of Scripture. Everything before Pentecost is viewed as antiquated and inadequate. Only Paul's writings and Luke's in Acts contain material on the abundant life. The Aramaic form of the original text of Scripture is the only accurate one. Even these are interpreted largely from an allegorical and spiritualizing perspective.

Trinity. According to The Way, God is one Person not three. Wierwille believes the historic doctrine of the Trinity degrades God and leaves humankind unredeemed. Christ is not God. He was only a man conceived by the Holy Spirit of God. Both the personality and the deity of the Holy Spirit are denied by Wierwille.

Virgin Birth. That Christ was born of the virgin Mary is rejected. Mary was a virgin at the time of her conception, but not at the time of Jesus' birth.

Salvation. The only visible and audible proof that a person is a child of God is believing and speaking in tongues.

Current Status

Currently The Way International's publishing arm is The American Christian Press. The group has an introductory course entitled "Power for Abundant Living." No official figures of devotees or members are ever released. It is estimated that there are between fifty thousand and sixty thousand members of The Way International.

Notes

1. Ruth A. Tucker, *Another Gospel* (Grand Rapids: Zondervan, 1989), 293.
2. David Barrett, *Sects, Cults, and Alternative Religions* (London: Blandford, 1996), 30.
3. Ananda Martreya Nayaka Thero, "Buddhism in Theravada Countries," in *The Path of the Buddha*, ed. Kenneth W. Morgan (New York: Ronald, 1956), 113–52.
4. Susuma Yamayuahi, "Development of Mahayana Buddhist Beliefs," in *The Path*, 153–81.
5. A. J. Bahm, *Philosophy of Buddha* (London: Rider, 1958), 38–48.
6. "Status of Global Mission," *PULSE*, 23 January 1998, 3.
7. Kenneth Boa, *Cults, World Religions and the Occult* (Wheaton, Ill.: Victor, 1990), 106–9.
8. Ibid., 112.
9. Barrett, *Sects*, 60.
10. Boa, *Cults*, 22.
11. Josh McDowell and Don Stewart, *Handbook of Today's Religions* (San Bernardino, Calif.: Here's Life, 1992), 289.
12. From *Atharva-Veda*, 10.10; in McDowell and Stewart, *Handbook*, 291–92.
13. "Status of Global Mission," 3
14. McDowell and Stewart, *Handbook*, 390.
15. "Status of Global Mission," 3.
16. Norman L. Geisler, *Bibliotheca Sacra* (January–March 1987): 82.
17. David Spangler, *Reflections on the Christ*, cited in ibid., 89.
18. Ibid., 93.
19. Benjamin Creme, *The Reappearance of the Christ and the Masters of Wisdom*, cited in ibid.
20. Marilyn Ferguson, *The Aquarian Conspiracy: Personal and Social Transformation in the 1980's*, cited in ibid.
21. Ibid., 96.
22. Ted Peters, "Post Modern Religion," in *The Religious Fringe*, Richard Kyle (Downers Grove, Ill.: InterVarsity, 1993), 286.
23. Boa, *Cults*, 246–56.
24. Elena S. Whiteside, *The Way: Living in Love* (New Knoxville, Ohio: American Christian Press, n.d.), 178.
25. McDowell and Stewart, *Handbook*, 106, citing *This Is the Way* (New Knoxville, Ohio: The Way International, n.d.).

Postmodernism as a Basis for Society?

by Paul R. Shockley

IN HIS WORK, *The Quest for God: A Personal Pilgrimage*, historian and journalist Paul Johnson writes:

> The existence or non-existence of God is the most important question we humans are ever called to answer. If God does exist, and if in consequence we are called to another life when this one ends, a momentous set of consequences follows, which should affect every day, every moment almost, of our earthly existence. Our life then becomes a mere preparation for eternity and must be conducted throughout with our future in view. If, on the other hand, God does not exist, another momentous set of consequences follows. This life then becomes the only one we have, we have no duties or obligation except to ourselves, and we need weigh no other considerations except our own interest and pleasures. There are no commands to follow except what society imposes upon us, and even these we may evade if we can get away with it. In a Godless world, there is no obvious basis for altruism of any kind; moral anarchy takes over and the rule of the self prevails.[1]

Johnson observes that even in one's own selfishness, some form of morality *always* creeps in.[2] Because modernist philosophy and its secular humanist religious component in Western culture have been dying a slow and painful death, *postmodernism* has inserted itself into the vacuum. So traumatic is this dying process that every aspect of our Western society has been altered.

The Essentials of Postmodernism

Postmodernism really is a simple set of ideas that has complicated repercussions.[3] It hangs on the framework of the belief that (1) *absolute or objective truth does not exist.* What is true for one individual may not be true for another. Therefore, (2) *reality is in the mind of the beholder.* Objective reasoning does not exist because (3) *humanity is molded or scripted by its own subcultures.* If absolute truth is bound in personal biases, then (4) *there is no objective, universal authority.* Postmodernism is marked by (5) *cynicism* and (6) *decision making on the ethical bases of feelings, emotions, and impressions.*

Though it is a simple set of ideas, it is very difficult to define.[4] In essence, postmodernism means "after modernism." To correctly explain postmodernism, then, one must first understand the central tenets of modernism.

The Essentials of Modernism

The worldview of modernism arose in response to the single most important social agent in the eighteenth century, the Enlightenment or "scientific revolution." This study is not concerned with *religious* modernism (classic liberal theology) but with modernism's *secular* dimension.[5] Within modernism, three dominant ideas prevail:

1. Reason is employed through the natural sciences to examine and comprehend all aspects of life. This means that absolutely nothing is to be accepted by faith.
2. The laws of human existence and nature can be discovered.
3. The scientific method can create progressively better societies and better people.[6]

External Forces in the Bankruptcy of Modernism

Today modernism is dying in Western culture. It has been superseded by a plethora of beliefs,[7] under the philosophical categories of existentialism, individualism, narcissism, materialism, hedonism, and nihilism, which flow into everyday life—"For as he thinks within himself, so he is" (Prov. 23:7 NASB).

Existentialism originated from the ideas of Søren Kierkegaard and developed along two avenues of thought, religious and secular. The framework for both branches involves a deep concern for humanity and a subjective and personal view of life. The existentialist acts in faith as much as from an apprehension and acknowledgment of truth. The mere act of acting out faith leads to an experience of God.[8]

Secular existentialism became the more popular view. Its subjectivism led thoughtful people inescapably to the awful but logical conclusion that all of life is meaningless. Despair, terror, and death are the plight of humanity. God is dead so there is no outside, ultimate reality by which to judge *anything*. Because there is no absolute truth, standards of morality are matters of personal preference; values become *invalid*. Therefore, an atheistic existentialist finds each human to be a meaningless machine with a totally unnecessary existence. There is no particular reason to choose one thing over another, or for that matter to make a decision about anything.

Alongside existentialism, postmodern emphasis is on individualism, relativism, narcissism, materialism, and hedonism. If there is no basis by which to judge anything and all ethical choices are equally valid, then only self-centered gain is important, since it provides self-satisfaction and personal comfort.

Individualism's chief priority is self-interest; relative truth and relative morality are necessary to accomplish individualistic gain. "You do what you want to do, and I do what I want to do. Just leave me alone." Individualism necessarily breeds narcissism's arrogance. Materialism becomes that which occupies narcissistic people's thoughts, affections, and identity as they strive to promote self-interest. This narcissistic self-interest hearkens back to the ancient Greek philosophy of hedonism. Hedonists believe that the ultimate good is what brings the most pleasure. One who seeks maximum pleasure and least pain is a wise and moral person. Proximal to all these factors is nihilism, which posits that there is no truth.[9]

Internal Forces in the Bankruptcy of Modernism

These views of life are not the only pressures that are crushing modernism, for modernism is not able to provide that solid foundation on which a society can depend.

Social science failed to produce progressively better, more just, and "evolved" citizens. Poverty, illiteracy, and homelessness have not dramatically decreased. Further, rational principles of modernity could not produce world peace—even through the United Nations!

Modernism claimed that humans were able to successfully choose their own directions and make their own plans. This does not seem plausible to Generation Xers, who face, in the United States for example, an overwhelming national debt and horrific shortages in the Social Security trust fund. Long-term prospects for economic freedom and the "progress" of prosperity seem uncertain.

Science and competition also have created awesome weapons of mass destruction that, since the fall of the Soviet Union, are available to Third World powers and terrorists. The future does indeed seem disheartening in a world where once stable Western governments now seem to be losing influence, sovereignty, and leadership to an often unpredictable United Nations.

In the realm of religion, it has been suggested that evangelicalism contributed to the failure of modernism because it did not offer a plausible worldview. Within evangelicalism, classical or normative dispensationalism,[10] for example, is thought not to best represent the Christian faith as a *viable option* for thinking people because the view depends on interpreting the Bible in its plain, normal, grammatical-historical sense, and this is a product of the eighteenth-century Enlightenment![11] It is neither appealing to postmodernists nor contemporary enough even for evangelicals. In fact, theologian Alister McGrath calls evangelicalism to "purge itself of the remaining foundational influences of the Enlightenment, not simply because the Enlightenment is over, but because of the danger of allowing ideas whose origins and legitimation lie outside the Christian gospel to exercise a decisive influence on that gospel. . . . This task remains a priority for the movement."[12]

Moreover, some who identify themselves as "evangelicals" believe that the rules of plain, normal interpretation of Scripture need to be expanded and redefined. They wish to allow theology the "breathing room" to expand, change, and develop under fewer restrictions. If there is no axis by which the wheel of development of theology is bound (i.e., a plain, normal interpretation method), then theology may develop where it wills, based on the prevailing ideas and influences of culture.[13] The School of Alexandria, whose allegorical interpretations deeply influenced theology by the third century, is a classic example of a school of thought rooted in Platonic idealism. It destroyed the boundaries of plain interpretation, leaving much of the medieval church with a nonliteral or subjective method of interpretation. And its effects unquestionably are still being felt.

The single most important factor in modernism's downfall as a general consensus in Western culture is its failure to fulfill the innate human need for authentic personal peace. Therefore, with the collapse of the Enlightenment, postmodern ideas dramatically emerged in a dynamic cultural shift. Now postmodernism, *in all its flexibility*, is viewed as a firm foundation on which to support humanity and its cultures.[14]

Manifestations of Postmodernism

Postmodernism was first recognized and labeled in the 1930s. It was more clearly observed on the fringes of society in the 1960s and has grown to become the general Western consensus of the 1990s.[15] Postmodernism is evident in arbitrary social laws, advertising, aesthetics, education, entertainment, language usage, media attitudes, political thought, and in religion and its theologies. Postmodern visions pervade mainline and even some historically evangelical churches.

The Cultural Shift of "Star Trek"

Theologian Stanley Grenz keenly observes modernism versus postmodernism through the comparison of the original "Star Trek" television series with that of its successor series, "Star Trek: The Next Generation." The definite philosophical shift can be clearly seen through the characters of "Mr. Spock" in the original series and "Data" in the sequel series. Spock represents the modernist ideal, a being of total logic, complete rationality, and little emotion. Data represents the incredible achievement of mechanistic modernism—a sentient robot or "android." But this mechanical man has the overwhelming desire to break free of his computer-bound limitations and endeavors to become human so that he may possess emotions, feelings, intuition, and even dreams.[16]

The Influence on Religion

Eastern mysticism is becoming increasingly popular in Western culture. Indeed, postmodernism claims that an individual must embrace spirituality to become a whole person. And since there is no one true religion, any spirituality will do. If all religions are equal, all gods are valid. If all gods are valid, there is no compelling reason to confine faith to one god over another. Feelings, impressions, opinions, and intuitions determine one's god or gods. To a consistent postmodernist, there is only one forbidden religion, lifestyle, or worldview—one that claims absolutes. This disfranchises historic Christianity, Judaism, and Islam. Moreover, law professor Philip Johnson states, "If God as Creator exists and cares about what human beings do, then metaphysicalism is true, and a common frame of reference for disputes about value and justice also exists. If God does not exist, and if there also is no platonic metaphysical realm of divine essence, then there may be no absolute reference point from which to judge competing interpretations of reality."[17]

In *The Death of Truth*, Dennis McCallum cites eleven examples of demonstrative postmodern influence.

1. The political correctness movement, an attempt by schools and corporations to control what students and employees say.

2. A ripening view that courts guard the privileges of the dominant culture—white males with wealth. Thus the legal system is inherently unfair to members of racial, ethnic, or sexual minorities or less affluent socioeconomic groups.

3. A reluctance among educational and parenting experts to correct, confront, grade, test, or group children, based on the "labeling theory" that labels damage children for life.

4. Tolerance to the extreme, as in the increasingly accepted view that no moral decision by another individual or culture should be questioned. All views deserve equal respect.

5. An educational deemphasis on mastering the literature, history, values, and philosophy of Western culture. There is, rather, a trend through multicultural education to allow students to set their own standards of literacy, accepting, for example, street English "ebonics."

6. New calls for segregation based on race or minority status, for example, at Afrocentric or "gay" schools.

7. The belief that every hurt is intentional and every accident legally actionable. Radical victimization marginalizes people of all kinds in a repressed-group psychology. Within such groups the only hope is to strip power from the dominant group—the "victimizers."

8. Historical revisionism, which purposely leaves out even major events of the past to further the agendas of feminists, gays, and other special interest groups.

9. Attacks on Christian world evangelism for its "destruction of culture."

10. The belief that "male" and "female" are socially created categories intended to enslave women to men. Mankind is said to comprise not two sexes but at least five genders: heterosexual women, homosexual women, heterosexual men, homosexual men, and bisexuals. These genetically rooted identities are to be affirmed by the educational system and protected by the courts.

11. Hostility toward science. When, for example, the Smithsonian

Institution's Museum of American History received money to add an exhibit on American science, the funding sources expected to see displays commemorating the achievements of science over the past century. Instead, they found mainly "a catalogue of environmental horrors, weapons of mass destruction and social injustice. Among all the displays of pesticide residue, air pollution, acid rain, ozone holes, radioactive waste, food additives, and nuclear bombs, there was no mention that the life expectancy in the United States has more than doubled in the last century, the period covered by the exhibit."[18]

Consequences of Postmodernism

Some of the major ramifications of postmodernism are as follows:[19]

1. All lifestyles, religions, and worldviews are equally valid.[20]
2. Criticism of a person's view or moral choices is the only real "crime."
3. Opinions receive equal weight with objective evidence.[21]
4. Reality becomes "virtual." Individuals create a personal reality.
5. Authority is regarded as the enemy.
6. Paganism is the acceptable religion.
7. Discrimination (age, ethnic, gender, and religious) is given a culturally acceptable and even laudable cloak.

Postmodernists believe that reason itself is a cultural bias of the modernistic, white, European male. If reason does not exist, truth is relative and all choices are equally valid. If all choices are valid, authority should be wholly rejected. Paganism will return, idolatry becomes practical, and discrimination is the norm. Therefore, *postmodernism is inherently unstable*. It breeds contradictions. Social and mental fragmentation cannot support *any* society. Indeed, the present society is a burden, the future a dread.

Potential Outcomes

If authoritative truth is rejected, manipulation, confusion, and chaos may be the overall results. Since postmodernists embrace opinions over facts, they are easily persuaded to believe what does not correspond to reality. This manipulation can lead anywhere.[22] In *How Should We Then Live?* Francis A. Schaeffer states:

Man no longer sees himself as qualitatively different from non-man. The Christian consensus gave a basis for people being unique, as made in the image of God, but this has largely been thrown away. Thus there tends, even with the good things, to be a progressive fracturedness in the practice of life as human life. Remember, too, that for a long time in philosophy, and popularly in some of the mass media, people have been taught that truth as objective truth does not exist. All morals and law are seen as relative. Thus people accept the idea of manipulation and are a bit more gradually open themselves to accept the practices of varying forms of manipulation.[23]

Whoever possesses power to control will make decisions based on selfish interests, and decisions impact others. The goal of doing things for the common good of humanity is lost, for it is a modernistic notion. With manipulation comes confusion. If people do not share basic common denominators, law and order cannot be exercised *democratically*. There will no longer be social cohesion, except under the rubric that postmodernism is the one absolute. And if everyone is truly "doing their own thing," chaos will be the norm.

But chaos cannot be tolerated in society because it disturbs people's selfishness and threatens personal welfare. Therefore, the questions that will arise out of this state of confusion are: What type of authoritative figure will rise to control the masses? What freedoms will society have to sacrifice in order to gain law, order, and preservation? Schaeffer asserts that "society cannot stand chaos. Some group or some person will fill the vacuum. . . . Who will stand in its way?"[24]

Additionally, relativism can be embraced theoretically, but it can never be lived out to its logical conclusion. This is because relativism does not correspond with reality. An apple will still fall from its tree because of the universal law of gravity, and one apple plus one apple will always equal two apples.[25] Hans R. Rookmaaker has correctly remarked: "The new generation begins to look for real humanity, to long for the fullness and openness and freedom to truth and real life. But after a while it finds only the same old thing, the thing it wanted to avoid, to escape, to change, to decry, in the first place."[26]

The Only Hope

Fortunately, the God of the Bible has revealed Himself and He promises that if we will trust in Jesus Christ, the Son of God, who died on the cross for our sins and rose again, we will possess eternal life. Legitimate spiritual expression must correspond to reality. God does! Though one cannot define God exhaustively, creation and its logical arrangements declare with Schaeffer that "He is there and He is not silent." Moreover, Jesus Christ, the Son of God, entered earthly time-and-space history, providing for a personal relationship with all those who will believe in Him as Savior. By nature humanity breeds sin, lawlessness, and rebellion.[27] And postmodernism is another manifestation of that self-autonomy that has been witnessed in the human race since Adam and Eve. However, humans are designed to be like God, to express dependency on the One who is infinite and personal.[28]

Naturally, the purpose of language was for God to reveal truth and for humans to express authentic religious affections creatively and reasonably toward Him who is the Author of those truths. To use language outside its normative sense departs into subjectivism. God gave the Scriptures to communicate, not to confuse or bewilder. Consequently, one should be aware of personal and cultural factors but not permit them to override the interpretation of the Scriptures.[29]

It is reasonable to claim that, though hermeneutics (the science of interpretation) has indeed been motivated and refined by the Enlightenment and by culture in general, the normal usage of language has indeed been around since God revealed Himself in Genesis. The influence of the School of Alexandria created a dramatic shift from plain interpretation of Scripture to an allegorical method of interpretation.

Just as modernism was not an adequate foundation on which a culture could build, neither is postmodernism. Its ideas warrant illogical conclusions that do not correspond to reality. In fact, postmodernism breeds contradictions and then chooses to say that all of these conflicting ideas are equally coherent and valid. However, to claim that mutually exclusive statements are equally true is to suggest that there is an absolute after all. Further, postmodernism is not a view that will meet the innate needs of people.

Yet the Bible remains, divinely preserved.[30] If we interpret the biblical text in its normal sense we will see once more that it truthfully meets the intrinsic needs of every person, since it was given by the unique Triune God, who is infinite, personal, and divinely authoritative. As Charles Hodge stated, "It is of great importance that men should know and feel that they are by their very virtue bound to believe in God; that they cannot emancipate themselves from that belief, without derationalizing and demoralizing their whole being."[31] Decidedly, "The Bible is the

Word of God in such a way that when the Bible speaks, God speaks."[32]

As has been stressed throughout *The God of the Bible and Other Gods*, the God of the Bible is the true and the living God. The security and stability people so desperately need and seek can only come from this God. Only He has extended to mankind His love and grace in Jesus Christ.[33]

Notes

1. Paul Johnson, *The Quest for God: A Personal Pilgrimage* (New York: Harper Collins, 1996), 1.
2. Ibid.
3. See Dennis McCallum, ed., *Death of Truth* (Minneapolis: Bethany House, 1996), for a clear summary of modernism, postmodernism, and their impact on health care, literature, education, history, psychotherapy, law, science, and religion. Also see Gene Edward Veith Jr., *Postmodern Times* (Wheaton, Ill.: Crossway, 1994).
4. Alister McGrath, *A Passion for Truth: The Intellectual Coherence of Evangelicalism* (Downers Grove, Ill.: InterVarsity, 1996), 184.
5. See Nancy R. Pearcey and Charles B. Thaxton, *The Soul of Science: Christian Faith and Natural Philosophy* (Wheaton, Ill.: Crossway, 1994), for an analysis of the remarkable relationship between the development of modern science and the Judeo-Christian worldview.
6. See George Ritzer, *The McDonaldization of Society: An Investigation into the Changing Character of Contemporary Social Life* (Newbury Park, Calif.: Pine Forge, 1993), for a captivating analysis of modernity by a distinguished social theorist. See also Max Weber, *The Protestant Ethic and the Spirit of Capitalism* (New York: Charles Scribner's Sons, 1958), and Eugene Kamenka, ed., *The Portable Karl Marx* (New York: Penguin, 1983).
7. Pluralism results in a loss of reason. See Ravi Zacharias, *Deliver Us from Evil: Restoring the Soul in a Disintegrating Culture* (Dallas: Word, 1996).
8. See C. Stephen Evans, *Existentialism: The Philosophy of Despair and the Quest for Hope* (Grand Rapids: Zondervan, 1984).
9. Mortimer J. Adler, *The Great Ideas: A Lexicon of Western Thought* (New York: Macmillan, 1992), 866.
10. Though the character of evangelicalism is in decay (see John H. Armstrong, ed., *The Coming Evangelical Crisis: Current*

Challenges to the Authority of Scripture and the Gospel [Chicago: Moody, 1996]), Mark Noll's *The Scandal of the Evangelical Mind* (Grand Rapids: Eerdmans, 1994) is extreme in its allegation that normative or classic dispensationalism is chiefly "responsible for the most disastrous effects on the mind" (p. 132). For a clear understanding of dispensationalism, see Charles C. Ryrie, *Dispensationalism* (Chicago: Moody, 1995).

11. McGrath, *Passion for Truth*, 166-79.
12. Ibid., 200.
13. J. Robertson McQuilkin and Bradford Mullen, "The Impact of Postmodern Thinking on Evangelical Hermeneutics," *Journal of the Evangelical Theological Society* 40, no. 1 (March 1997): 69-82.
14. This author is not suggesting that modernism no longer exists. For example, the post-World War II generation is still a force with which to reckon. However, its numbers are in decline. Therefore, with the overwhelming rejection of strong rationalism in the 1960s, 1970s, 1980s, and now the 1990s, the *ideas* of the "Enlightenment project" are no longer regarded as a stable foundation on which a society can rest. Additionally, capitalism, industrialization, and computerized technology are prime examples of "structural revolutions" that denote modernity. Modernism and modernity are culturally distinguishable. See Mars Hill Interview, "Calling, Postmodernism, and Chastened Liberals: A Conversation with Os Guinness," *Mars Hill Review*, no. 8 (summer 1997), 69-82.
15. Stanley J. Grenz, *A Primer on Postmodernism* (Grand Rapids: Eerdmans, 1996), 16.
16. Stanley J. Grenz, "Star Trek and the Next Generation: Postmodernism and the Future of Evangelical Theology," in *The Challenge of Postmodernism: An Evangelical Engagement*, ed. David Dockery (Wheaton, Ill.: Victor, 1995), 89-103.
17. Philip E. Johnson, *Reason in the Balance: The Case Against Naturalism in Science, Law, and Education* (Downers Grove, Ill.: InterVarsity, 1995), 124.
18. McCallum, *Death of Truth*, 14-15.
19. Jerram Barrs, "Postmodernity: Understanding Our Generation's Thought Life, Part 1," *Francis Schaeffer Institute Worldview* 5, no. 2 (autumn 1996).
20. See John Hick, *God Has Many Names* (Philadelphia: Westminster, 1982), and Joseph Campbell, *Transformations of Myth Through Time* (New York: Harper & Row, 1990).
21. See Daniel Taylor, *The Myth of Certainty* (Grand Rapids:

Zondervan, 1992), and John E. Thiel, *Nonfoundationalism* (Minneapolis: Fortress, 1994).

22. Adolf Hitler, *Mein Kampf*, trans. (Boston: Houghton Mifflin, 1943), and Eric Hoffer, *The True Believer: Thoughts on the Nature of Mass Movements* (New York: Harper & Row, 1951).

23. Francis A. Schaeffer, *A Christian View of the West*, in *The Complete Works of Francis A. Schaeffer* (Wheaton, Ill: Crossway, 1982), 5:237.

24. Ibid., 226.

25. Truth is that which exactly corresponds to reality, identifies things as they are, can be expressed in propositions, never fails or changes, and is derived from the thoughts of the Triune God, who is the Author of all truth.

26. Hans R. Rookmaaker, *Modern Art and the Death of Culture* (Wheaton, Ill: Crossway, 1994), 211.

27. See J. Dwight Pentecost, *Thy Kingdom Come* (Wheaton, Ill: Victor, 1990).

28. See J. Dwight Pentecost, *Designed to Be Like Him: New Testament Insight for Becoming Christlike* (Grand Rapids: Discovery House, 1994).

29. See J. Dwight Pentecost, "The Spirit and the Revelation of Divine Truth," in *The Divine Comforter: The Person and Work of the Holy Spirit* (Grand Rapids: Kregel, 1997), 21–34; Elliott E. Johnson, *Expository Hermeneutics: An Introduction* (Grand Rapids: Zondervan, 1990); E. D. Hirsch Jr., *Validity in Interpretation* (New Haven, Conn.: Yale University Press, 1967); and Roy B. Zuck, *Basic Bible Interpretation* (Wheaton, Ill.: Victor, 1991).

30. See B. B. Warfield, *The Inspiration and Authority of the Bible*, ed. Samuel G. Craig, with an introduction by Cornelius Van Til (Philadelphia: Presbyterian and Reformed, 1948); and Norman L. Geisler and William E. Nix, *A General Introduction to the Bible*, rev. ed. (Chicago: Moody, 1986), 33–200.

31. Charles Hodge, *Systematic Theology*, repr. ed. (Grand Rapids: Eerdmans, 1993), 1:201.

32. Zuck, *Basic Bible Interpretation*, 7.

33. For a similar but more in-depth analysis of the current plight of Western culture, see Harold O. J. Brown, *The Sensate Culture: Western Civilization Between Chaos and Transformation* (Dallas: Word, 1996).

Select Bibliography

Bavinck, Herman. *The Doctrine of God*. Grand Rapids: Eerdmans, 1951.

Colson, Charles. *Loving God*. Dallas: Dallas Theological Seminary, 1987.

Corduan, Winfried. *Reasonable Faith*. Nashville: Broadman & Holman, 1993.

Geisler, Norman, and Ron Brooks. *When Skeptics Ask*. Wheaton, Ill.: Victor, 1989.

Guinness, Os, and John Seel, eds. *No God But God: Breaking with the Idols of Our Age*. Chicago: Moody, 1992.

Miethe, Terry L., and Gary Habermas. *Why Believe? God Exists!* Joplin, Mo.: College Press, 1993.

Packer, J. I. *Knowing God*. Downers Grove, Ill.: InterVarsity, 1973.

Richards, Larry. *Is God Necessary?* Chicago: Moody, 1969.

Royal, Claudia. *Teaching Your Child About God*. Westwood, N.J.: Revell, 1960.

Schaeffer, Francis A. *The God Who Is There*. Chicago: InterVarsity, 1968.

Toon, Peter. *Our Triune God*. Wheaton, Ill.: Victor, 1996.

Tozer, A. W. *The Knowledge of the Holy*. New York: Harper and Brothers, 1961.

Zacharias, Ravi. *Can Man Live Without God?* Dallas: Word, 1994.

Subject and Name Index

Revelation
  natural 74
  special 75-76
Rice, Richard 119, 128
Richards, Larry 209
Ritzer, George 206
Robinson, John A. T. 9, 58
Rookmaaker, Hans R. 208
Rushdonny, Rousas J. 56
Ryrie, Charles C. 21, 72, 143, 157

Sagan, Carl 43, 44, 50
Salvation 39, 144-57
Sartre, Jean-Paul 41
Schaeffer, Francis A. 49, 63, 72, 203, 208
Schleiermacher, Friedrich 52
Scripture
  authority of 14
  canonicity of 14, 15
  Christ's news of 27-30
  doctrine of 38
  illumination of 17-19
  inspiration of 22
  interpretation of 18
  revelation of 13
Scriven, Michael 58
Showers, Renald E. 168
Sin, doctrine of 38
Sovereign plan of God 102-4
Sovereignty of God 97-101, 153
Spangler, David 196
Spinoza, Benedictus de 45
Steady-State Theory 65
Stevenson, Herbert F. 143

Taylor, Paul S. 72
Teleological argument 49-51
Theology of hope 54, 55
Tillich, Paul 54, 61
Tiplen, Derek 96
Toon, Peter 209
Tozer, A. W. 209
Transcendence of God 124

Trinity 86, 90-95
  economical 91
  ontological 91
Tucker, Ruth 195

Vahanian, Gabriel 58
Van Buren, Paul 58
Van Dusen, Henry P. 61

Warfield, B. B. 85, 208
Way International 175, 193-94
Wenham, J. W. 30
Westminster Catechism 35, 64, 102
Whitcomb, John 72
Whitehead, Alfred North 119
Word
  living 77-85
  written 77-85

Zacharias, Ravi 174, 206, 209
Zeller, George 168
Zuck, Roy B. 21, 208

Scripture Index

Handbook of Evangelical Theology
A Historical, Biblical, and Contemporary Survey and Review

A unique survey of nine key Bible doctrines and a review of the various positions within the evangelical church with respect to each doctrine.

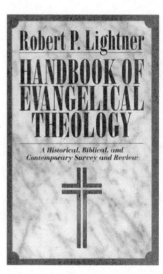

"I was impressed to see the breadth of views that he accepts as evangelical. Not only was I impressed, but I was encouraged to see the fairness in such a presentation. While Lightner is not afraid to affirm his own position, . . . he presents other positions with objectivity and balance."

—*Logos Review*

"An amazing example of succinct expertise. In a few hundred pages, Lightner has successfully presented the essence of systematic theology. Lightner's writings and lectures have established him as a perceptive and articulate thinker who is aware of the data and issues of theology and who can simply analyze and state them."

—*Moody Monthly*

0-8254-3145-x • 312 pp.

PUBLICATIONS

Grand Rapids, MI 49501

ALSO BY ROBERT P. LIGHTNER

Sin, the Savior, and Salvation
The Theology of Everlasting Life

With scholarship that is thorough yet accessible and a tone that is convincing but noncombative, Dr. Lightner explores the current confusion over issues such as: the vanishing concept of personal sin, the influence of the New Age, and the controversy over "Lordship salvation."

"This book crystallizes in clear, concise, and correct terms the essentials of the doctrine of sin and salvation better than any other book of its kind."

—Norman L. Geisler

0-8254-3153-0 • 320 pp.

kregel
PUBLICATIONS

Grand Rapids, MI 49501

A Biblical Case for Total Inerrancy
How Jesus Viewed the Old Testament

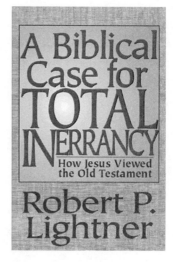

What does the Bible say about the doctrine of inerrancy, and what did Jesus believe about the authority of the Scriptures? Many contemporary answers to these questions disagree with traditional, orthodox views, and these divergent views claim to be a return to the theology of Jesus and the Bible.

This important study examines the biblical evidence regarding the Bible's inerrancy—what Christ Himself taught concerning the Scriptures. Lightner demonstrates that one's view of Christ cannot be divorced from what Jesus Himself believed to be true.

0-8254-3110-7 • 192 pp.

kregel
PUBLICATIONS

Grand Rapids, MI 49501

The Death Christ Died
A Biblical Case for Unlimited Atonement

A unique survey of nine key Bible doctrines and a review of the various positions within the evangelical church with respect to each doctrine.

"This book is priority reading for all, no matter what the extent of the atonement is held. . . . The author seeks to strike a biblical balance between divine sovereignty and human responsibility."

—*Joseph M. Stowell,*
President, Moody Bible Institute

0-8254-3155-7 • 176 pp.

PUBLICATIONS

Grand Rapids, MI 49501